DATE DUE

DEMCO 38-296

Sri Lanka is one of the few new Commonwealth countries to have had a strong democratic tradition and a vibrant electoral life since Independence. In this book Dilesh Jayanntha examines the basis for Sri Lankan electoral allegiance since 1947. He challenges the prevalent notion that caste is the basis for electoral allegiance and convincingly argues that the patron–client relationship is its primary determinant.

Following an introduction outlining recent Sri Lankan political history, Dilesh Jayanntha then examines electoral allegiance in three contrasting constituencies. Two of these are rural constituencies, the other an urban one. They differ from each other in various ecological, economic and social respects and they have a different history up until 1947. Yet, as the author demonstrates throughout, patronage networks based initially on private wealth and later on access to and control of state institutions determined electoral allegiance. Often the patronage network was congruent with caste. But as Jayanntha shows, where the patron–client tie cut across the caste tie it was the former which proved decisive in deciding electoral allegiance.

This is the first detailed comparative analysis of electorates in Sri Lanka. It addresses issues that are relevant not only to South Asia but to the developing world in general and will therefore be of interest to specialists and students of South Asia, comparative politics, sociology and anthropology.

CAMBRIDGE SOUTH ASIAN STUDIES

ELECTORAL ALLEGIANCE IN SRI LANKA

ELECTORAL ALLEGIANCE IN SRI LANKA

DILESH JAYANNTHA

The World Bank,
Colombo, Sri Lanka

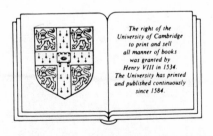

*The right of the
University of Cambridge
to print and sell
all manner of books
was granted by
Henry VIII in 1534.
The University has printed
and published continuously
since 1584.*

CAMBRIDGE UNIVERSITY PRESS

CAMBRIDGE

NEW YORK   PORT CHESTER

MELBOURNE   SYDNEY

Published by the Press Syndicate of the University of Cambridge
The Pitt Building, Trumpington Street, Cambridge CB2 1RP
40 West 20th Street, New York, NY 11011–4211, USA
10 Stamford Road, Oakleigh, Victoria 3166, Australia

© Cambridge University Press 1992

.......d 1992

Britain at
, Cambridge

in publication data

)ilesh
ıka – (Cambridge South
ies).
tics, history

320.9549'3

Library of Congress cataloguing in publication data
applied for

ISBN 0 521 34586 3 hardback

CONTENTS

ACKNOWLEDGMENTS

In producing this book, I owe a number of individuals and institutions a debt, and in a short note such as this, it is not possible to enumerate all of them. However, in facilitating my research, I owe a particular debt to my father, the late Mr C. A. K. Salgado, Mr Geoffrey Hawthorn of the Social and Political Sciences Committee of the Economics Faculty of the University of Cambridge, and the Smuts Memorial Fund. I also drew liberally on primary source material, principally from the Sri Lanka National Archives and the Office of the Commissioner for Co-operative Development. Last, but not least, I owe a debt to the numerous Sri Lankan political actors who provided me with valuable information and insights into the functioning of the polity and patronage networks of the country. Where appropriate, the names of people and of places have been changed.

PUBLISHER'S NOTE

It will be clear to the reader that it has been thought necessary to change various placenames. The names of certain individuals have also been changed. The author and publisher are confident that these changes in no way diminish the essential validity of this study and its conclusions.

ABBREVIATIONS

ADB	Asian Development Bank
AGA	Assistant Government Agent
APC	Agricultural Productivity Committee
ARTI	Agrarian Research and Training Institute
ASC	Agrarian Services Committee
CC	Cultivation Committee
CDN	*Ceylon Daily News*
CNC	Ceylon National Congress
CO	Cultivation Officer
CP	Communist Party
CSO	*Ceylon Sunday Observer*
CTB	Ceylon Transport Board
CWE	Co-operative Wholesale Establishment
DDC	District Development Council
DRO	Divisional Revenue Officer
GA	Government Agent
GOC	Government of Ceylon
GOSL	Government of Sri Lanka
JVP	Janatha Vimukthi Peramuna
LRC	Land Reform Commission
LSSP	Lanka Sama Samaja Party
MEP	Mahajana Eksath Peramuna
MP	Member of Parliament
MPCS	Multi-Purpose Co-operative Society
NWP	North Western Province
SLFP	Sri Lanka Freedom Party
SLN	*Sri Lanka News*
SLNA	Sri Lanka National Archives
SP	Sessional Paper
TC	Town Council
UC	Urban Council
UDA	Urban Development Authority
UF	United Front

ULF	United Left Front
UNP	United National Party
VA	*Vidane-Arachchi*
VC	Village Council
VLSSP	Vipalavakari Lanka Sama Samaja Party
WP	Western Province

1

Introduction

Caste, patronage and politics; the Pan-Indian background

It is tempting to study caste, patronage and politics in Sri Lanka in a Pan-Indian context. Certainly the country bears many similarities to her giant neighbour to the north. However, in several important respects a comparison has to be qualified. First, Sri Lanka is only a fraction of the size of India, and in terms of both area and population smaller than the average Indian state. This physical difference is compounded administratively, India being a federation of states many with their own particular identities, whilst Sri Lanka is a unitary nation. Thus any comparison of Sri Lanka should strictly be with a particular part of India rather than with the whole country. Secondly, even then it should be recognized that Sri Lanka, despite its geographical proximity to India, has had very different historical antecedents. The prevalence of Buddhism since the second century BC meant that the caste system was never so rigid and hierarchical as in most parts of Hindu India. Moreover, the Low Country was exposed to four-and-a-half centuries of Western influence in a way few Indian states were. This helped to undermine further what little caste hierarchy did exist in Sri Lanka.

However, the literature on India which is chiefly confined to particular provinces or districts does provide some sort of framework within which Sri Lankan politics can be studied. In particular there are several studies of patron–client relationships at the village and district levels.[1] It has been shown that these form the basis for political allegiance.[2] Although horizontal political links (between actors of the same social and economic status) tend to be intra-caste, vertical links between patrons and clients are intercaste.[3]

Some studies which suggested that caste groups in parts of South India formed an important base for political mobilization have been shown to

---

[1] Some good studies are Breman (1974) and Carter (1974).
[2] Carter (1974).   [3] Ibid.

be redundant.[4] Many of the regional caste categories (such as the *Reddi*, *Vellalla* or *Kamma*) represented no more than amorphous status blocs, lacking any form of social organization to support them and with no sense of community.[5] In the North too it was noted that 'beneath the veneer of theoretical categorization the *Kayastha* "caste" scarcely existed as an ongoing community and possessed little or no social reality'.[6] In the South it was the British who, with the extension of their administration, gave these categories a definable identity.[7] But even then they were not to be important as a means of social organization, let alone political mobilization.

Washbrook, Carroll and Baker have made an important contribution in questioning whether the mere use of a caste name in political rhetoric warrants the assumption of a group identity, still less implies it is a vehicle to support this identity in the political arena.[8] They have quite correctly stressed that we should look behind the rhetoric to examine the material interests and linkages of the so-called caste spokesmen.

Roberts, who has touched on this literature in the process of examining caste in Sri Lankan politics, has however criticized Washbrook's thesis. Roberts argues that Washbrook 'cannot conceive of corporate consciousness and communal solidarity without some concrete organizational foundations, whether in the form of marriage networks, panchyats, associations or interlocking patron–client networks . . . [and that] . . . his approach is characterized by misplaced concreteness and crude materialism'.[9] However, Roberts himself does not provide any alternative evidence for a 'corporate consciousness and communal solidarity' of any particular caste. He only argues that 'localized caste networks were penetrated and permeated by numerous indigenous channels of cultural transmission . . . [which included] . . . cultural brokers (such as wandering minstrels, story-tellers . . . troupes of actors . . . and . . . pedlars)'.[10] Yet the fact that such modes of cultural transmission existed is not evidence of their having created a 'corporate consciousness and communal solidarity'. Still less is it evidence of their having created a caste basis for political allegiance. In this context Washbrook's basic argument stands firm.

---

[4] Hardgrave (1969), Jeffrey (1974) and Jeffrey (1976) are instances of these (now redundant) studies.
[5] Washbrook (1975), pp. 168–9 and 172–4 and Washbrook (1976), pp. 126–7, 129–30, 133–4.
[6] Carroll (1975) and Carroll (1978).
[7] Washbrook (1975), pp. 181–4, Washbrook (1976), pp. 263–4 and see Hawthorn (1982).
[8] Washbrook (1975), Washbrook (1976), Carroll (1975) and Carroll (1978).
[9] Roberts (1982), pp. 201–2.   [10] Ibid., p. 196.

Thus an assessment of the literature of the Indian political scene does not point to caste-based electoral allegiances and intra-caste vertical ties. However the literature on electoral politics in Sri Lanka suggests that this is the pattern there, a point examined in the next section.

Electoral politics in Sri Lanka: a survey of the literature

The existing literature on politics in Sri Lanka is of two kinds. On the one hand there are some fairly general surveys of behaviour at an Island-wide level since Independence.[11] On the other, there are some very detailed studies of politics at the village level, over relatively short periods.[12]

At present there is nothing which bridges this gap. There are no detailed comparative studies of entire electorates over a period of time.[13] Thus, we are unable to explain why some villages in a given area voted one way, and other villages, in close proximity, another. We are also unable to explain why certain sets of villages have changed their allegiance over time. Finally we are unable to explain why some localities or electorates have produced some leaders, and others, others, the bases for their support, and whether these bases have changed over time (and if so how). In short, the determinants of political allegiance and leadership at the electoral level have not been examined.

This has meant that often some of the factors seeming to explain political allegiance at the village level have been assumed to explain allegiance at the electoral level too. Thus some fairly superficial, and sometimes misleading, explanations of the determinants of political allegiance have come to be accepted.[14] These explanations have something in common with the caste-based views of politics in India described earlier, which have been criticized by Washbrook.

Agriculture was, and is, the chief occupation of the inhabitants of the interior of Sri Lanka. The traditional cultivating caste, the *Goigama*, generally, but not always, produces the locally dominant landlord family in the area, the village elites who were dependent upon it, and the majority of the other inhabitants who were dependent upon these elites in turn. The locally dominant landlord families tended to produce

---

11 See for instance Jupp (1978), Kearney (1973), Wilson (1979), Woodward (1969) and Wriggins (1960). Critiques of the existing literature can be found in Moore (1978), Moore (1981a) and Moore (1981b), Appendices 6 and 7. See Farmer (1963) for a succinct historical introduction.

12 See for instance Morrison *et al.* (1979) and Robinson (1975).

13 There are only some descriptive studies of elections at the national level, lacking in analysis. See Jennings (1948), Jennings (1952), Jennings (1953), Weerawardene (1952), Weerawardene (1960) and Wilson (1975). There are also two short and superficial articles on by-elections, Jiggins (1974) and Phadnis (1969).

14 See, for instance, Jiggins (1979) and Ryan (1953), pp. 275–82.

candidates for election to the legislatures from 1931 onwards. In doing so they operated through traditional intermediaries, the village elites, who delivered them blocs of votes. As these village elites and most of their clients in turn tended to come from the landlord's *Goigama* caste, the fiction of a caste basis for voting emerged.

However, this was in reality only a special case of a more fundamental patron–client relationship. There is a vast literature on patron–client relationships in general and the terms have been used by different writers with different shades of meaning.[15] In what follows a patron is defined as an individual exercising control over a set of individuals (termed clients) over several years and often over several generations, in more ways than the mere monetary. In politics this control was exercised via a set of lesser influentials, termed intermediaries, who themselves acted as patrons to even poorer clients (see Chapter 2, pp. 32–3). The whole system of patrons, intermediaries and clients is defined as a patronage network. Patrons tended to live amongst clients of their own caste: *Karave* landlords and fish *mudalalis* along the coast; the *Goigama* in the interior; and the *Salagama* and *Durave* in isolated pockets. The fact that these patrons could later count on these clients for political support was not surprising. But the fact that these clients generally came from their own caste was dictated by a geographical coincidence: the tendency of a caste to congregate in, and numerically dominate, a particular village or locality, so that clients in the caste often tended to depend on patrons of that same caste. The clients' support for a member of their caste then was dictated by his having been their patron. Where the patron came from a different caste, he could just as surely draw their support. Thus where the patron–client tie cut across the caste tie, the former relationship proved more important in explaining political allegiance. The caste tie can therefore be said to have been important only in so far as it was congruent with a patron–client tie.

The point has been missed by several writers, notably Jiggins.[16] In all the electorates she has examined, the numerically largest caste has generally sent its representative to Parliament.[17] But in all these cases the numerically largest caste has also produced the leading patrons of the area. The importance of the patron–client tie is therefore not apparent, as it would have been had she chosen an electorate where a numerically minor caste produced one or more of the leading patrons and candidates for political office.

---

[15] For a review of the literature on patronage and some general discussion of the term see Eisenstadt and Roniger (1980), Eisenstadt and Roniger (1984) and Gellner (1977).
[16] Jiggins (1979).   [17] Ibid.

In the next section we shall try to show that there are several electorates in Sri Lanka which have, since Independence, returned members from numerically minor castes to Parliament. It can then be seen that this is a general phenomenon, and that membership of a numerically dominant caste is not a necessary condition for political success. Thereafter, the problem posed can be defined and the best means of approaching it assessed.

Our problem defined and an approach to it

An examination of the caste backgrounds of successful candidates of the eight General Elections to the Parliaments of Sri Lanka reveals that several have come from minority groups. As much as a fifth to a quarter of successful candidates in the Sinhalese seats have been from communities which in their constituency have been numerically exceeded by at least one other community (see Table 1).

In this context Jiggins' basic argument that 'caste identities . . . appear to be nearly always a necessary condition for voter, party manager and candidates alike'[18] deserves to be seriously questioned. This is especially so as most of the more general works on the subject also take caste as an important independent factor in determining voter allegiance.[19]

The problem then is one of trying to assess how true this is, if at all. This involves looking at alternative bases of such allegiance. Such a problem could be approached in two ways: either by focussing on a political party and trying to assess its bases of support nationally or within a particular district, or by focussing on one or more electorates and assessing the bases for support of the candidates contesting.

There are a number of reasons for adopting the latter approach. First, in Sri Lanka, political parties did not emerge for a long time. The first such party to be formed was the Trotskyist LSSP, which emerged in 1935. Several of its leaders were jailed during the war, and the party never assumed the sort of 'national' role representative of a wide cross-section of communities that the Indian National Congress did at this time. The first non-Marxist party, the UNP, was only formed on the eve of the 1947 General Election with the purpose of contesting it. Then too, in several electorates, the UNP ticket was given to more than one local patron, the philosophy being let the more influential man win. The 1947 and 1952 General Elections were not fought on party-ideological grounds. Instead, they entailed rival patrons mobilizing their different local networks. Focussing on an electorate thus enables us to study the

18 Ibid., pp. 152–4.
19 See, for instance, Kearney (1973), pp. 105, 106, 149 and 181–8 and Jupp (1978), p. 210.

Table 1   The caste of successful candidates for Parliament in relation to the caste compositions of their electorates (1947–77)

Number of seats where:	Election							
	1947	1952	1956	March 1960	July 1960	1965	1970	1977
The successful candidate's own community/caste is in a majority	40	47	50	89	92	95	97	99
The successful candidate's own community/caste is the largest, but not in a numerical majority	1	2	1	2	1	1	1	1
The successful candidate's own community/caste is equalled by another	8	6	6	3	2	2	2	2
The successful candidate's own community/caste is exceeded by another[a]	16 (25%)	18 (25%)	16 (22%)	27 (22%)	26 (21%)	23 (19%)	20 (17%)	33 (24%)
Non-Sinhala electorates (Sinhalese forming less than 60% of the total population)	30	22	22	30	30	30	30	33
Total	95	95	95	151	151	151	150[b]	168

a Includes the cases of Muslims winning one of the two Kadugannawa seats in 1952 and 1956, one of the two Akurana seats in March 1960, July 1960, 1965 and 1970, the Galagedera seat in March and July 1960 and the Balangoda seat in 1977.
b Welimada uncontested.
Sources: GOC (1946), GOC (1959), GOSL (1976) and *CDN* (1947), *CDN* (1952), *CDN* (1956), *CDN* (1960), *CDN* (1965), *CDN* (1970) and *CDN* (1977).

relative strengths of these different patrons, and the various bases for this, in a way focussing on a political party does not. It also enables us to identify the bases of support from a very early period, before political parties had been formed.

Secondly, it enables us to study the growth of the State, and the way in which this undermined private patronage, in a way that focussing on a nationally based party does not. We can more clearly see how different State institutions emerged in particular parts of the electorate, and how this altered the local patronage networks of the area.

Thirdly, the national and international constraints restricting candidates can be more clearly identified and isolated in an electorate than in a party. This is because in an electorate we can more clearly assess the impact of world recession, inflation and national budgetary imperatives on local projects and the availability of goods and employment. The implications this has for the political sympathies of particular areas, and the ability of patrons to mobilize these sympathies, can be assessed area by area and village by village. This can be observed in an electorate in a way that focussing on a political party operating at the national level does not allow us to see.

Shortages of goods were felt by the public through the Co-operative system. After 1956 this institution became the sole official distributor of rice and basic consumer durables. After 1970, it came to be wholly State-controlled, its officials being Government appointees. Studying the Co-operative network enables us to see first, the use to which an important State body would be put in gaining or losing political support and secondly, the ways in which the nationally and internationally induced shortages of goods were felt by the public and the impact this had on political goodwill in particular areas. In choosing an institution to reflect the growth of the State, the use to which this was put, the constraints upon such use, and the political impact of such use, the Co-operative network is of prime value.

The Central Wholesale Depot of the Co-operative in Colombo sold commodities to local retail outlets, sometimes at heavily subsidized rates. These commodities were then supposed to be sold or distributed to the public on a quota or ration basis.

Meanwhile there were certain State projects in each electorate, which we have covered to some extent. Some of these were financed from the decentralized budget scheme, and each electorate's allocation was Rs 2.4 million. Some of these were financed partly from the decentralized budget, and partly from national and/or international sources. Some were financed wholly from national and/or international sources.

By focussing on more than one electorate the way in which the national standing of the parliamentary representative was able to influence the benefits secured will be shown. A senior Minister was able to secure funds for a national project in his electorate which an ordinary MP was unable to do. He was thereby able to influence the proportion of the national budget going to his electorate in a way an ordinary MP was not. However, once these proportions were decided upon, he was no more influential than an ordinary MP in deciding upon disbursement within the electorate. (This is described in Chapters 4 and 6.)

To conclude this section: in the Sri Lankan context, the bases for political allegiance can be better studied by focussing on one or more electorates than on a particular political party. This is done in the next section where the reasons for choosing these electorates are discussed.

The electorates chosen: where and why

To assess the relative importance of the identity of caste and the power of patronage in political allegiance at least two rural electorates should be chosen which are as similar as possible in terms of all variables which could possibly explain electoral support, but only different in the castes of their political leaders. In this way one can ensure that any differences in the types of leaders emerging are not due to an accident of history, or some discrepancy in the social structures prevailing in the two areas.

For this reason this study has been restricted to the Sinhalese Low Country, excluding the Tamil and Kandyan constituencies. The latter have had very different histories to the former, with far less exposure to Western influence. The caste structures prevailing there are far more hierarchical, and the patterns of economic and political patronage underpinning them are also very different. They cannot be realistically compared with the patterns of patronage operating in the Sinhalese Low Country.

Within the Low Country three electorates have been selected, two rural and one urban. One of the rural constituencies, Bluville, has been traditionally dominated by a patronizing family from the numerically minor caste, the *Karave*. It has returned a member of this family to Parliament at six of the eight legislative elections since Independence. This same member was successful in securing a majority for his party at the 1982 presidential and referendum polls as well.

The other rural constituency, Greenville, lies in a coconut-growing area. It is numerically dominated by the *Goigama* caste, and has traditionally returned members from one of two patronizing families of this caste to Parliament. Greenville is one of several constituencies studied by Jiggins.[20] By focussing on it more closely than she did, the aim is to show that, although dominated numerically by the *Goigama*, and returning a member of the caste to Parliament, this political success was due to factors other than caste identity *per se*. Economic ties of dependence through land and the *Mudaliyar* system were, as in Bluville, more important.

The third constituency, Red Town, is a suburb of Colombo. In terms of population density in 1970, the electorate as a whole was not classified

[20] Jiggins (1979), Chapter 3.

as urban or quasi-urban by Wilson.[21] However, as early as 1947 it contained more industrial ventures and a greater proportion of white- and blue-collar workers than many electorates within the large towns of the country. These characteristics were accentuated as the country developed. Thus, in terms of patronage networks contrasting with those in our rural constituencies, it is a more useful electorate to study than some of the more densely populated ones classified as urban by Wilson.

In each of our three constituencies the status and power of the dominant families of the area by 1947 have to be explained. It is then necessary to trace how the growth of the State affected this. So, focussing on the pre-Independence period is essential in explaining the patronage that prevailed thereafter. Focussing on the period 1947–56 itself is less helpful. First, little happened then to alter the patterns of dependence established earlier and secondly, there was no major extension of the State. The social and economic relationships established in the pre-Independence era continued to persist unaltered until 1956. So the events of this period itself are themselves less important for the argument than the contrast between the events of the entire pre-1956 era and those of the years after 1956.

Moreover there is a dearth of source material on the period 1947–56. This is because there were no major Government or private programmes which significantly altered the patterns of patronage disbursement in the areas, so that there is little published or unpublished material to consult. *Kachcheri* records also became more sketchy after the British withdrew, so that there is little here which covers the mundane day-to-day activities of the regions. Also, the major actors who have been interviewed are very hazy in their recollections of this early period and can say little about it.

For these practical and methodological reasons, there is relatively little on the actual events of the period 1947–56. Relatively more space has been devoted to explaining how the dominant families in these areas came to exercise the dominance they did at Independence, and then at looking at how this dominance was undermined and the bases for it changed with the growth of the State after 1956.

To sum up, this study focusses on three electorates; Bluville, Greenville and Red Town. Chapters 2, 3 and 4 cover Bluville, 5 and 6 Greenville, and 7 and 8 Red Town. Chapter 9 examines the role of communal minorities, political dissidents and the JVP insurgency in each of the three electorates. Chapter 10 summarizes and concludes the entire work.

[21] Wilson (1975), Appendix 2.

2

Bluville: the constituency and the patronage network of Doctor Ay (1947–1959)

Introduction

Bluville is a coastal electorate. In 1946 the boundaries of this constituency stretched fourteen miles along the coast and about five miles into the interior at its northernmost point.[1] It comprised parts of Grey *Pattuwa* and Purville *Korale*.[2] In 1959 the constituency was redrawn to exclude Grey *Pattuwa* and to include a larger part of Purville *Korale*.[3] The southern coastal boundary was limited to only ten miles.[4] The new northern boundary lay about eight miles into the interior.[5]

These changes are unlikely to have significantly altered the caste composition of the electorate. There may have been a slightly larger proportion of the economically dominant *Karave* (fishing) caste in 1959 (25 per cent) than in 1946 (20 per cent), but the proportion of the *Goigama* is likely to have remained about the same at 50–60 per cent. So the *Goigama* community's numerical dominance in this electorate has been maintained since Independence.

The Bluville electorate of 1946 consisted of parts of two Revenue Divisions: Grey *Pattuwa*, which accounted for just over half of the constituency's population and Purville *Korale*, which contained the remainder.[6] Each Revenue Division had, until 1938–46, been administered by a *Mudaliyar*. These *Mudaliyars* had been the most senior native officers serving in the British Provincial Administration. Their positions had often enabled them to build up considerable patronage networks in their areas of jurisdiction. These networks significantly influenced patterns of political allegiance in 1947 and after and will be examined in detail later.

The main economic activities of the people of Bluville electorate in 1947 were fishing and agriculture. There were a few large estates devoted to the cultivation of tea, rubber and coconut, and, to a lesser extent, cinnamon and citronella.[7] Paddy, of which there was about 5,000 acres in

---

[1] GOC (1946). [2] Ibid. [3] GOC (1959). [4] Ibid.
[5] Ibid. [6] GOC (1946). [7] Ferguson's (1946).

the electorate,[8] was largely a smallholder's crop and, for various ecological reasons, did not yield a significant economic return at the time. Most of the paddy (nearly 4,000 acres of it) lay in the catchment area of the Cocos River, in the east of the electorate of 1947. There were no large estates within a mile of the coast, these being largely in the interior. The best tea and rubber lay three or more miles inland. The patronage networks which operated in the interior were therefore very different from those which operated along the coastal belt. In the latter case they operated through institutions such as schools and temples, and through individuals such as fish *mudalalis* and traders, who were undermined by the reforms of 1956–65. In the interior, private patronage networks were estate-land-based and survived until the Land Reforms of 1972–5.

Evidence for the contention that the *Karave* caste was the economically and socially dominant caste at the provincial and district levels in the area by 1947 shall now be adduced. As in most other non-socialist developing and agrarian countries, the main form in which wealth was held in Sri Lanka was land. So we shall take the extent of land owned as our main index of economic dominance. Of the nineteen estates of over 500 acres belonging to Sinhalese in this province in 1940, eleven belonged to members of the *Karave* caste, two to members of the closely related *Salagama* caste, and six to members of the *Goigama* caste, whose economic dominance was more pronounced in other parts of the Island.[9] Five of the six Sinhalese-owned estates of over 1,000 acres belonged to members of the *Karave* caste, and one to a *Goigama*. There can be little doubt then that the *Karave* predominated amongst the large-scale native landowners of the province.

Further, the land owned by the *Karave* was concentrated in the hands of a few families. This was not so in the case of the other castes. Nine of the eleven *Karave* estates of over 500 acres belonged to members of four families: the Bees, Cees, Boos and Coos. Moreover all these families were closely linked to each other by marriage ties, often many times over. The Bees, who owned a total of 5,477 acres in this province alone, were linked by marriage to the Cees, the Coos and the Boos, who owned 2,591 acres, 2,686 acres and 1,735 acres, respectively. Eldy Bee's youngest sister (Amy) married Doctor Ay, a future MP and Minister, grandson of *Mudaliyar* Coo, whose largest estate, Tiger Land, comprised 870 acres. Another sister married Frani Cee who owned the Green Acre estate of 1,306 acres, and the third married Arti Dee, who was Frani Cee's first

---

[8] Readings from Ordnance Survey Maps (Survey Department, Sri Lanka, published periodically) provide details of all crop extents quoted in the book, unless otherwise stated.

[9] Ferguson's (1941) for details of landholdings, and the basis for the next five paragraphs.

cousin, and whose sister had married Sir Arthur Boo's son Robin Boo. Meanwhile, Frani Cee's daughter, Linnie, married *Mudaliyar* Coo's other grandson, Tyrrel Ay, Doctor Ay's brother. The Cees were thus linked to the Ays twice over, Frani Cee's wife being Doctor Ay's sister-in-law (Amy Bee's sister) and his daughter, Linnie, being another sister-in-law (brother Tyrrel's wife).

This was to have important implications for Doctor Ay's bases of political support over the period 1947–59 for he did not have significant landholdings in the Bluville electorate of that time and had to rely largely on the land-based networks of his in-laws. Most of his land, a half share of Tiger Land, lay in a neighbouring electorate until 1959, and what support he drew from Grey *Pattuwa* was through the Bee and Cee patronage networks.

The Boos too were closely linked to these families. Doctor Ay's aunt (father's sister) had married Sir Arthur Boo, and another uncle (father's brother), had married Sir Arthur's sister. Thus the Boos too were linked to the Ays twice over by marriage. They were linked again to the Cees, Sir Arthur's brother, Bertie, having married Frani Cee's sister Martina.

Meanwhile, the wealthy *Goigama* families of the area were far more atomistic, and not linked to each other in quite the same way. The six estates of over 500 acres in this province belonging to the *Goigama* belonged to six different families. Moreover, only two of these families were later to be linked through a marriage, and then too this was to come very late and form the only connection.

The result was that the *Karave* formed a more united economic and social bloc than the *Goigama*. There was considerably more scope for a *Karave* candidate to have utilized land-based patronage networks to garner support than for members of the *Goigama* to have done so. Even if a *Karave* candidate's immediate family did not own land in an area, there was every likelihood that his wife's or an in-law's relations did. This was not true for the *Goigama*. Indeed, because of their marriage connections, *Karave* election campaigns were often closely co-ordinated. When Doctor Ay contested Bluville in 1947 and his brother-in-law, Eldy Bee, contested a nearby electorate that year, the latter was of considerable assistance to the former.

A candidate from a leading *Karave* family, then, had a slight advantage over one from a leading *Goigama* family. When one also considers that the chief philanthropists of the province, the Bees and the Coos, were *Karave*, the considerable political leverage candidates from this background could wield (via their economic strength and social cohesion) becomes apparent.

These *Karave* families were also socially dominant at the district and provincial level in this area. The dominant *Karave* landlord was addressed by the deferential title of *Hamu-Mahatmaya* (or Revered Sir) by dependent and poorer members of all other castes, including the *Goigama*. His house was called the *Walauwwa*. And it was to this *Walauwwa* that tenants and villagers would travel to offer the traditional *bulat-hurulle* for some favour granted, or to receive blessings and gifts on festive occasions. Further, many *Karave* held, and had held, *Mudaliyar-ships*, both administrative and honorary, in this area.[10] And as Peebles had noted: 'A *Mudaliyar* would [have been] unable to [have] carried out his administrative duties, without [having had] local power and prestige. For this reason one can assume that high local status would [have been] a pre-requisite for entrance into the *Mudaliyar* system.'[11]

Some of the larger *Goigama* landlords had only emerged as economically powerful during the early years of the century.[12] Their families did not therefore enjoy the same degree of social prestige attendant on land-ownership that some of the older *Karave* families, like the Coos, did. One of the largest *Goigama* landowners in the province, Melahamy, had been a cook. He built up a friendship with *Mudaliyar* Coo, the dominant *Karave* in Bluville town, and was often invited to the latter's holiday home in Bandarawela. On such occasions, if the *Mudaliyar* were dissatisfied with the food he was served, he would often joke with Melahamy, saying that the latter should teach his cooks a lesson. Such jokes were as much an index of the social 'superiority' *Mudaliyar* Coo would have felt in Melahamy's presence as of the friendship existing between the two parties.

That *Mudaliyar* Coo enjoyed high social prestige in the locality, being the dominant patron there, was undoubted. He was always addressed by the deferential title *Hamu-Mahatmaya* by other townsfolk, including the *Goigama*. His house, 'Peace Haven', was known as the *Walauwwa* and those who passed it always removed their shawls, as a mark of respect.

The largest Buddhist vernacular school on the Island at the time, Augusta College, had been founded by him.[13] Augusta was not a fee-levying school and soon after its foundation, in 1894, many lower-caste children began attending, sitting with the others. This angered the parents of some of the higher-caste children and they sent a deputation to the *Mudaliyar's Walauwwa* to complain. The *Mudaliyar*, after listening

[10] Appointments have been checked via the Dutch Tombos and *Blue Books* in the Sri Lanka National Archives.
[11] Peebles (1973), pp. 64–5.
[12] Ferguson's (1880–1946).   [13] Abeysooriya (1928).

to the complaint, promised to rectify the matter. He instructed that a special enclosure be constructed with lower stools at which the lower castes, as well as his own daughter and a relation, should sit. When this was effected the other higher castes were amazed and accepted the lower castes immediately. Thereafter the latter were allowed to sit with the higher castes.

The fact that a deputation of parents of the higher castes had gone to the *Mudaliyar* was not simply because he was the manager and proprietor of the school. It was also an index of the high social prestige he enjoyed in the area.

Many minor conflicts arising within Bluville town went to him for arbitration. Solutions to these conflicts, as to the above school incident, could not have been effected and accepted as just by the parties involved if the *Mudaliyar* had not been the dominant patron in the locality: a patron of all castes who transcended these parochial barriers.

The above examples have been used to show that the economically and socially dominant families in the province came from the *Karave* caste. The idea of a patron–client relationship transcending caste barriers is more useful in explaining ties of dependence and the likely future bases of political allegiance than that of a caste leader and his following. This second point will become more apparent as patron–client relationships established in Bluville during the end of the nineteenth and early part of the twentieth centuries are traced.

The patronage network of *Mudaliyar* Coo and his grandson, Doctor Ay: the historical antecedents (1894–1947)

In this and the next chapter the patronage network of the two main actors in the Bluville political arena of the post-Independence era, Doctor Ay and Dee Foo, will be examined. Doctor Ay (hereafter referred to as the Doctor) is probably the more dominant of the two having held this seat for thirty-one of the forty-two years since 1947 (1947–56, 1960–70 and 1977–88). Dee Foo (hereafter referred to as Dee) captured the seat on only two occasions, 1956 and 1970. Then too he entered largely on the coat-tails of his party, these two elections having been landslides for the SLFP. Nevertheless, certainly in the earlier years, both candidates relied largely on family-based patronage networks, which had been laid during the latter part of the nineteenth and early part of the twentieth centuries.

The Doctor comes from the numerically small *Karave* caste. His community is unlikely to have accounted for more than a fifth of the electorate's population in 1946, and a quarter in 1959, and these are liberal estimates. However, his grandfather, *Mudaliyar* Coo, was the dominant patron in Bluville town and a part of the network of leading *Karave* landowning families of the province, as described earlier. He owned over a thousand acres in the district and his brothers too were large landowners.[14]

The *Mudaliyar* was noted most for his various philanthropic activities. On numerous occasions when natural calamities had struck he had rendered assistance to those affected. When a village, about a mile from Bluville town, had been flooded in 1889, he had rushed food, clothing and provisional shelter to the area. Later he had constructed a bridge to prevent a similar occurrence and loss of life. In addition, he had constructed and financed two schools and a hospital in the area. Throughout his lifetime he had made a number of contributions both in cash and kind to institutions and individuals in need. One writer speaking of the *Mudaliyar* in 1928 described most of 'his benefactions [as being] carried on with a secrecy [and] not known to the public'. The *Mudaliyar*'s philanthropy and popularity within Bluville were such that after his death in 1943 a local legend emerged of his having been reborn as a god and of his visiting the largest temple in Bluville town which he had patronized. He is still remembered with affection in the area.

The patronage networks the *Mudaliyar* created and sustained, as augmented by other *Karave* relations, provided the main sources of political support for his grandson, the Doctor, in future years. These networks rested on four main institutions: (1) the schools, (2) the temples, (3) the local notables and (4) the estates. Each of these institutions will be examined in turn.

The schools

Mudaliyar Coo founded two schools, Augusta College in Bluville town, and a girls' school in Okerville, about four miles further east along the coast. Of these, Augusta College was the larger, and more famous. Indeed, as late as 1928, it was the largest vernacular school on the Island. It was formed at a time when Christian missionaries were founding schools all over the Island to propagate their own religion, and was designed in many ways to cater to the indigenous Sinhala Buddhist population. Teaching was in Sinhala and the imparting of a Buddhist

14 Ferguson's (1941).

education was regarded as a major part of the school's functions by the *Mudaliyar*. Consequently it was welcomed by the Sinhala Buddhist inhabitants of the area.

The *Mudaliyar* financed the construction and the maintenance of the school, meeting the salaries of the teachers and the minor staff out of his own pocket. Quite apart from the popularity these measures earned him, the school offered a very real means of building up a support base for himself and his family; a support base which was to embrace all castes and communities of the area. By 1940, the school had over 2,000 students coming from up to ten miles in the interior. The *Mudaliyar*, who personally managed the school until his death in 1943, and then his grandson, the Doctor, had the final say in the choice of subjects taught, and the emphasis to be given to factors like the role of their family in the history of the area. Their economic and social leadership of the region was thereby given a moral sanction.

Moreover, the wide geographical spread from which teachers came gave the Doctor contacts in villages he may otherwise have had little influence in. For instance, a *Goigama* teacher at Augusta College was also secretary of the rural development society of his home village, where the Doctor's family was not all that influential in its own right. The teacher was able to use this position to build up a support base for his patron in the area, even getting the society to organize election meetings there.

At election time the teachers and older students could be used to help in the campaign: canvassing, distributing leaflets, addressing mail, sticking up posters and the like. In 1947 the school played a key role in generating support for the Doctor. In 1952 and 1956 some teachers worked against him, clandestinely. But the very fact that they behaved in such an underhand and insincere manner, distributing leaflets as instructed on the one hand, but speaking against him in private on the other, meant their losing respect and influence in their localities. The fact that because of his personal wealth the Doctor was able to continue patronizing the schools, temples and local notables in the area, even after his defeat in 1956, was a key factor in his political comeback in March 1960.

Augusta College, like other private schools, was taken over by the Government in 1962, and thereafter could not be used to generate political support, in the way it had been used earlier. Government teachers for instance are debarred from taking part in political campaigns. However, a portrait of the *Mudaliyar* and one of his wife still hang in the main hall of Augusta College, and to this day young students know the part he played in initiating Buddhist education in the area; and the Doctor of course benefits through the goodwill generated.

The temples

The main temple in Bluville town is the Bluville Temple, founded in the eleventh century, and renovated and financially assisted by *Mudaliyar* Coo. The *Mudaliyar*, and later other members of his family, were the *Chief-Dayakayas* of this temple. They saw to its upkeep, the *Mudaliyar* constructing a new Preaching Hall and meeting the day-to-day needs of the priests. They also managed the lands which they had gifted to it.

The fact that the temple did not own extensive land in its own right, as many of the Kandyan religious institutions did, had two important implications for the political influence it could wield. First, the priests could not, and would not, pursue a role independent of that of the *Mudaliyar* in any political conflict, let alone oppose his grandson in an election. This was because, owning little land and having even this managed by the *Mudaliyar*'s family, they were heavily dependent on the latter for their day-to-day needs. Moreover, as there were no other wealthy *Dayakayas* in Bluville town, the priests had little scope to play upon any intra-*Dayakaya* friction for their own ends, as in Red Town. They were almost totally dependent on the *Mudaliyar*, even their promotions having to receive his ratification.

The second major political implication of the Bluville Temple not owning extensive paddy land, as the Kandyan temples did, was that its scope for antagonizing tenants, on the lines described by Evers, and thus losing public goodwill, was circumscribed.[15] Instead, the priests of the Bluville Temple provided free Sunday school education, *ayurvedic* services for the poor, and facilities for meetings of the local rural development societies. These latter bodies were formed largely on local initiative and that of the head priest of the temple in the area, and incorporated a number of youths who cleared jungle lands, constructed rough roads, and performed other such acts of public service. The priests of this temple then were regarded as public servants, rather than as social parasites, as those of the Lankatilleke *Maha-Vihara* (described by Evers),[16] or indeed those of Red Town, were. They were regarded with affection and respect, rather than hatred and distrust. Consequently, their scope for generating goodwill amongst the local inhabitants was enhanced. They were to be a useful support base for the *Mudaliyar*'s grandson, the Doctor, when he contested the Bluville seat in 1947 and subsequently.

There were two smaller temples constructed by the *Mudaliyar* in the area, which were to prove important support bastions for the Doctor.

[15] Evers (1972).   [16] Ibid.

The first was on the western outskirts of Bluville town. The second, close to his largest estate, Tiger Land, lay outside the Bluville electorate until 1959, when the second delimitation occurred. But, in the meantime, the Doctor and his grandfather consistently supported these three institutions. Every *Wesak* about two to three thousand of the poor would be fed at these centres, and after the election of 1947 Government funds were used to expand these activities.

The three temples patronized by the *Mudaliyar* catered to all castes in the locality, but the priests were drawn from the *Karave* caste. There were two temples, one in Bluville town, and another about three miles north, which were of the *Siam Nikaya*, where the priests were drawn exclusively from the *Goigama* caste. These two temples had been patronized by the Foo family. However, the latter not being as wealthy as the Coos, nor as generous, did not match their bounty, and these two temples had to survive without electricity for a long while. Their priests were also envious of the priests of the Bluville Temple as the latter had electricity and better accommodation and toilet facilities than they did. Consequently, they have traditionally supported the Foos against the Coos.

The third main support base on which the Doctor relied consisted of a number of local notables. These notables could often deliver blocs of votes in their areas. However, after 1956, with the extension of various State institutions which cut into their power bases, their influence was undermined. The first set of local notables described are the fish *mudalalis*.

The local notables

The fish mudalalis[17]

The fish *mudalalis* used to buy fish from the fishermen, have it frozen and packed, and then despatched to their retail outlets in other parts of the Island. The *mudalalis*' chief power lay in the quasi-monopoly they wielded in the fish market. Generally there was only one fish *mudalali* in a fishing hamlet and he was the only man the fishermen could sell their produce to. Where there were two or more *mudalalis* they almost always acted in concert. The fishermen did not have the capital to pack, transport and market their produce; only the *mudalali* had. Consequently he

---

[17] Alexander (1982) portrays the fish *mudalalis* as being slightly less powerful than they are portrayed here. This is partly because of the different climatic and agro-ecological background of Gahavalla. The continuous year-round rain there precludes a migratory season, and so undermines the scope for the fish *mudalali* to exert the sort of influence as he does in Bluville.

could deliver a whole bloc of votes in his village merely by the implicit threat of refraining to purchase the fish caught by the villagers.

The *mudalali* also wielded control through being the sole source of credit for the fishermen and by maintaining the latter in a perpetual state of indebtedness. However, after the formation and extension of the People's Bank in 1961 this power was circumscribed.

During the period of the South West Monsoon, between April and August, fishing in outrigger non-mechanized boats was difficult. The *mudalali* could then persuade fishermen to migrate to the eastern coast where fishing was easier during this period. He would provide the fishermen with the transport in lorries overland to the Eastern Province, a fishing camp on the coast, a daily supply of food to it and a cash advance (often with a small bonus at the end of the period) in return for the fishermen selling their produce to him at a pre-arranged price. The fishermen, whilst in the Eastern Province, would often spend heavily on novel consumer goods from the area, for personal and commercial use: rush mats, hand-woven sarongs and sarees, honey, paddy and dried venison. Being relatively short of cash the fishermen would turn to the *mudalali* to finance their spending spree and so by the end of the period in August they would be heavily indebted to him. This was therefore an inducement for them to work for the same *mudalali* during the following season.

In this manner each fish *mudalali* could create a personal clientele of fishermen around himself; a clientele which looked to him for leadership on many issues, and over many years. This leadership was augmented in other ways. Many *mudalalis* were relatively generous, giving credit on easy terms to those in dire need, and helping clients with cash gifts at funerals and weddings. Again, they would generally pay a handsome compensation if one of the fishermen who depended on them were killed or seriously wounded in an accident, especially if it had occurred when they had gone on an informal contract to fish for the *mudalali* in the Eastern Province. In this way their economic control over these fishermen received a softening veneer. The bond was not excessively exploitative and exhibited a strong flavour of paternalist condescension. It was often reinforced by ties of kinship between the *mudalali* and his clients. Thus the *mudalali* was able to exercise a moral as well as economic leadership over his clients. At elections he could deliver whole blocs of votes, sometimes numbering a few hundreds, to the candidates of his choice.

This choice was the Doctor, not because of any caste affinity the *mudalalis* had with him (for many of them were *Goigama* and *Durave*), but because of the patronage networks established by his grandfather and in-laws. The Bees had built two temples in their home town, a largely *Durave* area. They had also helped finance another temple and a *Devale* nearby. The priests in these temples were able to wield political influence on behalf of the Doctor, on the lines those of the Bluville Temple did, though not on the same scale, because of their smaller size. The Bees had also founded a school in the area, which had benefited the local fisher-men. *Mudaliyar* Coo had founded a temple in the area and the school he had built in Bluville town, Augusta College, had improved the edu-cational prospects of the progeny of the local fishermen. The *Mudaliyar* had also built a girls' school in Okerville, about four miles east of Bluville town, with similar effects. Though this village lay outside the electorate until the delimitation of 1959, it provided an important source of imper-sonators. Several families from Okerville registered themselves im-properly in Bluville and others came and voted in the names of deceased individuals.

In the early elections of 1947, 1952 and 1956, it was these coastal villages which formed the important bastions of the Doctor's support. And, of the coastal villages, those which had been patronized by the Doctor's family networks tended to give more support than those which had not been so directly affected. Some of these villages had sizeable blocs of non-*Karave* fishermen, and the Doctor drew their support irrespective of caste.

The Doctor tended to appeal to the fish *mudalalis*, who then delivered blocs of votes in their villages. The fish *mudalalis* and the richer fisher-men had been the first to benefit from the generosity of the Bees and Coos. After all it was their children who could most easily afford the clothes, sandals, textbooks and the time to attend the schools founded by these families. The poorer sections were unable to afford these items for a long time to come, and indeed free textbooks were not issued until 1978.

Having benefited from the bounty of these families, the fish *mudalalis* anticipated even further gains, if one of their representatives (like the Doctor in 1947) could get into Parliament. They therefore worked very hard on his behalf, organizing gangs to escort villagers to the polls, instructing them where to place their 'cross' on the ballot paper and supervising the whole operation. Many villagers were ignorant of the voting procedure in 1947 and even in 1952.

These *mudalalis* believed that the Doctor would be appointed to the Government, and therefore expected him to be in a position to reward them for the support they had given him. In the event, he was given a number of junior ministries and finally a ministry in the early 1950s.

The Doctor was able to use these positions to help the *mudalalis* (who had delivered him their bloc vote) in various ways. During the early period (1947–56), and especially after 1952, he was able to construct roads in the area, introduce electricity, and also found post-offices, schools, maternity centres and a base hospital (1951). Such public utilities were of particular benefit to local notables such as the fish *mudalalis*. After all, when electricity and piped water were introduced into these areas, it was they who could most easily afford these for their houses; not the poorer sections to whom these services were still luxuries. Similarly, new tarred roads had their greatest impact on the *mudalalis*, reducing their fish transport costs, but had a relatively marginal effect on the poorer sections. Again the introduction of outboard motors and nylon nets instead of cotton benefited the richer fishermen and *mudalalis* first.

The Doctor also helped the fish *mudalalis* in a number of informal ways; arranging bank loans and facilitating matters if they fell out with the police. Many of these fish *mudalalis*, like other minor notables of the area, had gangs of thugs which would be used to enforce their wishes, recover debts, or whatever. They were therefore frequently in conflict with the law. Indeed, one of the most influential had once gone to jail for attempting to shoot a person. The Doctor was a powerful figure who could help them out in such situations.

The Doctor's family had a long tradition of patronizing these fish *mudalali* families; a tradition which the Doctor continued after his advent to office. These *mudalalis* in turn had a long tradition of patronizing their own villages. This was effected essentially through their quasi-monopsony in the fish trade and their quasi-monopoly of local credit and augmented by various acts of kindness. With the development of the Fisheries' Corporation and, more significantly, the People's Bank after 1961, their economic control was undermined, and their political influence circumscribed. But in the meantime, during these early years, they could, and did, deliver whole blocs of votes in their villages to their one patron, the Doctor.

The small landowners

Amongst the local notables there were a number of small landowners who could deliver blocs of votes. The number of votes they could carry, however, by virtue of their being small landowners, was limited. This was because large landowners controlled much greater blocs of votes than the small. Thus, where there were small landowners in the vicinity of the large, the influence of the latter swamped that of the former. Further, small landowners tended to be much more commercial in their attitude to the management and cultivation of their properties than large landowners did, thereby sacrificing the goodwill of the villagers in their area. Whereas a large landowner may have given the workers on his estate various fringe benefits, and even allowed the landless villagers in the area to take, say, coconut palms for thatch or husks for firewood, free of charge, the small landowner was unlikely to have allowed this. Thus a small landowner was often less popular in his locality than a large one.

But if a small landowner had the capital and was carrying on a subsidiary activity, such as coir processing or cinnamon oil production, he could exert some influence. For instance, in one area there was a certain small landowner who used to purchase coconut husk from small-holders and process this into coir products, such as mats, brooms or whatever. He would also purchase the cinnamon leaf from village gardens, distil this, and extract cinnamon oil. He was able to do this because he was the only man in the locality who had the capital to purchase and maintain the necessary stills.

There were other individuals who did likewise in areas which had been patronized by *Mudaliyar* Coo. Such individuals, like the fish *mudalalis*, were tied into the families' patronage networks and anticipated material gains for themselves and their clients if they were to support the Doctor. Consequently, they delivered him whole blocs of votes. They were able to do this because many villagers depended on them for loans, employment, purchase of their products and intermediation with the local administration.

The small landowner was often the only source of appropriate credit in the area. For many years (even after the formation of the People's Bank in 1961) credit failed to reach the small farmer, defined as owning less than two acres of paddy. This was because of insufficient liaison between him and the bank officers, his lack of knowledge about the facilities available and the procedure to obtain and repay loans, and, most important, the failure of the banks to provide loans at the precise time he needed them.[18] The small farmer generally needed money urgently at certain crucial stages of the production cycle, if his crop was not to be lost. He preferred to borrow at exorbitant rates from the local money lender, who was often a leading small-scale landowner in the area, to getting a cheaper loan from the bank after a long delay, if this was going to mean risking the loss of his crop.[19] Thus, long after the formation of the People's Bank in 1961, the small landowner continued to exercise some influence through his control of credit.

Meanwhile the ecological structure of the Bluville electorate and the economic activities pursued there were such that the scope for certain subsidiary activities, and so the emergence of influential small

[18] Tennekoon (1980).   [19] Ibid.

landowners, was severely limited. In another part of the province, for example, the more fertile and rain-fed terrain had enabled many small landowners to produce cinnamon oil and copra. They bought the raw material direct from the villagers for a pittance and processed it for sale at a good price. Many were also involved in rice ration book pawnbroking. They lent the poorer villagers money in return for their ration books, collected the rice and then, by cornering the market, resold it at highly inflated prices.

Such activities gave an enterprising politician great scope for creating goodwill. In the part of the province described, the president of the local Multi-Purpose Co-operative Society (MPCS) from 1954 to 1956, broke into these trades. He initiated a policy of purchasing coconut husk, coir and cinnamon leaf at relatively reasonable prices directly from the villagers, and processing it himself. The MPCS also extended loans to fishermen, brickmakers and vegetable producers, impairing the local money lender's monopoly of credit. It entered the rice ration book business too, extending loans in return for the books, but on easier terms. At the same time the existing pawnbrokers were raided and their rice ration book hoards confiscated. In this way the local money lender's economic stranglehold over the villager was undermined.

In Bluville, however, these activities had never been as prevalent as in the area described. Even where they were pursued, many villagers had sources of subsistence other than those secured through the local notables. Thus the latter's control was less marked than in the area described. The scope for a politician to break into such activities, thereby creating goodwill, was consequently circumscribed.

Meanwhile the small landowner was also generally less influential than the coastal fish *mudalali*. This was because his clients generally had alternative sources of subsistence and were not as heavily dependent on him for their livelihoods. Even if he refrained from purchasing their coconut husks, they could subsist through consuming and selling their vegetable produce, paddy, or whatever. The small landowner's monopolistic control over his clients was less than that of the fish *mudalali* and his political influence correspondingly more limited.

The small landowner, where he was influential, was influential by virtue of his control of credit and capital or, more significantly, the local headmanships. If not the headman, he was almost invariably closely related to him. As such, he had access to the local administration and this gave him considerable scope for building up a clientele in the area. The small landowner could by virtue of a headmanship (or links with the headman) influence 1,000 or more voters though, by virtue of his landholding and personal wealth alone, he would have been unable to have influenced more than twenty to thirty or so voters. But as a headman he came under the patronage network of *Korale-Mudaliyar* Foo and so tended to support Dee against the Doctor. His role in this context will therefore be examined in the next chapter.

But, even then, the influence of headmen was limited in the region of the large estates. In the Tiger Land estate area although a certain village headman worked against the Doctor for many years he was unable to deliver Dee many votes. Even then, the little influence he did exert was by virtue of his headmanship, his control over land not being a factor at all.

Thus in Bluville the small landowning notable's scope to exert influence by virtue of his landholding was limited. This was because the agro-ecological and economic structure of the electorate circumscribed the number and scope of activities pursued by such notables, and also meant the dominance of the larger estates. As such, what influence the small landholder did wield was by virtue of his access to the local headmanships and the provincial administration. This administration was supervised by *Korale-Mudaliyar* Foo, so that those in it came within his patronage network. As such the small landowners who were village headmen were by and large more important in supporting Dee than the Doctor. They were never as significant a support base for the latter as the fish *mudalalis*, estate staff and, to a lesser extent, the priests and teachers.

The bus magnates

Another set of local influentials who supported the Doctor was the bus magnates. These individuals owned fleets of buses and had the monopoly of public motor transport on the roads. Until the 1930s magnates had competed with each other on given routes. But, thereafter, one company was given the monopoly over, and restricted to, a particular area. In some cases these companies were owned by single individuals and in others by groups of former magnates who had operated in the area previously.

In the Bluville region, the dominant bus magnate was a certain Mr Gou. He exercised influence partially through his monopoly of public (road) transport and the fact that he could generate goodwill by giving fare concessions to priests and school children. But the chief factor in his influence was the manpower his bus company offered him. He had over 2,000 employees in his control (if those working in his garages were included), and these men could be used to work at election time for any candidate he supported. These bus workers were notorious for the often crude and brutal methods they used, assaulting rival candidates, disrupting election meetings and threatening those who offered hospitality to UNP opponents.

The Doctor himself, like many of the other candidates, never condoned such activities. Indeed he always acted in a very fair and gentlemanly fashion towards his opponents. However, at the village level, many of the intermediaries he operated through, including the fish *mudalalis*, often used heavy-handed means of generating support. Such tactics sometimes backfired. When, in 1947, an Opposition politician, campaigning for his party's candidate in a neighbouring electorate, appeared on an election platform, bearing the wounds of an assault (by Gou's thugs), it aroused a wave of popular sympathy for him.

The influence these bus magnates wielded was generally contingent on the degree of unionization within their companies. Some magnates who faced weak unions continued to be influential until 1957, when their companies were nationalized. But in Gou's case, the Communists penetrated the ranks of his workforce soon after the 1947 Election; so much so that on one occasion in 1951 they assaulted their employer himself. Gou was unable to use his workforce as a political weapon in 1952, as he had been able to in 1947.

It should be noted that the bus magnates were generally fairly wealthy individuals in their own right. Gou for instance did not depend upon *Mudaliyar* Coo and fall into his patronage network, in the way the fish *mudalalis* and certain small notables did. His support for the Doctor was largely due to the latter belonging to a political party, the UNP, which would have protected his business interests. When (after 1956) these interests were better served by supporting the SLFP, he switched to the latter.

The estates

The fourth main support base on which the Doctor relied was the large estates owned by his wife and in-laws. As only a part of his largest holding, Tiger Land, lay in the Bluville electorate until the delimitation of 1959, and as during this early period (1947–59) he relied heavily on the patronage networks of his in-laws, his family's links with the Bees and the Cees will first be briefly examined.

An alliance between the Bees and the Coos had been discussed as early as the 1920s. There had been efforts to arrange a match between the Doctor's sister, Dotty, and *Muhandiram* Bee's eldest son, Eldy, in 1922. The Bees were keen on the match but, for certain reasons, *Mudaliyar* Coo forestalled it. The objections raised to this marriage did not preclude

another alliance however. In 1936 the Doctor married Eldy Bee's youngest sister, Amy, and in 1945 his brother Tyrrel married another sister's
daughter, Linnie.

Linnie's father's family, the Cees, owned the 1,306-acre Green Acre
estate which lay on the north-western edge of the old Bluville electorate.
The estate employed nearly 2,000 people. As the family was wealthy it
was able to offer the estate employees a number of fringe benefits which
smaller landowning groups would have been unable to: free coconuts
(although tea and rubber were the main crops grown), repairs to houses,
permission to keep a cow on the estate and cultivate a small garden,
(later) assistance with books and clothes to school children, festival
allowances, medical facilities and the like. This generated popular goodwill towards the family. So when Frani Cee's daughter's brother-in-law,
the Doctor, contested the Bluville seat, he was able to draw heavily on
this goodwill.

Another large estate in this area, comprising 452 acres, and belonging
to the Doctor's wife's first cousin operated on much the same principles
as Green Acre and was also able to offer considerable support.

The adult dependents of the workers from these two estates would
have been able to vote. If they too are counted we could estimate that the
area would have delivered well over 2,000 of the 11,000-odd votes the
Doctor secured in 1947. The Doctor and some of his close associates
assert that at this election they secured over nine-tenths of the votes from
this area, and a proportion almost as high in 1952 and 1956; this despite
the area having been almost solidly *Goigama*, with a negligible proportion of the Doctor's own *Karave* community.

Given however that these estate workers lay within the patronage
network of the Doctor's relations, their voting for him was not surprising. There were no other large estates in the area representing alternative
sources of land-based patronage. The large size of these estates relative to
others in the area was, then, one factor in the magnitude of their
influence.

The second factor lay in the types of crops grown: tea and rubber.
First, these were highly labour intensive. Whereas one can operate a
fifty-acre coconut holding with about three men, a tea or rubber estate of
this size would require seventy-five to 100. Thus a large estate like Green
Acre, devoted to tea and rubber, generated considerably more employment, and so potential votes, than holdings of a similar size in say
Greenville, devoted to coconut. Secondly, tea and rubber require a
highly disciplined, permanent workforce, unlike coconut which requires
periodic labour. Whereas coconut requires a lot of labour only every two

months for manuring and picking, tea and rubber require a force working continuously every day and throughout the year. The labourers on a
tea or rubber estate were then permanent employees and they were
therefore more dependent on their employer, the landowner, than villagers who worked casually for a coconut estate owner. Consequently, the
type of control a tea or rubber estate owner could exercise over his
employees was more vigorous and thorough than a coconut estate owner,
with the same acreage under cultivation, could wield.

The Superintendent, his assistant and *Kanganies* ensured a good
attendance at the early morning muster on polling day. They then
instructed their workers on voting procedure, telling them where to
place their 'cross'. The last time such voting had taken place had been
twelve years previously in 1935, so that most of the older voters would
have forgotten the procedure and the younger never partaken in it. They
were marched off in batches to vote at their respective booths and this
operation was supervised by another estate administrator. Support for
the Doctor from these areas was thereby assured. Such support would
have been more difficult to organize on a coconut estate, where most
labourers would not have been permanent employees.

The only opposition to the Doctor may have been from a very few
small landowners in this area. These landowners may have felt that the
large estates were pampering workers who would otherwise have worked
for them for lesser wages in cash or kind. But opposition was numerically
negligible and politically insignificant. The Doctor was able to carry the
area in 1947, 1952 and 1956 because his wife's relations had been
benevolent landlords and at the same time exercised a tight organizational control over their labour force.

However, it should be stressed that such organizational control was
unlikely to have altered the way in which individuals would have voted
once in the polling booth. In other words, it is unlikely that individuals
were forced to vote against their wishes. Rather, many workers did not
understand the voting procedure and may not have bothered to have
turned up at the polling booth if they had not been organized by the
estate administration. But ordinarily they would have supported their
master due to the benevolence his family had shown them. This can be
seen by the fact that in 1977, even after Land Reform, the Tiger Land
area, which had been patronized by *Mudaliyar* Coo, voted overwhelmingly for the Doctor. This was despite the family having lost three-
quarters of its land there.

There are a few other isolated areas where the Doctor's relations
owned land: Elephant Walk, a 190-acre estate owned by his father's first

cousin, and Ant Hill a 321-acre coconut and paddy group north of Okerville, owned by his own cousins, the Hous.[20]

However, these estates were on the whole much smaller than those of the Bees, the Cees and the Coos. Moreover the crops grown did not generate as much employment, or give the same degree of influence, as tea or rubber did. For instance, a large proportion of both these estates was devoted to coconut. The fifty acres of coconut in Elephant Walk would not have employed more than three to five people, whereas fifty acres of rubber would have employed 75 to 100.

Further, coconut lands invited intrusions and thefts in a way tea and rubber lands did not. In the case of tea or rubber, the product, green leaf or latex, had to be processed using special machinery involving skilled labour not available to the ordinary villager before it could be consumed or sold. Coconuts on the other hand could be plucked straight from the tree and consumed or sold by any untrained villager, without having to be processed using special machinery or skilled labour. Consequently it was quite common, especially in densely populated areas such as Ant Hill, to have villagers intruding and stealing coconuts; a phenomenon which did not occur in the case of the large tea and rubber estates in relatively secluded areas, owned by the Bees and the Coos. The Hous took a very harsh approach to such intrusions and thefts, punishing culprits severely. This lost them goodwill in the area. Indeed the Communist Party was able to penetrate Ant Hill (which would otherwise have been a stronghold of the Doctor) during the 1950s and 1960s, largely because the Hous had been relatively harsh landlords there.

The type of exchange relationship between the landowning patron and his client also had implications for the extent to which political support could be generated. Unlike tea, rubber and coconut, paddy land was generally leased out on an *ande* (crop sharing) basis to tenant cultivators. The Hous' 135 acres of paddy in Ant Hill were leased out in this manner. This meant that there was considerable scope for bitterness and conflict between patrons and client tenants over what was regarded as the latter's fair share of the crop. This scope for bitterness did not exist in the case of tea, rubber and coconut holdings. The Paddy Lands Act of 1958 limited the patron-owner's share of the produce to a quarter, but field studies show that in most areas tenants continued to pay well over half.[21] In many cases this was due to fear of eviction, though in some cases owners compensated by providing 'collateral help' in the form of other inputs.[22] However, in the Colombo District over a quarter (28 per cent) of the

---

[20] Ferguson's (1941).   [21] ARTI (1975).   [22] Ibid.

tenants paying a half share of the produce felt that the rent they paid was excessive, and the proportion of tenants who thought this rose as the quantum of collateral help offered declined.[23] There was little likelihood of tenants feeling well disposed towards relatively harsh landlords such as the Hous. Consequently, the scope of the latter to generate support for the Doctor by arousing 'goodwill' was limited.

Further, as their tenants did not form a cohesive well-disciplined labour force in the way those working on the Bee, Cee and Coo tea and rubber estates did, they could not organize and deliver their votes in the way these landowners could. Moreover, as the Hous were often out of Okerville and did not maintain a close personal face-to-face relationship with their tenants, they could not identify the latter easily and intimidate them into voting for the candidate of their choice, as the fish *mudalalis* could.

The influence of these relations in generating support for the Doctor by virtue of their having been landowners is therefore likely to have been very limited. They owned relatively small extents in areas where many others owned estates as large as, or sometimes larger than, their own; and these large landowners were patrons in their own right.

Moreover, the local headman was often more influential than the medium-sized (coconut) landowner. For instance, although the Elephant Walk estate supported the Doctor, the village headmen of the area, who fell within the patronage network of *Korale-Mudaliyar* Foo, opposed him. Their influence proved considerable as the area has traditionally given Dee more support than the Doctor.

We have seen, then, that during the period 1947–59 the main areas from which the Doctor received estate support were Green Acre and a small part of Tiger Land. In 1959, the Bluville electorate's boundaries were redrawn and Grey *Pattuwa*, in which Green Acre fell, was excluded.[24] Instead, the more northern and eastern parts of Purville *Korale* were incorporated. This meant that the area in which the Bees' 674-acre Wild Land estate and the Doctor's own 870-acre Tiger Land group fell were incorporated. Thus, after 1959, what estate support the Doctor drew was largely from this area.

Mudaliyar Coo, and later the Doctor and his brother, Tyrrel, had been very generous landlords, offering their workers a number of fringe benefits similar to those given on Green Acre. Moreover, they took an almost paternal interest in their labour force. Tyrrel and his wife ran a dispensary and milk feeding centre for their workers on the estate. If

---

[23] Ibid.
[24] GOC (1946), GOC (1959), Ferguson's (1958) and a study of Ordnance Survey Maps form the basis for this paragraph.

specialized medical treatment were required, they would offer free transport and meet any necessary expenses at the closest general hospitals. Such a personal interest on the part of an estate owner in his workers was very rare. The latter generally needed a letter from the estate dispensary certifying that it did not have the necessary drugs and/or facilities for their treatment before they could be admitted to a general hospital. As the estate dispensaries received State grants, they were generally unwilling to admit being poorly stocked. Thus securing a letter from them, let alone travelling to the district general hospital, was difficult for most.

Meanwhile the villagers in the Tiger Land area had benefited from *Mudaliyar* Coo's generosity. He had built a temple for them, constructed roads in the vicinity and given them donations in cash and kind during periods of misfortune. Moreover, the school and other institutions he had founded in Bluville town had benefited these villagers as much as it had those in other parts of the area. Further, the two other large estates in the vicinity, although *Goigama*-owned, belonged to friends of the *Mudaliyar*. They never worked against the Doctor. Indeed, the Superintendent of one, and a grandson of the owner, was to campaign actively on the Doctor's behalf in 1965. Meanwhile, as tea and rubber were the main crops grown, discipline over the labour force and the delivery of votes was easy to effect.

This area, then, which was predominantly *Goigama*, has, since its incorporation into the electorate in 1959, been a significant support base of the Doctor's. The latter, and some of his election agents, estimates that it has consistently given over nine-tenths of its votes to him. As late as 1977 fully a fifth of the Doctor's votes came from this area alone.

We have seen, then, that caste *per se* played relatively little part in explaining the political allegiance of an area. What did explain this was first, the degree of control exercised over individuals by various patrons and secondly, the relative strength of these patrons in their particular area. This in turn was determined largely by the size of landholding and the nature of the crop grown.

Sometimes patronage networks clashed. In one area, for instance, the Doctor's influence, through the ownership of a small plot of land, was rivalled by *Korale-Mudaliyar* Foo's network of village headmen. The Doctor's family owned a 25-acre coconut block there. The family was relatively generous, allowing villagers living in the vicinity to use palm leaves for thatch, husk for firewood, and to cultivate subsidiary crops and graze their cattle on the land. On festive occasions they even allowed some villagers quotas of the nuts themselves. However the villagers living further away from the estate, who did not benefit from this generosity, were more influenced by their headmen. For reasons to be

elaborated later, these headmen came under the patronage network of
Korale-Mudaliyar Foo. Consequently the area has tended to support
Dee.

Sometimes a political leader, weak in a particular area, tried to use the
minor influentials in neighbouring areas under his patronage to establish
a bridgehead in the locality and build up a support base for himself there.
The Joland episode illustrates this. Joland was an eight-acre plot of land
behind *Mudaliyar* Coo's house in Bluville town. The town was by and
large for the Doctor, having benefited significantly from his grandfather's bounty, the school and temple particularly. The inhabitants of
Joland had benefited from these institutions too, and also in other special
ways. *Mudaliyar* Coo had constructed a well for their use, assisted them
with their cultivation and a conversion of a part of their grass field to
paddy land, and given them handsome gifts in cash and kind during
times of need. The area was a strong support base of the Doctor's, but a
village headman who lived some distance away supported *Mudaliyar*
Foo. In 1947, the *Korale-Mudaliyar* tried to use this headman to establish
contacts with the villagers of Joland and to campaign for his nominee,
Joo. But this attempt failed dismally when he was driven out of the area.
The incident reveals the way in which one faction, the *Korale-Mudaliyar*'s, attempted, albeit unsuccessfully, to penetrate a locality dominated by its opponent using a bridgehead (the village headman), which it
had there.

We have seen how in this early period (1947–59), when most of the
estates owned by the Doctor's family fell outside the then Bluville
electorate, he relied heavily on the land-based patronage networks of his
in-laws. But it was not only through estate labour that these relations
were able to help.

The Bees were undoubtedly the premier family of Grey *Pattuwa*. They
had built, and continued to finance, the largest school in the area. They
had also built, and continued to patronize, a number of temples in this
part of the province.

More significantly, Eldy Bee, the Doctor's brother-in-law, had
founded, and until 1962 continued to lead, the local District Buddhist
Education Society. This institution managed thirty-four Sinhala and
four English schools in the area and, at the time of the 1962 takeover,
accounted for over 20,000 students and 500 qualified teachers. Eldy Bee
had also established a network of *Dharma* schools, designed to spread
Buddhism.

The political influence he could and did wield through these schools
and temples on behalf of his brother-in-law, the Doctor, during the

period 1947–59, was considerable. The precise way in which such influence was exerted was similar to the way it was exerted by *Mudaliyar* Coo's schools and temples. The Bees also owned shops in several townships in Grey *Pattuwa*, which they leased out to traders.

Through their ownership and control of these shops, schools and temples, they exerted political influence over a number of intermediaries to whom the ordinary villagers tended to be under obligation: in particular, traders who were tenants of the Bees who sold on credit, fish *mudalalis*, who benefited from the schools and temples built there, the teachers in their schools and the priests in their temples. However, neither the traders, teachers nor the priests could deliver as many votes as certainly as the fish *mudalalis* and estates could. Nevertheless, the patronage networks operated in a manner similar to those in Bluville town itself.

Conclusion

In this chapter it has been argued that, politically, the important dimension of social stratification in this province was that between a patron, his intermediaries and his clients. A patron was generally a large landowner having holdings of over about 500 acres, covering two or more districts. His family intermarried with those of equivalent status often from other districts and sometimes from other provinces as well. He was often a major philanthropist at the provincial and district levels. The intermediaries whom he consulted in the dispensation of patronage (and later the garnering of political support) had more circumscribed spheres of influence. They were small-scale landowners, seldom owning more than twenty-five acres or so, estate superintendents, traders, teachers, priests and fish *mudalalis*. They were dominant at the village level having several clients dependent on them and often monopolizing headmanships. But their landholdings or fishing operations were generally restricted to their own village and their administrative jurisdiction likewise circumscribed. Despite marrying those of equivalent elite status from other villages, their ties seldom cut across district or provincial lines. Their spheres of influence were therefore more circumscribed than those of their patrons. The final set of actors were their clients, the landless or near landless villagers, the estate workers and the ordinary fishermen who constituted the large mass of voters, dependent on the intermediaries and larger scale patrons in varying degrees.

We have argued that the dominant patronizing families in the region came from the *Karave* caste and that their clients came from all castes including the *Goigama*. It has thereby been shown that politically the patron–client tie was the most important dimension of social stratification, and as this tie cut across caste lines, caste itself was not important as a dimension of social stratification.

We have gone on to argue that this patron–client tie provided the basis for political allegiance in 1947 and thereafter. A patron tended to be surrounded by members of his own caste, as *Mudaliyar* Coo was in Bluville, so that he could carry this vote easily. But where he had landholdings in, say, *Goigama* areas such as that surrounding the Green Acre and Tiger Land estates, he could just as easily garner this support. Thus although the patron–client tie was often congruent with a caste tie, suggesting a caste basis for voting, where it cut across this tie it proved just as effective in drawing political support. We therefore reject the idea that a candidate had to be of a numerically dominant caste to achieve political success, and show that economic dominance and identity with a patronizing family were more important. It was this economic dominance and identity with a patronizing family which underlay the Doctor's electoral successes in Bluville during this early period.

Finally, we have argued that the different economic and ecological conditions of different parts of the electorate had implications for the extent of economic control exercised, goodwill generated and political support derived. The patron–client tie of dependence tended to be stronger in the fishing villages than in the non-estate agricultural sector. And in the agricultural sector some crops, such as tea and rubber, permitted a greater labour force acre for acre, tighter discipline and control and less scope for theft than others such as coconut. The political support garnered by owners of land devoted to the former crops was therefore greater than that garnered by those cultivating the latter.

3

Bluville: the patronage network of Korale-Mudaliyar *Kit Foo* and his son, *Dee* (1947–1959)

Introduction

The patronage network of the Doctor's chief political rival, Dee Foo, will now be described. Dee comes from the *Goigama* caste, which is numerically dominant but economically weak in terms of land owned at the district and provincial levels in much of the area and Bluville in particular.[1] He is closely related to the leading *Goigama* families of the Greenville region, to be described in Chapter 5. These families, although large landlords in these areas, often owned virtually nothing elsewhere.[2] However, members of these families, by using the influence of relations close to the Governor, had sometimes been able to acquire *Korale-Mudaliyarships* in areas where they owned relatively little land and were economically and socially not dominant.[3] Dee's father, Kit Foo, for instance, owned only fifty-three acres of rubber in the entire province, certainly not a large holding.[4] However, his wife's relation being the *Maha-Mudaliyar*, was the native headman closest to the Governor, and had been able to secure Kit Foo the post he had coveted. Like the other *Korale-Mudaliyars*, who did not own large tracts of land in the areas they had administered, Foo wielded political influence largely through the office he held and the influence this gave him over lesser officials.

In the 1947 election he campaigned actively on behalf of Joo, a former teacher at one of the schools founded by the Bees. Joo came third. The *Korale-Mudaliyar* had sponsored Joo as an Independent to assess the sort of following his son could muster at a future date. In the event, he believed this following to be sufficiently large to encourage his son to stand in 1952, and subsequently.

Dee then has been the Doctor's traditional rival, but has generally been the weaker candidate, winning the seat on only two of eight occasions, 1956 and 1970. Both these elections represented landslides for

---

[1] Statement based on a study of Ferguson's (1880–1946).
[2] Ibid.
[3] For details on the criteria used in appointing *Korale-Mudaliyars* see GOC (1935).
[4] Ferguson's (1941).

the SLFP nationally. So his victories may have been more a product of such national factors than an index of his local influence *per se*.

This was especially so in 1956. The first three General Elections were staggered over several days, for administrative reasons. The election of 1956 was spread over three days: thirty-seven constituencies returning 42 members on the first day; twenty-two constituencies returning 23 members on the second day; and thirty constituencies returning 30 members on the final day.[5] Results were declared after each day's poll. A party which could establish a clear lead on the first day generally enjoyed a band-wagon effect thereafter. Marginal opportunistic patrons who controlled blocs of votes in electorates polling on subsequent days tended to switch support to such a leading party. In 1947 and 1952 this had worked to the UNP's advantage but, in 1956, it was the SLFP which benefited. After the first day's poll, the SLFP–MEP coalition held twenty-eight seats to the UNP's eight.[6] The following day Mr S. W. R. D. Bandaranaike declared that 'there was no question now that [he] would have to be Prime Minister'.[7] Thereafter the UNP was unable to win a single seat. Bluville polled on the second day and many marginal opportunistic groups, which anticipated a SLFP landslide after the first day's poll, turned against the Doctor. Dee's election victory in 1956 was probably more the result of this than of any very strong grass-roots base he had in Bluville at the time. This is discussed further in Chapter 4, pp. 52–3.

The village headman's system will now be described as it functioned in low-country Ceylon during the nineteenth and early twentieth centuries, focussing on Bluville in particular. This system was to prove the basis for *Korale-Mudaliyar* Foo's patronage network and his son Dee's political following.

The *Korale-Mudaliyars* and the village headmen's system (1833–1963)

By 1833 one could distinguish four types of administrative *Mudaliyars*.[8] *Gate* and *Guard Mudaliyars*, including the *Maha-Mudaliyar*, were attached to the Governor personally and were largely from the Western Province. They served as interpreters and translators to the Governor and as courtiers and other high officials. The third group, the *Atapattu Mudaliyars*, served as *Kachcheri* officials. The fourth and perhaps most

---

[5] *CDN*, 5 April 1956. [6] *CDN*, 7 April 1956. [7] Ibid.
[8] Peebles (1973), Chapters 3 and 4 form the basis for this paragraph.

influential group, to which *Mudaliyar* Foo belonged, the *Korale* and *Pattu-Mudaliyars*, administered territories of various size and population. Their duties were largely concerned with agriculture, *raja kariya* and Government revenue.

During the late nineteenth and early twentieth centuries, a number of honorary *Mudaliyarships* and *Muhandiramships* were created by the Colonial Government.[9] This was done as a means of bestowing public recognition on great philanthropists and influential landlords of particular areas and of enlisting their support in various ventures.[10] The Doctor's grandfather, Coo, fell into this category, having been made an honorary *Muhandiram* in 1889, and an honorary *Mudaliyar* in 1919.[11] He had been offered a *Korale-Mudaliyarship*, but had refused this. So, unlike *Mudaliyar* Foo, he did not have any formal administrative duties.

Under the *Mudaliyar* administration, each village or group of small villages was placed under the supervision of a minor headman, generally known in the Low Country as a *Police-Vidane*, Police Officer or Police Headman. Above these came the *Vidane-Arachchis*, and above them, the Chief Headmen or *Mudaliyars*.[12]

The *Police-Vidanes* and *Vidane-Arachchis* tended to come from the same social, cultural and family background, an experienced *Police-Vidane* being promoted to *Vidane-Arachchi* in his later years. They both represented segments of the village elite. They both tended to be small scale landowners, owning up to twenty-five acres each, in different parcels. Thus, they represented a fairly distinct landowning stratum, dominant only at the village level, and with few economic or social links cutting across provincial boundaries. As such there was a social gulf between these lesser headmen and the *Korale* or *Pattu-Mudaliyars* such as Foo. The latter tended to come from provincially and nationally prominent families. They often had landholdings outside their immediate areas of jurisdiction and had social and administrative links with other *Mudaliyar* families elsewhere on the Island.

The duties of the lesser headmen will now be described in order to illustrate the wide scope of their influence.[13] The *Police-Vidane* had duties in the fields of crime, public health, education, land settlement, surveying, excise, agriculture and irrigation, rubber and tea control, elections, village committee administration, the licensing of guns, motor vehicles and carts, estate duty work, cattle care, the registration of births, deaths and vaccinations, the supervision of Crown lands, wells,

---

[9] Ibid. [10] Ibid. [11] Abeysooriya (1928). [12] GOC (1922).
[13] GOC (1935), Appendix F, forms the basis for this paragraph and also the next.

pits and roads, the care of lepers and lunatics, the reporting of cases of rabies and sudden deaths, the licensing of opium holders and paupers, and the assisting of the fiscal department.

The *Vidane's* policing functions in the field of crime gave him enormous scope to create goodwill amongst the local inhabitants and to intimidate and coerce opponents. He could, if necessary, adopt a lenient approach towards offenders and allow certain shady trades, such as the illicit distilling of liquor, the felling of Crown timber and encroachments upon Crown lands, to flourish. Again, his role in pointing out and demarcating Crown land gave him scope for favouring select individuals, as did his duties in the preparation of lists of Village Committee tax payers. At the same time, these powers could, if necessary, be used to intimidate and coerce those who opposed him in any way whatsoever. This meant that the local *Police-Vidane* was a major power at the village level. He could, through a mixture of favours and threats, encourage other inhabitants to follow his dictates.

The *Police-Vidane's* administrative duties at elections reinforced this power. These duties involved the revision of voters lists, the publication and serving of notices advertising the elections, the preparation of polling booths and, most important, the identification of voters on the day of the poll. In many geographically remote areas the *Police-Vidane* also received the poll-cards identifying each voter, which he was supposed to distribute around his village. An unscrupulous *Vidane* could desist from registering villagers known to be sympathetic to a candidate he disliked, or fail to deliver their poll-cards once they had been so registered. In this way he could impede their voting for a candidate of their choice. At the same time, he could permit others to vote in the names of deceased individuals for a candidate of his choice. Thus, he could materially influence an election result, in a way few other villagers could. Consequently, any candidate seeking political support in the first ten years after Independence went to these intermediating headmen first.

The *Vidane-Arachchis* and *Patabendi-Arachchis* represented the group of (lesser) headmen, slightly superior to the *Police-Vidanes*.[14] They had wider, more general, powers than the latter, and their locus of jurisdiction was also greater. In 1938, there were fifteen *Vidane-Arachchis* and perhaps twenty *Patabendi-Arachchis* within Purville *Korale*, an area of almost 130 square miles. In his locus of jurisdiction the *Vidane-Arachchi* had to supervise the *Police-Vidanes*, co-ordinate relief work when floods or epidemics occurred and assist the police and excise departments in their duties.

---

[14] Ibid. and SLNA 26/331 forms the basis for this paragraph and the next three.

The *Vidane-Arachchi*'s power to disburse patronage flowed from his comprehensive set of responsibilities in appraising wealth at the village level. It was his duty to issue Security Reports of below Rs 500 (those above this sum being issued by the *Mudaliyar*). He also had to report on the conduct of individuals and their financial positions when requested to by the Government. He had to assess properties (for purposes of the assessment tax), appraise paddy crops (in connection with the *Huwandi-ram-Rents*), and recover rates and taxes due. The *Vidane-Arachchi* also had to furnish valuation reports for land and trees acquired and report on applications for a change of ownership of land or exemption from any tax. He had to be present at Inquiries or objections raised by landowners to acquisitions, land transfers or taxes levied. He was in charge of issuing permits for sweet *toddy* licences (and checking trees in this connection). In coastal areas he had to register *madel* fishing nets.

These duties gave the *Vidane-Arachchi* considerable scope to place villagers under obligation to him. He could create ties of dependence and build up a personalized clientele of influential followers. These followers could be influenced at elections to vote for a candidate of the *Vidane-Arachchi*'s choice.

The *Vidane-Arachchi*'s ability to effect this was reinforced by his electoral duties. He was in charge of supervising and preparing voters' lists, identifying voters at the polling booth and assisting Returning Officers at Inquiries into objections and claims regarding the election. It has been alleged that in parts of Bluville electorate, as elsewhere, *Vidane-Arachchis* permitted double voting in dead people's names and actively 'supervised' the booth so as to swing the election towards the candidate of their choice. It was for this reason that whole villages tended to vote more or less en bloc for one candidate or another during this early period (1947–60).

The *Vidane-Arachchis* and *Police-Vidanes* could swing villages to the candidate of their choice because of the enormous influence their administrative posts afforded them.[15] They had been able to build up personalized followings through a mixture of intimidation and favouritism. These followings had been retained for several generations as lesser headmanships tended to pass from father to son or uncle to nephew. The same families therefore monopolized lesser headmanships and patronized the same set of client families over several generations. This creation and sustaining of followings at the village level will be more closely examined in the next section.

---

[15] See GOC (1922) and GOC (1935) for the wide range of powers of, and influence wielded by, the lesser headmen.

The lesser headman's power and following in his locality

We shall first focus on the means by which lesser headmen harassed their enemies and thus cowed opposition, in particular on the forms of intimidation, both explicit and threatened, which were resorted to. A common phenomenon was of the lesser headman stealing produce from those he disliked or his connivance in his relations or friends doing this. A petition filed on 30 May 1938, for instance, accuses the *Vidane-Arachchi* of Bluville of stealing 105 coconuts, a *mammoty* and an axe from the petitioner's house. The *Vidane-Arachchi* is alleged to have had a grudge against the petitioner and so maliciously harassed him. He is supposed to have opened up the doors of the petitioner's irrigation channels, thereby issuing water to the fields the day after sowing, thus washing away the latter's seed paddy.[16] Meanwhile headmen could bring false charges against those they disliked, as a *Vidane-Arachchi* of the area is supposed to have done in a gambling case of 1910.[17]

The headman sometimes ran a shop, illicit *toddy* distillery or gambling den, encouraging villagers to become indebted to him and so further increasing his control over them. In 1915 a *Vidane-Arachchi* of the area was found to have run such a gambling den.[18] A petition to the Excise Department, followed by a raid, meant that in 1932 the *Vidane-Arachchi*, the *Constable-Arachchi*, and a *Police-Vidane* of the area were found to be illicitly distilling and selling *toddy*.[19]

Headmanships were thus used to expand one's financial interests, whilst consolidating the support of influential business colleagues. A petition to the *Mudaliyar*, dated 8 March 1937, described how the *Patabendi-Arachchi* of Bluville town formed a monopsonistic ring with some fish *mudalalis* to outbid others, but then failed to pay the amount promised, and used his position to prevent any penalties being imposed on his henchmen.[20]

Again, when a fish *mudalali* cum small time bus owner applied for the *Patabendi-Arachchiship* of Bluville in 1926, many residents petitioned the AGA to protest. They alleged that the applicant and his nephew (a local *Police-Vidane*) tried to bully individuals into travelling in their buses. They envisaged that his appointment as *Patabendi-Arachchi* would enable him to harass people more easily and expand his business interests unduly.[21]

Corruption was endemic. A petition of 1933 alleged that three local *Vidane-Arachchis* demanded more than the prescribed fee for the issuance

---

[16] SLNA 26/748.   [17] SLNA 26/685.   [18] SLNA 26/634.
[19] Ibid.   [20] SLNA 26/513.   [21] SLNA 26/512.

of cattle licences.[22] Indeed, fees would be demanded for the most routine of duties. Collusion in the operation of illicit gambling dens and *toddy* distilleries was also widespread, as described earlier. As the Headman's Commission of 1935 noted, the whole system was 'irretrievably corrupt ... the complaint [being] longstanding and persistent, and the conviction ... widespread and general ...'[23]

Of course, the headman's influence did not merely rest on his powers to intimidate and harass the villagers. He could use his position to favour friends and relations, thereby building up a clientele or following for himself. Thieving from Crown forests (or other villagers) would be overlooked, as would the widespread encroachments upon Crown lands. In February 1920 three *Police-Vidanes* of the area are supposed to have (illegitimately) failed to arrest a relation for a crime. They are said to have returned the warrant for his arrest, saying that he could not be found, when he could.[24]

Connivance in coral blasting, the dynamiting of fish, and the removal of sea sand for the manufacture of cement, were also widespread along the coast. The *Patabendi-Arachchi* of one hamlet (1947–60), and from a well-known family closely allied to the Foos, made himself very popular by allowing these infringements of the law.[25] Two *Patabendi-Arachchis* in Bluville, the father (1927–43) and his son, who succeeded him on his death in 1943, also made themselves popular by permitting such infringements.[26] Indeed, the latter had made himself so popular that when he was dismissed in 1945 about 200 villagers petitioned for his return.[27]

Lesser headmen also made themselves popular by overlooking Village Committee tax defaults. It was the lesser headman's duty to report whether defaulters were present in the village or not. Only when their presence had been thus ascertained could the Village Committee prosecute. Many headmen favoured their allies by reporting them as absent, even when they were not, thus getting the cases struck off the Village Tribunal book. Between 1936 and 1938, for instance, no less than nineteen *Police-Vidanes* in the Bluville region all stated that none of the Village Committee tax defaulters in their localities were present there and that their whereabouts could not be ascertained.[28] *Mudaliyar* Lou in a confidential note to the AGA said that he doubted the veracity of these statements.[29]

In these ways a lesser headman built up a clientele or following for himself. In the last analysis he needed such a following to enforce his rule at the local level. And almost every headman had some such following.

[22] SLNA 26/634.   [23] GOC (1935), paragraph 35.
[24] SLNA 26/634.   [25] SLNA 26/504.
[26] SLNA 26/513.   [27] Ibid.   [28] SLNA 26/532.   [29] Ibid.

To sum up so far, the lesser headman's office gave him wide-ranging powers and duties. He was generally the most influential man in the locality by virtue of this office and also because of his private wealth, which was large by village standards. He could use this office to build up, consolidate and sustain a following for himself in the village. This was done through a mixture of intimidation and favouritism.

The *Mudaliyar* as patron of the lesser headmen

Lesser headmen were appointed by the Government Agent of their district on the recommendation of the *Korale-Mudaliyar*. As they had to be men of some local influence and wealth, the choice was almost invariably limited to one elite family (or a very small number of elite families) of the village. These families thus monopolized headmanships over several generations.

In Hamville, the Bou family controlled the headmanships over several decades.[30] Kee Bou, *Patabendi-Arachchi* of Hamville (1923–36), was succeeded by his sister's son Ternie Bou (1936–47). The latter's resignation in 1947 led to the appointment of another relation, Zernie Bou (1947–60). At the time of his appointment, Zernie Bou's brother was headman of Hamville West and his uncle was headman of Hamville East. His father had at one time been the *Vidane-Arachchi* of Hamville town.

Ternie Bou's application for a headmanship similarly gives an idea of the family's connections. He had been born in December 1883 and his father had been the *Vidane-Arachchi* of Hamville until his death. His maternal grandfather had held the *Vidane Arachchiship* of Hamville before his father. At the time Ternie applied for the *Patabendi-Arachchiship* in July 1936, his brother was the *Police-Vidane* of Zanville, and his uncle the *Vidane Arachchi* of Lakeside, both nearby towns. As noted earlier, the *Patabendi-Arachchi* who created the vacancy that year by his resignation was his maternal uncle.

Thus the lesser headmen of particular localities formed a tightly knit bloc of village elites, closely related and connected to one another, though these relationships and connections seldom if ever stretched across provincial or district boundaries. The *Mudaliyars* of an area also came from a limited set of families. These families too had monopolized *Mudaliyarships* of particular *korales* over several generations. In Purville *Korale*, for instance, there had been Foo *Mudaliyars* as early as the eighteenth century.[31] From the late nineteenth century onwards, this

---

[30] SLNA 26/504 provides the basis for this paragraph and the next.
[31] See the Dutch Tombos in SLNA Lot 1.

family, and the Lous (to whom they were connected), had monopolized the *Mudaliyarship*. Fit Foo, Kit Foo's father and Dee's grandfather, had held the *Mudaliyarship* from 1883 to 1892. He had been succeeded by Merry Lou (1892–1915), and then by Kit Foo himself (1916–30).[32] The last *Mudaliyar* of Purville *Korale* had been Merry Lou's son, Perry Lou (1930–41).[33]

This type of monopoly of *Mudaliyarships* meant that these families were able to build up a clientele for themselves from amongst the village elites from whose ranks the lesser headmen were drawn. The *Mudaliyars* appointed men from these village elites to headmanships. They indulged the sort of corruption and bullying described earlier. In the event of disputes, petitions or complaints to the AGA the *Mudaliyar* almost always supported his headman. A close bond thus developed between these *Mudaliyar* families and those of the lesser headmen; a bond which was strengthened over successive generations; a bond which was to provide the basis of support for candidates from the *Mudaliyar* families seeking election to national office after 1931.

In Purville *Korale*, for instance, a close bond developed between the Foos and the Bous of Hamville. When Dee contested in 1947 and subsequently and his father (the ex-*Mudaliyar*), campaigned on his behalf, the Bous, who still retained lesser headmanships, were able to deliver whole blocs of votes to their former patrons.

Such support was forthcoming because in his day *Mudaliyar* Kit Foo had indulged these village elite families and the lesser headmen in particular. He had allowed the latter considerable scope for self-enrichment and defended them even when they were accused of the most serious of crimes.

In one such case in 1923, when a petitioner alleged that the local *Vidane-Arachchi* was involved in operating a gambling den, he was repeatedly blocked by *Mudaliyar* Foo.[34] First, the *Mudaliyar* attempted to dismiss the whole charge in a letter to the AGA. Thereafter, forced to call an Inquiry, he (perhaps falsely) alleged that the petitioner had failed to turn up to substantiate his case. This was the standard acceptable excuse for closing an Inquiry of this nature. Moreover, he amended some of the oral evidence which suggested that there may have been some gambling, so as to dispel this idea. The *Mudaliyar*'s Report was accepted and the AGA in a letter to the GA argued that 'the evidence [was] insufficient to take any action, and the *Vidane-Arachchi* [was] not to blame'.

---

[32] GOC *Blue Books* (1884–1942).   [33] Ibid.
[34] SLNA 26/685 forms the basis for this paragraph and the next three.

However, in a further petition, the petitioner alleged that he had indeed gone for the Inquiry but had been 'attacked [there] by the *Mudaliyar* using the following words, "Palayan Hora" [Get out you rogue], "Palayan Borukaraya" [Get out you liar] in the presence of the headmen and several others'. Thus the *Mudaliyar*'s assertion that the petitioner failed to turn up at the Inquiry seems to have been a deliberate untruth designed to close the case.

The petitioner went on to assert that he felt greatly aggrieved by the insulting words used by the *Mudaliyar* when he had done nothing deserving of such treatment and that 'if *Mudaliyars* were to side with their headmen, and insult those who bring [the latter's] wrongdoings to light, there [would] be no way of keeping the headmen in check from doing all sorts of wrongful acts'.

Doubting the justice of any Inquiry held by the *Mudaliyar*, the petitioner went on to request that the (British) AGA of the district personally look into the matter. Characteristically this new petition was dismissed by *Mudaliyar* Foo as 'frivolous and untrue', and thus the matter came to an end.

There were several hundred other petitions which were dismissed in like manner.[35] By these means, *Mudaliyar* Foo would defend his headmen, maintain their support, lessen his workload and create the impression amongst his colonial masters that the administration he headed was functioning smoothly, efficiently and fairly.

Certain *Mudaliyar* families traditionally patronized certain village elite families in distributing headmanships. The *Mudaliyar* would then tactfully permit his headmen to use their positions to accumulate wealth. In the coastal areas the illicit blasting of coral, removal of sea sand (for cement) and the dynamiting of fish were commonplace. In the agricultural interior, underestimation of the *Huwandiram-Rent* on the paddy crop was popular.

Paddy was cultivated over nearly 5,000 acres of the electorate and was therefore a significant crop. Paddy land belonged largely to village smallholders who cultivated it together.[36] Due to the mode of operation of the Sinhala law of inheritance, fields tended to be infinitesimally divided and subdivided.[37] It was quite common for an individual to own an eighth of a share of one field, a sixteenth of another, and say a nineteenth of yet another, perhaps two miles away. This sort of

---

35 SLNA 26/205–26/236 inclusive; 26/311, 26/322, 26/328–26/331 inclusive; 26/352; 26/465, 26/474; 26/476; 26/486; 26/504–26/506 inclusive; 26/512; 26/513; 26/634; 26/685; 26/734–26/736 inclusive; 26/748.
36 For details on the mode of paddy cultivation see Obeysekere (1967).
37 Ibid.

scattering of holdings, which a given owner could not supervise simultaneously, and corporate ownership of particular fields led to the emergence of the *Vel-Vidane* or irrigation headman.[38] It was his duty to supervise the overall welfare of a given field. It was he who saw that the necessary irrigation channels were cleared, that each sector got a fair share of water and soil nutrients and that the whole was kept in good working order. In return he received a share of the crop, a share known as the '*Huwandiram*'.

By the twentieth century the right to collect this *Huwandiram-Rent* was being auctioned. However in practice the *Vel-Vidanes* continued to monopolize it. It was their duty to report the yield during a given season, this report providing the bench-mark for the upset price at the next auction. They invariably underestimated the yields. The yields reported until 1950 were always in the twofold to threefold range (or between two and three times the amount sown). Any paddy cultivator, grain tax assessor or provincial administrator would have recognized this as a gross underestimate, standard yields being in the tenfold to twelvefold range. Yet successive *Mudaliyars* of Purville *Korale*, including Kit Foo, chose to overlook this.

The *Vel-Vidanes* were allowed to underestimate the yield, ensure a low upset price for the *Rent*, and then secure this at the auction. Often they were the only bidders for the *Rent* in their areas, because others recognized the practical difficulties in outsiders collecting village paddy, and so kept away. The dearth of outside bidders made the *Vel-Vidanes* clinching of the *Rent* at a low upset price that much easier. The dearth was actively encouraged by the *Mudaliyar* who auctioned the rights to the *Rent* at an ill-advertised time and place. So the *Vel-Vidane* secured his right to the *Rent* virtually at the price he chose. And of course, he remained grateful to his *Mudaliyar* patron for the tacit assistance rendered him during the whole exercise.

Other widespread practices amongst lesser headmen were the illicit manufacture of liquor, the operation of gambling dens and the underestimation of the grain tax due. By permitting such activities the *Mudaliyar* earned the goodwill of his subordinates.

The only times *Mudaliyar* Foo consistently chastized his headmen were in cases of caste intolerance. Even here, however, he was generally compelled to adopt this attitude by his British superiors.

By the 1920s several *Nekathi/Berawa* people of the South had begun to wear shirts, use umbrellas and tile their house roofs. All these actions

---

[38] A study of the *Huwandiram-Rent* Records in SLNA Lot 26 forms the basis for this paragraph and the next two.

were against prevailing social traditions. In such cases, higher caste villagers, often led by headmen, are alleged to have assaulted them.[39]

The British took a very serious view of such actions. In October 1926, for instance, when a *Vel-Vidane* attacked a *Berawa*, and a police officer failed to report this, the AGA almost assumed the guilt of the lesser headman, and instructed the *Mudaliyar* to pursue some very detailed remedial measures.[40] He stated: 'If this complaint is true it must be stopped at once. Please enquire and report why the Police Officer failed to give a Report (which he obviously did not do), and also on the *Vel-Vidane*'s conduct. Also please give the petitioner a report to go to the Village Tribunal.' Such preemptory instructions from the AGA to the *Mudaliyar* were rare. And in such cases the *Mudaliyar* had to follow the dictates of his colonial masters and crack down (or at least appear to crack down) on his subordinates, if only to safeguard his own position. In this instance *Mudaliyar* Foo had to recommend 'that the Police Officer and *Vel-Vidane* ... be severely reprimanded, and warned that they [would] both be dismissed if trouble of this nature were to arise again in the village.'

Yet, even in this case the *Mudaliyar* attempted to defend his headmen by forwarding their explanations (which denied the charge); something which was not commonly practised. And of course although his Report asserted that he 'warned (them) severely', this phrase may have been used more to impress his superiors with his alleged zeal than to portray actual events.

When penalties were imposed for malpractices, these were invariably instigated by the British AGA, just as dismissal notices were issued in his name. The *Mudaliyar* was not directly involved. He chastized his headmen only in so far as this was necessary to safeguard his own position. Otherwise his role was very much that of their indulgent patron.

This situation was modified from the 1930s onwards. The patronage network of the *Korale-Mudaliyar* began increasingly to clash with that of certain rising private landowners. In the districts being studied this took the form of a conflict between the *Mudaliyars* of Grey *Pattuwa* and Purville *Korale* and the Bee and the Coo families. In 1933, for instance, some of the Coos on the Bluville Urban Council made a determined effort to have additional headmen appointed for their area and placed under the Council's control, rather than that of the *Mudaliyar*.[41]

---

[39] SLNA 26/1369–26/1371 inclusive.
[40] SLNA 26/1369 provides the details of this episode, and forms the basis for this paragraph and the next.
[41] SLNA 26/735.

In November 1932 a bill was introduced in the State Council proposing that 'headmen appointed for areas within the limits administered by Municipalities and Urban District Councils be discontinued' and another bill that 'a Commission be appointed to look into the question of the Headmen's system'.[42] These bills presaged the formation of the Headmen's Commission of 1935, referred to earlier, and the eventual dismantling of the system.

With the rising debate about, and public condemnation of, the Headmen's system during the 1930s, *Mudaliyars* of the decade had to be more exacting in the disciplining of their subordinates.[43] Perry Lou, who succeeded Kit Foo as *Mudaliyar* of Purville *Korale* in 1930, tended to be far stricter with his headmen than his predecessor. Sometimes he would force *Vel-Vidanes* to revalue their rents,[44] and dismissal was far more frequent than previously.[45] When the *Mudaliyar* was replaced by a Divisional Revenue Officer (DRO) in 1941, this 'hardened' attitude became even more marked.[46] DROs were even further removed from the local village elites because they had few economic, social or historical links with their area of jurisdiction. Moreover, they never tended to stay in an area for as long as the *Mudaliyars* had done. The year following *Mudaliyar* Perry Lou's resignation saw three DROs in succession in Purville *Korale*.

For these reasons, Kit Foo's successors never established the sort of personal rapport with their headmen that he had enjoyed. He was probably the last of the indulgent *Mudaliyars*; the last great patron of the lesser headmen of Purville *Korale*.

The *Mudaliyar*, the headmen and elections (1947–63)

The *Mudaliyars* themselves did not survive Independence.[47] Following the recommendations of the Headmen's Commission of 1935, the posts of *Mudaliyar* were suppressed from 1938 and finally abolished in 1946 (though some continued till 1951). In 1958 the Government decided that the posts of *Vidane-Arachchi* would be discontinued with the retirement of those in office at the time. In 1961 the remaining *Vidane-Arachchis* were compulsorily retired, and in 1963 the *Police-Vidanes* suffered the same fate.

42 *Hansard*, 1933.
43 SLNA Lot 33 forms the basis for this paragraph.
44 SLNA 26/311; *Mudaliyar*'s Diary, July 1941.
45 SLNA 26/311; 26/352; 26/476; 26/486; 26/748.
46 SLNA 26/311; 26/352; 26/465; 26/504; 26/513.
47 Tressie-Leitan (1979) forms the basis for this paragraph.

During the transitional period from 1947 to 1963, when the lesser headmen remained, the *Korale-Mudaliyar*, although he had ceased to hold office, still exercised a significant degree of control over them. His word carried enormous weight with his former clients.

This was because first, these headmen were under a moral obligation to him for their appointments. True they had often paid him 'gratifications', but these had generally been regarded as conventional gifts: 'a part of the ancient custom of presenting after appointment, an offering of *bulat-hurulle*' in the words of the Headmen's Commission Report of 1922.[48] Moreover, when the lesser headmen in turn had extorted bribes from the villagers the *Mudaliyar* had always stood by them. We have seen how Kit Foo facilitated their corruption, glossed over their breaches of conduct in his Reports to the AGA and intimidated villagers who raised questions regarding their conduct. Numerous witnesses before the Headmen's Commission of 1935 asserted that the *Mudaliyar* always stood by his appointees, however corrupt the latter had been.[49]

Moreover the various *Mudaliyar* families had a long-standing tradition (going back over two centuries and more) of patronizing certain leading village families.[50] So when headmanships in these areas fell vacant, a Foo *Mudaliyar*'s preferences would be known. When he toured villages with the GA to question inhabitants about the moral character of candidates, objections would seldom, if ever, be raised against his 'favourite'. Villagers were afraid to do so, as, in the words of the 1935 Report, 'that man favoured by the *Mudaliyar* was always chosen'.[51] This was as much an index of the way the *Mudaliyar* would stand by, and advance his nominee, and of the consequent personal tie between the two, as of the fear he aroused in the villages. Families thus favoured by the *Korale-Mudaliyar* tended to remain grateful and loyal to him long after he had lost office. They worked actively on his son's behalf when he contested in 1952, and subsequently.

The second reason for the continuing influence of the *Mudaliyar* after Independence is that many of the lesser headmen may well have believed him to have been more powerful than he really was. They had had an exaggerated idea of his power whilst he held office. The Report of 1935 stated that '[lesser] headmen dared not refuse [to pay the *Mudaliyar* gratifications] because they believed that he had the power to deprive them of their appointments'.[52] This belief was misplaced. If the *Mudaliyar* did wish to deprive a lesser headman of his appointment, he had to follow a fairly complex procedure involving the GA to effect this. He did

---

48 GOC (1922), paragraph 22.   49 GOC (1935), paragraphs 31 and 35.
50 See SLNA Lot 26.   51 GOC (1935), p. 34.   52 Ibid.

not have the power to arbitrarily, and on his own initiative, get rid of the man. But such misconceptions were rife amongst these lesser officials, and it is quite possible that even after the *Mudaliyar* ceased to hold office they had an exaggerated idea of his power, and behaved accordingly.

Thirdly, even after 1945, the *Mudaliyar* could still exercise *some* leverage through his relations and friends working in the local *Kachcheri*. *Korale-Mudaliyar* Foo had many such relations and friends working in the local *Kachcheries*. As late as 1963, a *Police-Vidane* needed to be on good terms with such *Kachcheri* officials, in order to maintain access to the GA and thereby safeguard his own position. Consequently it was not in his interests to have displeased the *Mudaliyar*, whose relations and friends these were.

For these three reasons, long after they had lost office, *Korale-Mudaliyars* (such as Kit Foo) maintained influence amongst the lesser headmen they had appointed. Their word was still law for these officials. So, when *Mudaliyar* Foo sponsored Joo in 1947, and his son, Dee, contested in 1952 and 1956, many lesser headmen in the interior of Purville *Korale* supported these candidates too. And they delivered whole blocs of votes in the village they controlled. This was easy as, retaining office until 1963, they continued to maintain a stranglehold over villages in ways described earlier, and their electoral duties also gave them wide powers.

However, the *Korale-Mudaliyar*'s control of his headmen was not absolute. In many areas patronized by the Coos, headmen whom Kit Foo had appointed worked for the Doctor. In the next section we shall try to explain why this was so, by clearly defining the limits of the *Korale-Mudaliyar*'s influence.

The limits of the *Korale-Mudaliyar*'s influence

There was little scope for electoral conflict between leading Sinhalese families until 1931. So, when a *Korale-Mudaliyar* such as Kit Foo appointed lesser headmen, it is unlikely that he had any clear intention of using them to build himself a political base as such.

Moreover, even if he had nurtured such an intention, it would have been difficult to have realized it everywhere. This was because the *Mudaliyar* had to please his British superiors by ensuring an efficient administration. An efficient administration required a lesser headman who knew his area, a man of some wealth, standing and local influence. In areas where *Mudaliyar* Coo had built schools, hospitals and temples, or those villages surrounding his Tiger Land estate, these men tended to fall within the latter's patronage network.

Indeed, their wealth and influence was largely the product of Coo largesse. The Dous for instance, an influential family in the Bluville area, had received generous grants of coconut land and houses from the old *Mudaliyar*.[53] One Dou brother worked as a teacher in Augusta College (founded and maintained by the Coos) before rising to the prestigious post of headmaster. So when another brother, following family tradition, was appointed *Patabendi-Arachchi* of Bluville in 1946 this was more a recognition of his, and his family's, status in the area than a significant addition to it. The Dous were to work for the Doctor in future years.

In Bluville, the most influential families were those of the fish *mudalalis* and richer boat owners. As this was the main economic activity in the village, and the lesser headman's duties entailed its supervision, a knowledge of the trade was essential. When the *Patabendi-Arachchiship* of the village fell vacant in 1928, all three candidates who were 'highly recommended' for the post to the AGA by the *Korale-Mudaliyar* were influential fish *mudalalis*. The candidate finally chosen was chosen as he was regarded as the most 'influential' having sold a market to the Village Council on very favourable terms, and financed and organized the rescue of fishermen in distress.[54] Often, candidates would be marked as 'unsuitable' if they were not influential fish *mudalalis*, as happened in Okerville in 1945,[55] and in Bluville in 1951.[56] Lesser headmanships in many fishing villages therefore tended to be monopolized by fish *mudalalis*. And for reasons elaborated earlier, these men, especially in Bluville, its environs and Okerville, fell within the Coo patronage network.

Such men were to work hard for the Doctor's political advancement. When he first entered local politics in 1933, it was expected that he would be returned uncontested.[57] However, a certain Jek Lou is supposed to have encouraged another individual to run against him. In the event, the Doctor won resoundingly, but the headmen of Bluville town who supported him never forgave Jek Lou for the act he was believed to have committed. Years later, in November 1941, when Jek Lou attempted to contest a ward in the Bluville UC elections they worked hard against him.

Such headmen owed their wealth and influence primarily to the Coos. Their appointments were more a recognition of this position than the basis for it. Consequently their loyalty to and dependence upon the Coos took precedence over any tie to the Foos. In such cases, *Mudaliyar* Foo's ability to count on their support after 1947 was limited. Throughout Bluville, in areas of Coo patronage, these headmen worked for the Doctor and against Dee.

[53] SLNA 26/513 forms the basis for this sentence and the rest of the paragraph.
[54] SLNA 26/505.   [55] SLNA 26/506.   [56] SLNA 26/513.
[57] SLNA 26/748 forms the basis for this paragraph.

Conclusion: the role of caste in elections

In this chapter we have focussed on a patronage network based on the relics of the old British provincial administration. As shown, much of this survived into the early 1960s, and it is argued that this constituted the basis for Dee Foo's political support.

Like other *Mudaliyar* families, the Foos were traditionally the patrons of certain village elite families within their domain. Dee's father, like his grandfather (and other ancestors) before him, had appointed headmen from these families. He had defended them in times of crisis, and indulged their corruption. So, even after he had lost office many remained grateful, and worked for his nominees at elections. He also continued to exercise some real influence, after Independence, through the *Kachcheri*, and some headmen may have over-estimated his power. Thus, in areas not patronized by the Coos, his power prevailed and he continued to carry his former subordinates with him. The latter's control over the villagers and duties at election time enabled them to deliver whole blocs of votes to his son well into the 1960s.

Once again, therefore, it is clear that caste *per se* played little, if any, role in drawing political support on the lines Jiggins has suggested.[58] The caste bond was only important in so far as it was congruent with a patron–client bond, and in the single-caste village structure of low-country Sri Lanka (where a particular patron often lived surrounded by his own caste) such congruence was not uncommon. What may have appeared to be a caste bond was, in such cases, really a manifestation of a patron–client bond.

This can be clearly seen by the fact that when patronage networks cut across caste ties, as they did in many parts of Bluville, it was the former ties of dependence which determined the basis of voting. Of the twenty-one headmen who were fairly solidly for the Doctor in 1947, no less than fifteen represented villages, the majority of which were not members of his own *Karave* caste. So, about two thirds of the Doctor's support seems to have come from non-*Karave* sources. Of this two thirds about half (represented by six headmen) came from the patronage networks of the Green Acre and Tiger Land estates, and the remainder from the private acts of charity concentrated in certain hamlets and Bluville town. Dee also drew support from outside his own caste. Most notable were his *Durave* support blocs in areas unpatronized by the Coos, where the headmen had been appointed by his father. In addition, Dee was able to count on the depressed castes, where they resided near, and were dependent upon, certain *Goigama* village elites which had been patronized by

[58] Jiggins (1979).

his father. Both candidates penetrated areas in Grey *Pattuwa* where their castes were not always numerically dominant, through school teachers, priests, village elites and other such intermediaries.

However, until 1970, the *Karave* caste voted consistently and over-whelmingly for the Doctor, and according to many this was due to a caste identity. Indeed, in most fishing villages, over nineteen of every twenty people voted for him; a proportion that was almost always greater than that of any agricultural village voting for a candidate of its choice. The fishing communities' tendency to support the Doctor, however, was in one way due to their proximity to the Coo residence and the long tradition of Coo patronage they had benefited from. Their tendency to vote en bloc for the Doctor to a greater degree than most agricultural areas did for any candidate of its choice was (in our view) dictated by the nature of the economic activity pursued. Fishing being the only activity pursued, it was easier to satisfy the interests of village intermediaries, notably the fish *mudalalis*, than in an agricultural area where different activities meant conflicting group interests. Moreover, the land scarcity in the fishing villages meant that most villagers had no alternative source of income. They depended on one activity, fishing, and one local patron, the fish *mudalali*, for their livelihood. Thus, the local patrons in the fishing villages (the fish *mudalalis*) exercised a tighter control over their clients than their counterparts did in the agricultural hinterland. This meant that the delivery of vote blocs was easier in a fishing village, than an agricultural; hence its greater incidence.

To conclude then, the nature of the patron–client bond determined the degree and extent of political support rendered. Both candidates drew support from a wide cross-section of castes. But the patronage system underlying the Doctor's support was more fundamental and enduring than that underlying his rivals. It was based on the tangible control of land and capital resources, whereas that of Dee was based on the relics of a colonial administration that was fast disintegrating. More-over, the Doctor's appointments to Government enhanced his capacity to disburse patronage and reward intermediaries. He was thereby able to consolidate his already substantial support base in the area, and emerge as the dominant political figure in Bluville by 1956. With the extension of the State after 1956, the role of State patronage in underpinning political allegiance, was to increase further. It is to this that we shall now turn.

4

Bluville: the growth of the State (1956–1982)

1956 and after

The 1956 General Election was staggered over three days. After the results of the first day's polling were announced it was clear that Bandaranaike's MEP coalition was heading for a landslide victory, having won twenty-eight seats to the UNP's eight.

Bluville polled on the second day, and many marginal opportunistic groups, anticipating an SLFP victory, turned against the Doctor. The Muslims of Zoville, numbering just over 2,000, were the chief such group. Previously they had voted solidly for the Doctor, but they now believed that their interests as a minority community would be better served by an MP of the governing party – and a close relation of the future Prime Minister at that! Consequently, for the first and last time, they voted en bloc for Dee. Even their women were made to turn up at the polling booth; a phenomenon never witnessed in Bluville before.

There were other marginal opportunistic groups which did likewise. Some teachers at Augusta College, who saw the SLFP's *Swabasha* policies as offering them greater access to Government jobs and prestige, campaigned clandestinely against the Doctor. And certain local influentials, such as a prominent *ayurvedic* physician, did likewise. However, they did not control whole blocs of votes in the way that some fish *mudalalis*, village headmen and small landowners did. The impact of these teachers and *ayurvedic* physicians was largely on the younger generation of new voters. They mediated between the upper ranks of the SLFP and this group, helping to organize the campaign in a small way.

Meanwhile the group of new voters voted as a bloc, as they were to do in several future elections. In Bluville there were about 4,000 new voters, about four-fifths of whom voted. Except for some of the fishing villages and estate areas, where the youth tended to follow in the footsteps of their fathers and get closely tied to the local patrons, most of the new votes went to Dee. The Doctor retained his firm base of support from the fish *mudalalis* and estates. The drop in support of 2,800 from his total of 1952 was largely the result of the switch in allegiance by the Muslims.

However, this was the only major switch in Bluville. Both candidates had a solid core of support based on their different patronage networks. And these cores of support, and the patronage networks sustaining them, were to persist for many years more.

Yet, the post-1956 era saw a major extension of the State. This was to mean State wealth replacing private wealth as the source of political patronage. It was to change the bases on which patronage was to be disbursed and the type of intermediaries who were to emerge.

The extension of the State was also to mean a greater premium being placed on the acquisition of the party ticket as the party came to be seen as the main vehicle by which State power could be captured, patronage disbursed and political goodwill engendered. The party therefore gradually came to attract votes independent of a candidate's personal resources. However, it is difficult to identify this in terms of votes in Bluville as, after July 1960, no candidates there contested as Independents. As such, it is impossible to trace the gradual erosion in Independent support in Bluville and the growing importance of the party ticket in terms of votes, as is possible in Greenville.

Meanwhile, the extent to which minor patrons or intermediaries could deliver blocs of votes was circumscribed. This was due to the electoral reforms of 1956–65, and their effective implementation with a strong well-organized Opposition. These reforms have thus to be explained.

The electoral reforms of 1956–65

Between 1956 and 1965 a number of such reforms were introduced.[1] These, as implemented until 1982, circumscribed the power of local influentials to supervise the delivery of vote-blocs. Double voting, impersonation, thuggery and intimidation were made more difficult to effect by these legal reforms and due to the emergence of a stronger and relatively independent Elections Administration and a well-organized Opposition.

Yet, although supervision at the poll could not be carried out as before, the local notable retained some influence, as will be shown later. He could still ensure that a solid core of villagers worked for a particular candidate and turned up on polling day to vote for him. And so, the notable's ability to deliver these votes, although undermined by his incapacity to supervise the poll, remained until well into the 1960s. The way in which supervision of the poll was circumscribed can be examined under four heads, reforms regarding: (i) voting qualifications, (ii) the

[1] See GOSL (1972a).

registration of electors and revision of registers, (iii) the conduct of elections and (iv) the use of wealth.

(i) *Voting qualifications*: The main reforms here concerned the tightening up of residence requirements. No one could be on the electoral register of a district unless he had been ordinarily resident in that district on the first day of June in the year of the register.[2] Again, no individual was entitled to have his name entered or retained in any address, other than that at which he was on the first day of June of that year.[3]

There were also restrictions on plural voting. No person was entitled to have his name entered or retained in more than one register[4] or more than once in the same register.[5] An individual voting in more than one constituency at a General Election, or any other election, or asking for a ballot paper for this purpose, was deemed guilty of an illegal practice.[6]

These rules made it more difficult for two or more village headmen to have their supporters registered in more than one place, and so, enjoy two or more votes. It also made it more difficult to register voters from outside the electorate in that electorate itself, as had been common earlier. Nevertheless these practices continued, but on a lesser scale than previously.

(ii) *The registration of electors and revision of Registers*: was made more thorough. First, polling districts were made smaller and more manageable, so that each such district contained not more than 1,500 electors unless the Commissioner of Elections decided otherwise.[7] This enabled the new Elections Department to supervise the poll much more rigorously than in the past. With an impartial police force, and a well-organized Opposition, the intimidation, thuggery and impersonation which local notables had connived in previously was curtailed.

There were also provisions for individuals to object to the inclusion of the names of others in the Register if they suspected them of not being entitled to be in the Register.[8] The Registering and Revising Officers were empowered to check these claims, and punish and control offenders.[9] Provisions for the punishment of village headmen and officials conniving in the offence or distorting information requested by the Returning Officer and for the revision of incorrect Registers were also made.[10]

Detailed rules had already been set on the method of revising the register and preparing a list of dead persons and others disqualified from voting.[11] However, the village headmen, whose duties these were, had

---

[2] Ibid., Sections 4.1(c) and 4.2.
[3] Ibid., Section 6.   [4] Ibid., Section 8(1).
[5] Ibid., Section 8(3).   [6] Ibid., Section 8(2).   [7] Ibid., Section 10(2).
[8] Ibid., Section 15(3b).   [9] Ibid., Sections 15(5)–15(14) inclusive.
[10] Ibid., Sections 16(6a)–16(6c) inclusive.   [11] Ibid., Section 18.

not followed these rules and abuses had continued. So, new provisions were made for the Registering Officer to question and object to these lists if he had any suspicions about them,[12] and to hold a Public Inquiry into the matter if he deemed this necessary.[13] He was also empowered to act upon his findings and alter the lists if needed.[14]

(iii) *The conduct of elections*: A number of reforms were introduced regarding the conduct of elections. To help prevent impersonation, provisions were made for the issue of an official identity card for each voter.[15] This had to be produced by the voter before he was issued a ballot paper.[16] New, more stringent measures were introduced for checking the identity of voters. Where the Presiding Officer or a Polling Agent doubted the authenticity of identity, the former was empowered to request the voter to sign a declaration of identity, and to refuse a ballot paper to any voter refusing to make such a declaration.[17] It was also stipulated an offence to wilfully furnish a false declaration, and provisions were made for punishment in such cases.[18]

As an added precaution against double voting, it was decided to mark each voter with indelible ink on the left finger of one hand, just prior to his voting.[19] The checking of each voter's hand was taken as a check against double voting. Those refusing to accept this check, or refusing to be marked, or found to be marked on being checked, were deemed not eligible to receive a ballot paper.[20] Provisions were laid down for the listing of their names.[21]

There were new rules concerning the distribution and format of poll-cards. Prior to 1956 these cards had been sent to headmen who had been responsible for distributing them to the voters in their area. These cards had carried insufficient information about the voter, his polling station, and the like, so that impersonation had been facilitated. Moreover, many headmen only distributed cards to those villagers who supported the candidates they did, withholding them from known supporters of the rival candidates. Sometimes these headmen had used these withheld cards to help impersonators vote several times over. This had tended to militate against the left-wing parties.[22]

Provisions were now made for more detailed poll-cards so as to help prevent the card of one elector being used by an unscrupulous headman

---

12 Ibid., Sections 19(1)–19(3) inclusive. 13 Ibid., Section 19(4).
14 Ibid., Section 20(1). 15 Ibid., Section 22.
16 Ibid., Section 43A. 17 Ibid., Section 43(1).
18 Ibid., Section 43(3). 19 Ibid., Section 42(2c).
20 Ibid., Section 42(2A). 21 Ibid., Section 47(1d).
22 *CDN*, 5 February 1960 describes the protests of the leaders of the LSSP, CP and MEP regarding this just before the March 1960 General Election.

for another elector's vote.[23] It was also stipulated that this official poll-card be sent direct to the elector by ordinary post to reach him at least seven days before the date of the poll, or retained at the post office until called for.[24] Stringent penalties were also laid for unauthorized individuals found to be in possession of these poll-cards.[25]

These measures undermined the headman's power by removing him from his role as the official local distributor of the poll-cards. He could still intercept these if he had connections at the local post office, as many headmen did. However, the penalties for unwarrantedly being in possession of these cards being so stiff, most headmen were deterred from attempting this.

Meanwhile, there were provisions for the Presiding Officer, rather than the village headman, to mark the ballot paper or papers of a blind or other such physically disabled voter in the manner directed by him, and to cast this in the ballot box.[26] This further restricted the headman's influence at elections as he had traditionally performed this function.

New measures were enacted to ensure that all voters had a fairly clear idea of the choice before them, and to preclude the sort of farce that occurred in Greenville in 1947 (see Chapter 5). It was stipulated that a notice be displayed in a conspicuous place outside each polling station showing the name of each candidate in Sinhalese, Tamil and English and the symbol allotted to him before the commencement of the poll.[27]

It had been common for various forms of intimidation to occur at the polling booth. Wealthy candidates would hire gangs of supporters, often led by loyal village headmen, to 'supervise' their interests at the poll. Many of these thugs posed as 'polling agents' and cowed known supporters of the rival candidate into not turning up to vote for him. Others acted as 'counting agents' and interfered with the counting of votes.

New legislation now limited the number of polling agents and counting agents a candidate could have.[28] There were also measures to help prevent intimidation at the poll. Individuals were prohibited from certain forms of canvassing within the precincts or a quarter of a mile of the polling station on the day of the poll.[29] There were also restrictions on advertising between the day of nomination and the day of the poll,[30] and the use of megaphones and shouting on the latter day.[31]

In some areas polling stations had tended to be so completely under the control of one candidate that a free vote could not be guaranteed. New legislation now empowered the Commissioner of Elections to alter the

---

[23] GOSL (1972a), Section 35A(1).
[24] Ibid., Section 35A(2). [25] Ibid., Section 35A(3).
[26] Ibid., Section 42(5). [27] Ibid., Section 37(1).
[28] Ibid., Section 39(b). [29] Ibid., Section 52(1A and 1B).
[30] Ibid., Section 52(B). [31] Ibid., Section 52(1B).

location of any polling station from that previously advertised, or the date of polling, if he deemed this necessary.[32]

Intimidation had been facilitated before 1956 because secrecy of the ballot had not been efficiently maintained. New legislation now decreed that every officer, clerk, candidate or agent, authorized to attend at the counting of votes, sign a declaration promising to maintain the secrecy of the count.[33]

Meanwhile, precautionary measures were introduced to help prevent the stuffing of ballot boxes. Detailed specifications were given for the layout of the ballot paper,[34] and its issuing to the voter.[35] There were also provisions for recording the ballot papers in each ballot box before the count.[36] Moreover, the Presiding Officer now had to despatch to the Returning Officer the duplicates of the official identity cards entrusted to him,[37] and a statement specifying the number of ballot papers entrusted to him, accounting for them under the heads of (i) ballot papers issued to voters other than spoilt ballot papers, (ii) spoilt ballot papers and (iii) unused ballot papers.[38] These measures meant a greater accountability regarding the ballot papers issued and used, so that the stuffing of ballot boxes became more difficult.

Finally, a comprehensive list of election offences was enumerated and minimum punishments stipulated for those convicted of such practices.[39]

(iv) *The use of wealth*: Several measures were enacted to directly circumscribe the power of wealthy candidates to patronize local influentials and others during the election itself. Most of these measures were introduced only after the Trotskyist LSSP had gained places in Government in 1964.

Many employers had been able, overtly or covertly, to coerce their employees into voting for a particular candidate. New legislation now defined certain forms of such coercion as 'undue influence', making the employer liable to prosecution.[40] Further, an employer was mandatorily required to grant leave to any employee who requested in writing leave to vote, such leave without loss of pay, for not less than four hours on the day of poll.[41] Those failing to comply with this provision were deemed guilty of an offence and liable to punishment.[42]

The treating of voters to food, drink or entertainment, bribery, and the use of undue influence or force had already been declared corrupt

---

[32] Ibid., Section 35(3A and 3B).
[33] Ibid., Sections 53(2)–53(5) inclusive.   [34] Ibid., Section 40 (2 and 3).
[35] Ibid., Section 42(2).   [36] Ibid., Section 47(4).
[37] Ibid.   [38] Ibid.   [39] Ibid., Section 52.
[40] Ibid., Section 57(4).   [41] Ibid., Section 91.   [42] Ibid.

practices.[43] Now more stringent sentences were prescribed for those found guilty of committing these offences.[44]

Rich candidates had been able to hire large cohorts of election workers, under various guises, to assist them in their campaigns. New legislation now provided for their each appointing an election agent,[45] and for him to have certain clearly defined duties regarding the appointment of polling agents, clerks and messengers.[46] A limit was also placed on the number of individuals a candidate could employ to assist him in his campaign.[47]

A limit on election expenses of Rs 5,000, or 20 cents for each elector on the Register, was also imposed.[48] It was further declared illegal knowingly to furnish a false declaration as to such expenses, and provision was made for the punishment of those so doing.[49]

Rich candidates had also had an advantage in transporting their supporters to the polling booths in estate lorries and private cars. Now such travel was debarred and individuals were only allowed to proceed to the booths by foot or public transport.[50] The sole exceptions were those who satisfied the Returning Officer that they were physically disabled, and so unable to proceed in this manner.[51] It was declared an offence to travel, or assist others to travel, to the polling booth by private means and provisions were made for any District Court to requisition any vehicle used in the commission of such an offence.[52]

Richer candidates had also enjoyed an advantage over the poorer in the printing and distributing of literature about themselves and against rivals. Often such literature had been scurrilous in nature. The publishers' and printers' names not being advertised, it had been difficult to trace their origin and institute legal action, if required. New legislation now required that these details be specified in any election literature distributed.[53] The publication of false statements regarding a candidate was also declared illegal and those found responsible for such publication were made liable to punishment.[54]

In order to give poorer candidates a better chance of distributing literature to voters, a new measure was introduced. Each candidate was now entitled to send each elector on the Electoral Register of his district a postal communication by ordinary post, free of charge, during the period between nomination and the seventh day before poll.[55]

These measures, by helping to reduce the importance of private wealth in campaigns, also helped to increase the importance of the party ticket.

[43] Ibid., Sections 55–7 inclusive. [44] Ibid., Section 58(1).
[45] Ibid., Section 59. [46] Ibid., Section 61. [47] Ibid., Section 68(1).
[48] Ibid., Section 66(1). [49] Ibid., Section 68 (B). [50] Ibid., Section 67(4c).
[51] Ibid., Section 67(4d). [52] Ibid., Section 67(6).
[53] Ibid., Section 68(A). [54] Ibid., Section 58(A). [55] Ibid., Section 92(c).

The party with its links with Government (or an alternative government) came to be seen as a more reliable disburser of patronage than an individual. This became more so with the extension of the State. Two other measures also worked to this effect. First, provisions were made for no more candidates than there were members to be returned in an electoral district to have the certificates of official party candidature.[56] In practice the policy of parties to give more than one local notable the official ticket had atrophied after 1947. But it still continued in some isolated cases, and this reform put an end to it. Secondly, it was decreed that the official candidates of a recognized party had to deposit only Rs 250 as security, whilst an Independent candidate had to provide Rs 1,000.[57] This move was designed to discourage a multiplicity of candidates with little local support contesting and draining the National Exchequer, as had occurred in March 1960. In the long run it encouraged the emergence of an essentially two-party system, and helped to give more stress to the party than the individual in the outcome of an election.

To review, the chief forms of voting irregularity and inequity in rural Sri Lanka have been: (i) the stuffing of ballot boxes; (ii) impersonation and double voting; (iii) intimidation, thuggery and deceit, as in Greenville in 1947, and (iv) the unfair use of wealth.

The reforms summarized above, coupled with the wider powers given to the Commissioner of Elections and the establishment of a new independent Department of Parliamentary Elections, made the stuffing of ballot boxes almost impossible to effect after 1964.

Nevertheless, impersonation, double voting, intimidation, thuggery and fraud, continued. In Bluville, this was particularly so in the fishing villages where the tightly knit social and geographic structure facilitated bloc voting. Moreover, the effective implementation of the reforms required not only an independent Elections Department and Police Force but also a well-organized Opposition. In areas where a candidate lacked polling agents to supervise his interests, impersonation, double voting, intimidation and thuggery were facilitated. In 1965, 1970 and 1977, both parties vying for power were relatively well organized and evenly balanced, so that this problem was not significant. But in October (and to an even greater extent December) 1982, the Opposition to the Government was totally disorganized. In several areas the Opposition did not even have the Polling Agents to supervise their interests, a point admitted by Government supporters. In this context, Opposition politicians have alleged that at the Referendum Poll in December 1982 impersonation, double voting, intimidation and thuggery were carried

[56] Ibid., Sections 28(F) and 35(C).   [57] Ibid., Section 29.

out on a major scale, not witnessed previously. Whilst it is difficult to categorically estimate the validity of this statement, or the scale of impersonation, one point remains: for the first time the fairness of a national poll in Sri Lanka has been called into question.

To sum up then, the reforms as implemented until and including July 1977 were reinforced by a strong well-organized Opposition. This meant that it became more difficult for intermediaries to supervise the poll and guarantee the delivery of vote blocs. It also became more difficult for a wealthy patron to harness support, either directly, or through these intermediaries, at the election itself. Support therefore became less reliable. But such support still needed to be given because, long before the campaign proper began, a wealthy patron could still patronize traditional intermediaries and they in turn could favour their own set of clients.

The growth of the State during the SLFP periods of Government, between 1956 and 1965, and then again between 1970 and 1977, eroded the power of private sources of patronage. Aspirants to political office had to count less on private wealth and more on access to, and control of, important State institutions. However, the successful amongst these aspirants still tended to come from the older families of wealthy patrons. This was because it was these families which held political office, or were the alternative or Opposition candidates at the time of the growth of the State, and therefore had the easiest access to these institutions. This will become clearer in our next section when we look at the way these institutions developed in Bluville, and especially in the important fishing sector.

The growth of the State (1956–65)

Soon after S. W. R. D. Bandaranaike's election in 1956, the transport services were nationalized. This eliminated the power of the bus magnates. But in other fields the influence of many local notables, through whom the Doctor and Dee Foo operated, remained. This was especially true in the case of the village headmen and fish *mudalalis*.

Dee Foo had always been anxious to break into the power base of the latter group. As noted, it had traditionally been one of the chief cores of support for the Doctor. In 1956 the SLFP government initiated a nationwide policy of mechanization and modernization of the fishing industry. Dee Foo saw this as his opportunity to win support amongst the fishermen.

Three modes of fishing could be distinguished in Bluville at the time. Inshore fishing was the least lucrative, and tended to be carried on by very poor fishermen who had little capital. Deep sea fishing was more profitable and *madel*, or beach seining, the most. These last two modes of fishing required equipment: canoes in the first case and nets in the second.

There existed a set of equipment-owning *mudalalis* who lent these items to clients in return for a part of the catch. They accounted for about a twentieth of the total population of any one fishing village. They seldom participated directly in the fishing operation itself, thereby enhancing their local status.[58] But they were the powerholders in the fishing villages, with capital, and the ability to bind clients to them. It was they who enjoyed a quasi-monopsony of the fish trade and a quasi-monopoly of the credit market. It was they who sent out sets of clients to the Eastern Province, during the monsoon, when the latter could not secure any returns in Bluville. And it was they who helped these clients during times of need and kept them in a state of perpetual indebtedness and obligation.

They formed the economic and social elite of the area. Amongst them were a select semi-educated category which directed the fishing operations in a managerial capacity. Often the sons or nephews of the older equipment-owning *mudalalis*, they were the ones who, besides captaining the canoe crews and supervising the hauling of the nets, acted as the office bearers in the local Co-operative Societies (formed in 1948). They undertook the accounting and financial management of these bodies.

They, together with the other equipment owners, formed the village elite. They owed much of their status to the Doctor's grandfather, *Mudaliyar* Coo. It was the *Mudaliyar* who had given many of them their small landholdings from which they derived a subsidiary source of income. It was the *Mudaliyar* who had built the schools to which they sent their children and the temples at which they worshipped. And it was the *Mudaliyar* who had helped them in times of need and patronized their social functions.

For these reasons, detailed in Chapter 2, these families helped his grandson, the Doctor, by delivering him blocs of votes in their areas. And they in turn were helped by the Doctor when he secured Cabinet appointment with prestigious white-collar jobs at State institutions, and the building of roads, bridges, hospitals and other infrastructural facilities in their areas. These families, therefore, were very closely connected to the Doctor.

Dee Foo recognized this fact. He saw his best chance of capturing the coastal vote, to lie in breaking the powers of patronage disbursement of

---

[58] Fernando *et al.* (1984).

these families of the fishing elite. Consequently, when the SLFP government introduced a national policy of modernizing and mechanizing the fishing industry, he sought to tailor it to these political ends.

The richest and most powerful of the Doctor's supporters had been the *madel* or beach seine net owners. Successful seining required long open stretches of sandy beach. The best such stretches were found in Bluville town and Okerville, both strongholds of the Doctor's. But there was always a shortage of them. In fact, the shortage of beaches was so acute that seining had to be done on a rotational basis, each net being allowed a particular section of the beach only for a certain period each day.

Dee realized this. He arranged to have a harbour constructed in Okerville, the second largest fishing town in the electorate. A bund was constructed in 1957, and 800 yards of the best beach were lost to the seine fishermen. This undermined their financial positions considerably. Meanwhile the Government introduced small mechanized boats, which could be operated by crews of four to five men over a range of thirty to forty miles. These were to be issued to fishermen on hire-purchase terms, which provided for the recovery of the capital over a period of five years.

In Bluville, Dee was anxious that the topmost rung of the fishing elite, the equipment owners through whom the Doctor mediated, be excluded from the receipt of the new boats. The Fisheries Inspectors were instructed to give preference to the poorer fishermen (forming the crews of the traditional craft) in the distribution of boats. Practical experience in deep sea fishing was made the criterion of choice of beneficiary. This, and the very small down-payment of Rs 1,000 requested, was designed to enable the traditional craft owners to secure the new boats. These beneficiaries were the clients of the village level patrons, though some were related to the boat owners and cannot be termed as having not been in the elite. (They were essentially on the fringe of the elite.) The first ten $3^1/_2$ tonners issued between 1958 and 1962 were all secured by them.

But the scheme did not work as planned. The weak (8–12 horsepower) engines issued and the absence of nylon gill nets meant that the catch was poor. The use of nylon gill nets was prohibited in the sea over a long stretch of the south-western coast until 1965. In addition, none of the fishermen had been given prior training in the repair of engines. Consequently, the skippers had to hire technicians from outside, at an exorbitant cost, whenever a mechanical fault arose. The investment failed to pay. Thus, the crewmen who had bought the boats were forced to mortgage them to the richer seine fishermen and *mudalalis* who remained in the villages. In many cases the richer traditional boat-owners secured control of the new mechanized craft in this way. By 1965, therefore, the composition of the village elite had changed only very slightly. True, as a class it was the boat owners and not seine fishermen who formed the topmost rung of this elite. But these new boat owners were generally former seine fishermen or their children or those of wealthy *mudalalis*. They tended to come from the same families that the Doctor and his grandfather had patronized in the past.

After the UNP's return to power in 1965, the Doctor was able to assist these families once again. Permission was secured to use nylon gill nets. In 1968 more powerful engines were introduced for their boats. These innovations meant that the catches increased markedly. The income and wealth of these families rose correspondingly. And, of course, except in one area which will be examined later, their bond with the Doctor was strengthened.

Meanwhile, the ties between these intermediary families and their clients took on a new form. They became less tight and binding than previously. Mechanization meant that the monsoon season now became the most profitable. The new $3^{1}/_{2}$-ton boats could travel into deep water, which the traditional craft had been unable to reach, during the monsoon. With the churning of the sea they could secure larger catches than during the non-monsoonal period. Consequently, the monsoon period became the best for deep sea fishing in Bluville. And so migration into the Eastern Province at this time, by sets of fishermen tied to particular *mudalalis* (along the lines described in Chapter 2), became far less common. This, and the emergence of alternative sources of credit from the People's Bank, weakened the hold many fish *mudalalis* exercised over their clients.

However, less rigid forms of bondage remained or developed. Scope emerged for a rich $3^{1}/_{2}$-ton boat owner to earn popularity and goodwill amongst his crewmen. Conventionally half the catch would be kept 'for the boat', and the remaining half shared out amongst the crewmen including the owner. A good owner could now only take his (half) share of the catch as a boat owner, allowing his share as a crewman to be distributed amongst the others. Similarly, a good $3^{1}/_{2}$-ton boat owner would now allow the fish caught by lesser boat owners and fishermen to be stored in his large refrigerator until auction time. And, of course, he would help such men financially and in kind, during times of need, as well as patronize their various social functions.

The quasi-monopsonistic power of the fish *mudalalis* in the purchase of fish continued as it still does today. The Co-operatives were unable to break this. Many local branches were formed and operated from 1948 onwards, but this was done by the richer fishermen and *mudalalis* themselves. So rather than exercising monopsonistic powers in a private capacity they now began to wield it through control of these bodies. In

1972 new regulations prohibited: (i) anyone in the fish trade from holding office in these Co-operatives and (ii) any one individual owning or controlling more than a fifth of any one Society's shares. These measures circumscribed the ability of fish *mudalalis* to exercise monopsony via these bodies. But, as such Co-operatives could not afford to run at a loss, they now left the field of fish purchasing, marketing and distribution. The *mudalalis* retained control of these functions, in a private capacity. Consequently, their monopsonistic power survived.

Thus the Doctor was able to continue to operate through these traditional intermediaries of his. In the elections of March 1960, July 1960 and March 1965 he maintained his support along the coastal belt. Dee's policies had merely antagonized the powerholders in the fishing villages, who were at that time (1960) still the seine net owners. Whilst alienating this group, he had not been able to build up support amongst the crewmen he had favoured. This was because the absence of nylon gill nets and powerful engines had reduced returns and forced many of them into bankruptcy. Dee was blamed. Even by March 1965, no significant improvement in yields could be discerned, and Dee continued to suffer the ill will of this group (and of those who had acquired boats through mortgages). Thus, at all three elections during this period the Doctor continued to retain his support along the coastal belt.

After his return to the Cabinet in 1965, the Doctor secured permission for the use of nylon gill nets, and also introduced more powerful engines for the new boats. Yields and income rose. As the Doctor was seen as responsible for this, he earned added goodwill amongst the fishermen. Dee faded into the realm of the forgotten. And the Doctor retained his hold on the coast. The only area where he lost support was in a certain part of Bluville town. This was due to his inappropriate handling of the State machinery in the late 1960s. This is the subject of the next section.

The use of State institutions (1965–77)

We have seen how the period of SLFP rule, lasting (with only a short four-month break) from 1956 to 1965, saw a great growth in the State network. The transport services were nationalized in 1957 as were schools in 1964. Augusta College and the Okerville Girls' School, founded by *Mudaliyar* Coo, now had their teachers chosen by the Department of Education from a national pool of qualified candidates. Those chosen were generally from outside the area and not tied to the Doctor as closely as their predecessors had been. Meanwhile, the last of the village headmen were retired in 1962.

But, as we have seen in the case of the fishing industry, the families of these local influentials maintained their economic dominance at the village level. It is true that access to, and control of, State and party institutions became more important as a means of disbursing patronage. But those who were most easily able to gain such access and control tended to come from the richer families providing the traditional clients of the larger patrons. Thus, although the means of patronage disbursement changed over this period, the personnel who disbursed this patronage, and through whom the two party candidates operated, remained (largely) the same. This is further substantiated on pp. 75–9. Meanwhile, however, the growth of the State afforded a discerning candidate the opportunity to break into an opponent's patronage network when he was out of power. An Opposition candidate's personal resources were relatively small and insignificant as compared to that of the local MP, who had the full backing of the (now expanded) State. The latter could therefore favour those aspiring to village elite level status and attempt to displace the traditional clients of his rival.

We have seen how Dee tried this in the coastal belt and failed. The Doctor too attempted this, but in a more subtle and discreet manner. When appointed a Minister in 1965, he initiated massive infrastructural improvements in areas which he had not carried solidly. In several inaccessible villages in the west of the electorate and also in parts surrounding Tiger Land Estate, roads and paths were constructed. These roads were not merely welcome because they offered connections previously not available, but also because they were constructed in such a way that they tended to be functional in the very worst of weather. Many of the old village paths had tended to get flooded during the monsoon.

The policy of road construction was designed partially to cultivate support in areas in which the Doctor was weak. Many of the locations in the west of the electorate had been Dee's strongholds.

Through road construction the Doctor gained goodwill in these areas, and cultivated new contacts. The *Vel-Vidane* of one hamlet became a staunch supporter of his. In another area he gained the affection of a fatherless family by giving two of the older sons jobs in his Ministry: the first as a store-keeper, the other as a driver. These two brothers were to help him to penetrate their village, which had consistently voted against him. It was partially due to their support that in 1977 he was able to secure about a third of the votes from the area. Meanwhile, the community of potters, which had tended to vote as the dominant *Goigama* village headman in the Hamville-Kudville area instructed them to, also benefited. They got easy credit, and State shops and boutiques for the sale of their products were opened on the main road. Both these measures helped break their dependence on the village elite (tied to Dee), which had controlled their votes. The *Kumbal* potters now form a fairly firm part of the Doctor's support.

However, during this period the Doctor made one major error. The main highway used to cut the railway line at two points. Those making the journey used to suffer long delays, having to wait at the rail motor halts for the trains to pass. At one of these points, Kudville, the *Kumbal* potters used to have a sales centre, and those motorists delaying at the halts used to provide good custom for their products. The Doctor failed to recognize this fact in a new road plan he drew up. Anxious to reduce the delays at the rail motor halts, and to create a pleasant driveway by the sea for visiting tourists, he arranged the construction of a new diversionary road. This road, later named Beach Way, ran from Kudville to Bluville town, hugging the coast for most of the distance. Its construction antagonized the potters, who saw reduced custom for their goods. More significantly, it antagonized some of the most powerful fish *mudalalis* of Bluville town who saw their lands, on which they used to beach their craft, acquired without compensation. These *mudalalis*, who had been some of the Doctor's strongest supporters, now became his enemies.

In a moment of indiscretion, the Doctor had publicly promised one of his supporters, Zee, nomination to the Bluville seat in 1970. Most of the fish *mudalalis* of the town now began to work for Zee, financing his meetings and promising him blocs of votes. Some switched over to Dee. To compound the problem, exigencies of State forced the Doctor, now a senior Cabinet Minister, to be out of the country and electorate for much of the time. During the 1969 floods he was unable to visit the place, and this gave his new found enemies ammunition in their campaign against him.

Close confidants now began to advise the Doctor against recontesting Bluville. In retrospect this appears to have been bad counsel. The Dee Foo of 1970 did not have the same personal standing as the Dee of 1956, owing to certain aspects of his conduct. He had lost the respect of many of the intermediaries through whom he had operated and, by 1970, was not regarded as a strong candidate. It is quite likely that if the Doctor had recontested Bluville on the UNP ticket in May 1970 he would have retained the seat. But his advisers thought differently. The Doctor therefore stepped down to contest another seat in which his Ministry had constructed many beneficial public works, and where a network of migrant shopkeepers from Bluville proved his intermediary supporters.

The new UNP candidate was the grandson of the owner of an estate, and its Superintendent. He had built up some support for himself by helping individuals in the area, transporting them to hospital during times of need, buying tea leaf from smallholders at favourable rates, and generally acting in a socially concerned manner. However, he did not enjoy the same economic and social status as the Doctor. The extent of his family's disbursement of patronage had also been on a far lesser scale than that of the Doctor's. So he did not have a personal network of intermediaries and clients except in the villages surrounding his estate. The votes from this region would have accounted for about 3,000 at the very most. Apart from this, all Zee's support was derived from Bluville town, its environs, and Okerville: areas which had traditionally gone to the Doctor and, if not for his construction of Beach Way, would have done so again. Indeed, about three quarters of Zee's votes would have been from these sources. All these coastal votes were given on a party basis. They came from the intermediaries and clients of the Doctor's; men who had become associated with the UNP over a period of over two decades as a result of the Doctor's link with the party. These men now felt obliged to support a candidate of that party, irrespective of his family background and personal connections. It would have been awkward for them to have switched support to a party and set of people they had always worked against. Thus, Zee's personal role as a patron in gathering this support was very limited. He did not have the stature and links the Doctor enjoyed. This, coupled with the national swing against the UNP, lost him the seat by a large margin. He was not even considered for renomination in 1977.

Dee's victory in May 1970 was to herald another major extension of the State in Bluville, with important implications for future modes of patronage disbursement. This was seen, first, in the growth of the Co-operative Movement. Isolated small-scale credit societies had existed as early as 1911 in parts of Sri Lanka, and, in 1942, consumer societies had been formed. In 1947, Co-operative Agricultural Production and Sales Societies, which involved a number of farmers clubbing together to purchase tools, fertilizer stores and sales outlets to be held and used in common, were established. But it was not until 1957 that the Co-operatives really began to intrude into the everyday life of all individuals. In this year the Co-operative Agricultural Production and Sales Societies were enlarged into Multi-Purpose Societies. With a controlled economy, these institutions began to monopolize the distribution of almost all essential items in a household budget: rice and basic foodstuffs, textiles, soaps, footwear, household electrical appliances and the vital kerosene oil needed for cooking and lighting, to name but a few. In addition to being near monopolists in the distribution of these scarce consumer goods, the Co-operatives were also the main marketing outlet for agricultural products, disbursers of agricultural credit and purchasers of agricultural products. Thus they intruded into the lives of every consumer and every farmer. In Bluville their conduct was to be especially significant in the paddy-growing smallholder-dominated western part of the electorate, which had traditionally supported Dee. However, during the 1960s their management remained relatively independent, appointments being made by the Commissioner of Co-operative Development. There was relatively little scope for an MP to interfere in the choice.

This situation was to change rapidly after the advent of the UF to power in 1970.[59] The new Government believed that all State institutions which were, or could be, sources of political patronage should be controlled by it, so that it could further entrench itself in strategic positions of power. New legislation now decreed that nine out of the fifteen directors of every Multi-Purpose Co-operative Society (MPCS) be nominated by the Minister for Co-operatives on the recommendation of the District Political Authority or MP of the area. Only five were to be elected by the members of the Society, and one by its employees. The managers of the different branches of this Society were then to be chosen by this Board.

The Purville *Korale* MPCS, which covered Bluville and a neighbouring electorate, had 196 such branches. Those in the Bluville electorate, accounting for about half this number, had their manager appointed largely on Dee's recommendation. These managers tended to be drawn from the ranks of Dee's traditional supporters (who had now begun to be closely identified with the SLFP as a party).

Unfortunately, most of these appointees were ill-suited for their jobs. They tended to regard the institutions they operated as the means for personal material enrichment, rather than one of consolidating their, or their party's, power. No less than 186 of these managers have now been interdicted for misappropriation of Society funds.[60] In one case a manager had misappropriated Rs 15,000, in another Rs 45,000. Between 1971 and July 1976 total leakages had amounted to Rs 1 million.

One MPCS, chaired by a supposedly close associate of Dee's, had bought goods from private traders at high rates and then sold them to the general public at lesser prices, getting the Society to bear the loss. By this means certain key officials in the MPCS had been able to favour those businessmen who had helped them in various ways. Often prices had been reduced by 25 per cent, and in one notable case by 90 per cent.

[59] Asiriwatham (1981) provides the basis for this paragraph.

[60] Commissioner of Co-operative Development (Investigations Department), Confidential Files of Inquiry into the Purville *Korale* MPCS (1970–7), form the basis for this paragraph and the next four.

In 1973 an official of the MPCS had sold 2,000 gunny bags to a private trader, known to him, at a low price without having called for tenders. In another incident that year, he had made a similar sale to a low bidder, again supposedly known to him, dismissing the higher tenderer. As a result of such deeds, the Contracts Section of the Society had sustained a loss of Rs 130,000. Building contracts had been given to favourites, and when costs had exceeded estimates, as occurred in the case of a new school and Paddy Marketing Board retail outlet, it was the Society which had to pay. Again, purchases of land and buildings had been made without the permission of the Commissioner of Co-operative Development, as required by existing legislation.

Meanwhile Society vehicles had been freely used by certain officials for their private travel. In 1974 one official had issued five vouchers totalling Rs 700 to subordinates, without mentioning the reasons for the trips or places visited. The officers inquiring into these activities after 1977 had been unable to pass these vouchers. And no action had been taken to check the misappropriations which had been occurring at the local level.

The Society had also been used as a means of favouring friends, relations and party supporters. It was these people who had been employed and received favoured treatment. Twenty-one such officers had been chosen and sent for training in accounts and management, without receipt of the necessary security bonds. Meanwhile, the money that had been taken as security had not been deposited in a separate bank account (as required by Society Regulations), but had been used for the general conduct of business.

Such activities meant that those working in the Purville *Korale* MPCS began to be permeated by an air of corruption. The misappropriation of funds, and selling of public goods to private traders, meant that there was a shortage of consumer items for general distribution. As the economy was so tightly controlled at the time, and as the Co-operative was generally the only place at which an individual could purchase his essential needs at reasonable prices, these shortages engendered great bitterness. Rumours abounded of textiles, oils and the like being sold to private traders cheaply, who would then sell them to the public at black-market prices. Many of these stories cannot be categorically substantiated, but that this was the general belief is certain. This, coupled with the fact that only a few favourites benefited, engendered much public bitterness.

The problem was especially acute in the smallholder-dominated paddy-growing western part of the electorate. This was because, unlike in the fishing villages, mismanagement in the Co-operatives here not only affected the inhabitants as consumers, but as producers too. The MPCS was the chief source of agricultural credit and inputs and the major (sometimes only legal) purchaser and seller of products. Mismanagement in the institution meant that there were shortages of vital inputs and credit, so that production was hampered. Moreover, the fact that farmers were legally obliged to sell their paddy and minor crops, produced under very trying conditions, to the Government at low official prices below black-market rates engendered much ill-will. It was therefore not surprising that Dee and the SLFP lost support in this traditional stronghold of theirs.

Meanwhile, the estates had been nationalized and were being run on similarly corrupt lines. Again, the villagers did not benefit in the way that they had done during the days of the private landowner. Most of the properties confiscated by the Government in Bluville had been planted with tea and rubber, and could not therefore be subdivided for distribution amongst the local inhabitants. They were run instead by a new group of so-called managers, who generally consisted of the close friends, relations or associates of the sitting MP, Dee. These individuals tended to be mercenary in their approach to management, in a way private owners had not been. Many would sell jobs in the factories, and expect bribes for promotions. Villagers in the vicinity were not allowed the fringe benefits of firewood, thatch and grazing rights, which they had been traditionally used to. And, of course, when ill they did not receive free transport, medicine and assistance, as in the past.

Thus, it was not surprising that when the Doctor came to campaign in northern Bluville in 1977 he was worshipped on the platform as a god. The treatment he had afforded these villagers as a landowner was very different to what they were receiving after the estate takeovers.

It was due to such treatment, and the mismanagement of these estates and Co-operatives, that the United Front (UF) Government lost so much support in Bluville and nationally too. True, there were external factors such as the oil price rise of 1973 and the long term decline in international tea and rubber prices which had weakened the payments balance. This had contributed to a depreciation of the rupee and domestic inflation, coupled with import restrictions and shortages of scarce goods. It was also true that the Government and local political actors were not wholly to blame for this plight. But, nevertheless, their inefficient and corrupt management of the overgrown State institutions accentuated an already serious problem. And in the public's eye it was this corrupt management, and not the intangible external factors, which could most readily be perceived, and the perpetrators of which could most easily be identified.

Meanwhile Dee's personal conduct had left much to be desired. This, and certain differences he had with the party leadership meant that he failed to secure SLFP renomination in 1977. Peeved and indignant, he spoke publicly in support of the Doctor. Some of the paddy-growing western villages, where he still had some degree of personal influence, gave a higher proportion of votes to the Doctor than previously (about half his total, on this occasion). But this may have been due more to the peculiarly acute way in which the mismanagement of the Co-operatives affected the farmers here, as explained before, than to Dee's personal influence *per se*. In addition, there was the national swing against the sitting Government.

The new SLFP candidate was a lawyer from a nearby town, with almost no personal ties in the electorate. Virtually all the votes he received would have been given on a party basis. Over three quarters of his votes would have been from the paddy-growing western part of the electorate (which had traditionally supported Dee), though the support here was, for reasons explained earlier, less forthcoming than in the past. This was because Dee's intermediaries had established SLFP branches in these areas and benefited from State patronage, and so come to identify their interests with those of the party rather than the individual. They, therefore, felt obliged to support the party candidate, even though Dee spoke against him. Moreover, by now the personal wealth of a candidate and his ability to disburse patronage were so small compared to those of the party and the State that there was little incentive for an intermediary or his followers to support an Independent candidate against a party nominee.

So in 1977, as in 1970, it was the party rather than the individual which really drew the votes. Organization at the local level was important, but national issues of inflation, unemployment and the management of State bodies were the key determinants of the result. Patron–client ties still existed, but as a result of the economic changes examined, and the electoral reforms implemented, they were far less tight and binding than previously. Indeed, in certain areas the traditional intermediaries of the candidates had switched allegiance. In the smallholding paddy-growing western part of the electorate the SLFP lost support it had previously enjoyed due to its mismanagement of the Co-operatives. And in Bluville town the fish *mudalalis* who had lost their lands for the construction of Beach Way, and had still not received compensation, supported the Communist Party candidate against the Doctor. (The Communist Party candidate also drew some support from the Okerville area, through certain family contacts he had there.) However, the clientele of the *mudalalis* were not so closely bound to them, for the reasons enumerated on pp. 60–4. Moreover, with the electoral reforms of 1956–65 detailed on pp. 53–9, supervision of the poll became that much more difficult.

With the long-standing ties between a patron and an intermediary and his clients being eroded in this way, voting has become far more atomistic. Individuals now vote much more according to their own dictates than those of others. This is one reason why the votes of particular villages are more evenly divided than before. The phenomenon of a whole area voting en bloc for a particular candidate is now much rarer than it used to be.

To sum up, these changes in voting behaviour were largely the result of the growth of the State coupled with the electoral reforms of 1956–65. We traced this growth between 1956 and 1977 in the key areas of economic activity in Bluville: fishing and agricultural co-operatives. We have seen how this helped erode the importance of private wealth in the disbursement of patronage and helped create new, looser ties based on State institutions (though the same families tended to remain as patrons and intermediaries). We have tried to show, however, that it was not mere control of these State institutions but their appropriate manipulation which could help build up political support. We have mentioned three noteworthy cases: (i) the construction of Beach Way and the mismanagement of (ii) the Co-operatives and (iii) the nationalized estates, where the use of the State actually undermined the popularity of the sitting MP. Nevertheless, we have also seen that in other cases State patronage could be used to reward supporters, strengthen one's intermediaries against those of a rival, cultivate new contacts and, if necessary, harass one's opponents.

The extension and consolidation of political support via the State, and the constraints faced (1977–82)

As we have seen, during the period 1965–70, the Doctor had not actively attempted to bully those who had worked against him, as Dee had done in the case of the *madel* owners. Rather, he had sought to strengthen his political base by cultivating new contacts in areas he was weak in.

This policy was continued after 1977. The fish *mudalalis* who had lost their lands for the construction of Beach Way, and had worked against the Doctor, received prompt cash compensation. In Kudville, where again the construction of Beach Way had engendered ill-will, a pottery centre was established for the manufacture of ceramics. About Rs 500,000 were invested in the venture and thirty individuals provided with employment. As noted, both the fish *mudalalis*, and to a lesser extent the potters, had swung against the Doctor in the late 1960s with the construction of Beach Way. These new programmes helped win them back.

Meanwhile, in one traditionally difficult area for the Doctor, a new fertilizer factory was established at a cost of Rs 46.2 million. About thirty acres were acquired for the project, and cash compensation promptly paid to the owners. (The memories of Beach Way may have still been vivid.) Eight hundred individuals from the area were provided with employment. Even before the factory commenced operations, the Doctor's commitment to the area won him new supporters. This, and perhaps the knowledge that the UNP with a five-sixths majority in Parliament was likely to last its full six-year term and so control the disbursement of State patronage over the period, may have induced individuals to switch allegiance to the Doctor's nominees at the 1979 local government polls. At these elections virtually the whole area voted for the UNP, whereas in 1977 only about a third had done so.

Meanwhile, in another area, which had been fairly evenly divided in its support for the Doctor, a factory for the conversion of coir into yarn was established in January 1981. Fifteen unskilled workers were given primary employment and three apprentices were hired to be trained as machine operators. A market was also provided for green husk suppliers, with a standing order for 8,000 husks per day. With the increased atomization of voting, the Government's policy was to cultivate goodwill amongst as wide a section of the populace as possible. Consequently, spinning sets were directly loaned to 125 families for the spinning of yarn. The finished product was to be bought back by the State at a piece rate, and each family was expected to make about Rs 25 daily by these means. In this way the State further replaced the powerful private trader as the chief monopsonist for the products of the poor and monopolist in the distribution of credit and capital goods.

Areas of traditional support were not neglected in these schemes. In one village bordering Tiger Land estate, twenty-six acres were acquired from the Land Reform Commission, and a large workshop for the repair and assembly of buses was established. An investment of Rs 10 million was made and employment provided for 700 individuals. In the Okerville harbour, various improvements were embarked upon, with the construction of a breakwater, a slipway for the repair of boats and ice-rooms for the storage of fish. A fisheries bank (under the auspices of the People's Bank), for the extension of easy credit to fishermen, was also established.

Three workshops for the training of carpenters, each catering for about forty individuals, and one sewing centre to train forty girls, were also established. Employment creation and the fostering of special skills were the objectives of these schemes. The aim was to curtail the large and growing number of arts graduates who were unable to find jobs appropriate for their qualifications and thus swelled the ranks of the leftist JVP.

Meanwhile, two more general infrastructural schemes were initiated. The first was one of rural electrification, benefiting a wide cross-section of society directly, and also helping small-scale industries (such as rice milling). Between 1977 and 1980 inclusive schemes were completed in eleven villages.

The second major infrastructural scheme still being implemented is the Cocos River Basin Project. At present the 8,500 acres of paddy in the Cocos River's catchment area, of which nearly 5,000 acres fall in Bluville electorate, yield a very low annual return. This is because constant floods allow the fields to be cultivated during only one season per year. Moreover they also suffer from an inflow of briny water (through the river) with the tide. This lack of control over irrigation has meant that the yields from these fields have been in the region of fifteen to twenty-five bushels per acre per year. The proposed scheme involves the construction of bunds and the widening of the river and subsidiary canals, so as to allow greater control over the water flow. This, and the prevention of the present inflow of briny water into the fields, is expected to allow double-cropping and nearly triple yields to sixty bushels per year. The farmers of several villages in the electorate should benefit from this scheme.

As with the electrification scheme, there has been no discrimination on grounds of party loyalty. In fact the Cocos River Basin Project should benefit those who have traditionally supported Dee more than it should other sections of the electorate. This has reinforced the Doctor's image as a very fair, just, and non-partisan, figure, and earned him widespread goodwill.

However, such goodwill was, and is, highly dependent on national and international factors. Nationally, the abolition of the rice rations harmed many paddy smallholders. Whereas in the past, they had received a higher real return on their investments selling their produce on the black market at inflated prices, or trading their ration quotas for consumer durables, they were unable to do this after 1977. Indeed this was a significant factor in the swing of 5 per cent or so against the Doctor and the UNP, at the October 1982 Presidential Poll. Even areas bordering the Tiger Land Estate (which had traditionally been a stronghold of the Doctor's) gave him only about half its votes at this poll. With the Doctor's exit as an important landowner in the area, national factors assumed greater prominence.

Again, many projects undertaken relied heavily on foreign aid and overseas markets for their success. The Cocos River Basin Project, financed by a consortium of Western donors, was temporarily halted in 1981 with the cuts in foreign aid in these countries. The electrification scheme, financed by the ADB was also slowed down when the finalization of the second stage of the loan was delayed. The yarn factory established in 1981 was unable to expand as planned due to increased protectionism in the West and the market constraints (abroad) this entailed. Meanwhile, the incipient textile industry in the area was also threatened with competition from imports as the economy was liberalized.

The national and international factors constraining these projects were then, doubtless, important in explaining the limits to goodwill engendered. They were factors in the swing against the Doctor in October 1982. They have become even more important with time, as far-flung rural areas have been integrated into the national and international economy and more exposed to changes in overall investment policies and world trade and aid patterns.

Meanwhile, with the extension of the State, and the integration of the rural economy into the national and international nexus, the patronage networks of old have changed their character. It is this to which we shall now turn.

The new patronage networks (1977–82)

The new patronage networks which have emerged in Bluville are based on access to the Doctor in his public role as a senior Government Minister. Whoever has such access stands to gain a State office. Such a man then acquires the potential to become a patron in his own right.

Close members of the Doctor's own family, by virtue of their social and physical proximity to him, have some advantage in this. Soon after the 1977 elections, the Doctor's brother, Tyrrel, secured the chairmanship of a major State Corporation and began to start rewarding those known to him with State jobs. About forty to fifty individuals were given posts as clerks, drivers, cleaners and security guards in the Corporation. The beneficiaries were from six villages surrounding the Tiger Land estate and tended to be from the families of traditional clients. Rumours began to circulate that Tyrrel was attempting to consolidate and expand his clientele so that he could pave the way for his son to contest the seat at a future date.

Tyrrel's most notable act was his decision to site the employment-generating Provincial Corporation factory in Bluville, rather than the district capital. This project, financed by the West Germans was designed to help decentralize the final manufacture of a Corporation product to the regions. Although the Germans and five of the seven Board members argued that the district capital was a more appropriate location, having better infrastructural facilities, Tyrrel, as Chairman, vetoed the proposal, and was able to establish the complex in his home electorate of Bluville. Some accused him of being politically motivated in this decision by the desire to create a clientele for himself in the area. It earned him much unpopularity at Board level, and eventually forced his resignation. But, be this as it may, these activities during his chairmanship of the Corporation indicated the extent to which he, as a member of an old landed family, was forced to rely on the State (rather than personal resources), in the attempt to create and maintain a political base in his home area.

This expansion of the State at the expense of private wealth has made for a greater equality of opportunity in politics (and the economy). A poor man may now rise far through personal access to a powerful Minister, and thereby State bodies. Thus, many of those who are now rising in Bluville are, or have been, the fairly humble employees of the Doctor.

The man who is presently regarded as most likely to succeed him began life as a servant boy, rose to be his Estate Superintendent, and thereafter the organizer of an estate labourers' union. After the Doctor's return to office in 1977, this man was appointed Superintendent of a 900 acre State plantation which included the nationalized portion of Tiger Land estate. As such, he exercised control via the State of an acreage and labour force far in excess of anything the Doctor had ever controlled as a private landowner. Moreover, he was able to use this office to further expand his estate workers' union, and then get elected as leader of the UNP branch in the area. Thereafter, he was able to use party (and perhaps State) funds to favour individuals in various ways. He purchased a van, which was used to transport sick workers to hospital, and was a regular (and generous) visitor at weddings and funerals. He also used the financial resources at his command to have a number of pictures of himself printed and distributed freely in the area. In this way, he has used his access to the Doctor and State to lay the basis for a political career.

Another man mentioned as a possible candidate is the Doctor's current Private Secretary. He was a one-time employee of a Corporation and used this position to help the fishermen of the region. He was until recently the chief link between the Doctor and his constituents, and not long ago was mentioned as a possible UNP candidate for the chairmanship of the local District Development Council (DDC).

Meanwhile, other employees have become intermediaries, somewhat in the way the fish *mudalalis* and small-scale landowners were in the past. But, whereas the latter used personal wealth to gain control of State bodies, these new intermediaries use their access to the Doctor to gain entry into these institutions and thus augment their personal wealth. In one case a labourer on Mrs Amy Ay's estate was able to join the local party branch, secure employment as a Ministry chauffeur and then (by supposedly questionable means) lease four acres of land and cultivate this, whilst also securing a post for his non-graduate wife as a teacher at a Government school. He is now trying to secure a post for his sister as a sales assistant at a Sri Lanka position abroad which comes under the purview of the Doctor's Ministry. This same man now has his own lorry and driver used for the transport of the produce from the leased land. His total income now exceeds Rs 3,000 a month, far more than the paltry Rs 1.10 a day he received as an estate labourer.

Two other former labourers on Tiger Land Estate, both brothers, have been able to gain houses through their links with the Doctor. One is now a Ministry chauffeur, the other the manager at a prestigious State institution. Neither would have enjoyed anything like the wealth and position they now do if not for their personal access to the Doctor, party, and thereby, State.

Using their access to the Doctor to augment their wealth and positions has meant some of these intermediaries accepting bribes. In such cases they have been unable to build up political goodwill as such. Indeed, they cannot be said to have created a clientele for themselves, as intermediaries of the past had.

Yet, even where favours have been granted regardless of such incentives, the ties binding these new intermediaries to their clients are far less tight and binding than in the past. This is because, first, there is no strong institutionalized element of economic dependence in them as before and secondly, the ability to supervise and coerce at the polling booth has been eroded.

The ties between a patron and an intermediary have also become far less binding than previously. This is because a patron now exercises influence only in so far as he is in control of State institutions and not by virtue of his private wealth and ability to dispense private patronage. As stated before, when appointed Chairman of a State Corporation, Tyrrel Ay began to distribute jobs to those from Bluville personally known to him. Amongst others, his personal driver, Leelo was given a post as the Corporation Chairman's chauffeur, at a salary much above his previous one. Leelo's dependence was now not upon his master personally but upon the State, and whoever held the chairmanship of the Corporation. When Tyrrel Ay lost this position in 1979, Leelo stayed on as the Corporation Chairman's official driver. Later Tyrrel Ay offered him his former post back at the former salary, but Leelo refused it. Indeed, he was even unwilling to work for his old master on a part-time basis at weekends, on the grounds that he would then be losing valuable overtime pay. Thus, clients and intermediaries have become dependent on State officials, rather than on private patrons *per se*. The latter often still wield influence but (like Tyrrel Ay) only in so far as they control State institutions. When they lose such control they lose their influence and to a certain extent a part of their former clientele, as Tyrrel Ay lost Leelo.

This phenomenon is the result of the expansion of the State at the expense of private wealth. With the fifty-acre limit on landholdings, and other restrictions on business expansion, few individuals have the personal resources to create and maintain large personal clienteles. This can only be done by seizing control of the all-important State network. With the curbs on Independent candidates (Chapter 4, pp. 53–9), their poor electoral performances since Independence and, most important, the need for links with Government ministers and the Colombo Administration for the implementation of popular local projects, the party is seen as the main, or only, vehicle by which such control can be achieved. Thus the premium placed on securing the party ticket in any electoral contest has grown.

In the process the influence of party branches and considerations of party welfare, have increased. At present some associates of the Doctor (including his daughter) wish to develop some land close to Okerville as a tourist resort. This same spot has been eyed by local villagers for a housing complex and, because of UNP branch pressure, the Doctor is now reconsidering the position. This sort of grass-roots opinion would not have been channelled through a party branch to such effect in the past. But because the party is the all-important vehicle by which State power can be captured and retained, branch opinion has to be considered. And considered it is. The Okerville branch of the UNP argues that, if the tourist project were to materialize, this would create so much ill-will in the area that the far left JVP would gain support. The Communist candidate did have a network of friends and relations in the area (which was able to give him about 1,000 votes in 1977), so that the left has some base on which to build in this area. The Doctor, as an astute and experienced statesman, will consider these facts before coming to a decision. The present chances are that the tourist project will be halted.

The party therefore wields an influence independent of that of the individual candidate. And to a very large extent, the candidate now wields influence only in so far as he has control of party and/or State bodies, rather than through his personal wealth *per se*. However, the establishment of a party branch seldom, if ever, signifies the commitment on the part of the founders to any particular political ideology. Rather, it represents a desire to gain State patronage for themselves and their area. Thus, there has always been a tendency for the ruling party to see the number of its branches in any particular electorate increase during its tenure of office. In Bluville the number of UNP local branches rose from 74, just before the July 1977 election, to 130 at present.

To sum up this section, the new patronage networks which have emerged in Bluville are based on access to the State via association with a political party. As such, personal or familial ties based on private wealth have been eroded. The new political actors often have some background of a client relationship to the patrons, but they are from a wider social compass than in the past. The new ties between a patron and intermediary, and intermediary and client, are far more temporary and loose in nature than originally in the past.

The 1982 Elections

The greater importance of party policies and national issues was clearly seen in the Presidential Poll of October 1982. A major factor working against the SLFP were the memories of the long queues for essential items seen in the 1970–7 era, and the fears that these would be revived if the party were returned. Other important factors were the divisions within the party, the absence of LSSP backing and the associated poor organization at the grass-roots level. In several parts of Bluville, the SLFP organizer, Arti Ay, a second cousin of the Doctor, did not even have Polling Agents. In such cases the possibility of impersonation cannot be ruled out.

Nevertheless, the UNP and the Doctor saw their support fall from about 55 per cent of the total vote in July 1977 to about 50 per cent in October 1982, and the SLFP share rise from about 35 per cent to about 45 per cent. The major factors in this were, first, the swing against the UNP in the paddy-growing areas (Chapter 4, p. 74), and secondly, the loss of traditional support in Bluville town and Okerville. This loss of support was due largely to the unpopularity of the Doctor's new intermediaries, and the fact that some of them took bribes and acted arbitrarily and arrogantly (p. 77). Moreover, in Okerville, Arti Ay, a lawyer, had built up a clientele for himself by appearing for several fishermen in legal cases, without charging costs.

In October the UNP's share of the vote represented a median performance in the district. The Doctor, recognizing this as a setback, campaigned actively at the Referendum Poll. For the first time since 1959/60 he went personally to meet constituents at pocket meetings.[61] At the same time, the SLFP candidate of July 1977 (and a key party figure in

---

[61] Pocket meetings cover a set of houses within a village. They number not more than fifty people or so and thus enable a closer rapport between speaker and constituents than normal election meetings of several hundreds. In December 1982, the Doctor also had a question and answer session at the end of each pocket meeting.

the area) crossed over to the UNP bringing 2,000 party organizers with him.

The Opposition's utter disarray facilitated widespread intimidation and impersonation. Although electoral legislation debarred the advertising of the lamp symbol and use of party colours, this rule was openly flouted by Government supporters. They put up green flags and posters with the lamp symbol around their own homes (and those of opponents too, warning the latter of dire consequences if these were removed). Villagers in areas known to have supported the SLFP in October were warned against turning up to vote again. This may explain the lower turnout in these areas than elsewhere. Finally, the Opposition organizer failed to find Polling Agents for several booths. In such cases impersonation would have been facilitated.

These factors assured the Doctor's resounding victory at the Poll in December 1982. Securing the highest vote in the district and nearly the highest in the province, it represented one of his greatest victories, on paper.

Conclusion: the new framework

In this chapter, we have traced the growth of the State in Bluville in the two key areas of economic activity there, fishing and agricultural co-operatives. The growth of State bodies was at the expense of private wealth and made their control the criterion in determining one's ability to disburse patronage and succeed in politics. This had implications for patterns of political recruitment because it meant greater and wider access to politics for the masses. Fairly poor individuals now had greater chances of rising to prominence through their work for, and control of, various State organizations and networks, as in the case of the Doctor's Estate Superintendent and Private Secretary. True, those coming from the elite families of patrons and intermediaries still enjoyed an advantage by virtue of their closer access to established notables and the deference they could sometimes inspire. But this advantage could be lost through clumsy handling of the State machinery, as in the case of Tyrrel Ay's handling of a State Corporation.

Meanwhile, the growth of the State, at the expense of private wealth, had three major implications for patterns of political allegiance. First, it weakened the ties of economic dependence of clients upon intermediaries, and intermediaries upon patrons. We have argued that this, coupled with the electoral reforms of 1956–65, made the delivery of vote blocs much more difficult than in the past. Electors became more atomistic, voting as individuals and considering national issues. Thus, especially after 1965, villages became more even in their distribution of support for a particular candidate than before. Secondly, with the increased role of the central Government in disbursing patronage, the need to have an MP with contacts in Colombo rose. This, coupled with certain electoral reforms, helped in the demise of the Independent candidate and the institutionalization of a two-party system. Allegiance then began to be more to a party than to any particular individual candidate. And the candidate began to exercise influence only in so far as he was a party or State official, rather than in his own personal right. Dee's inability to switch his vote bloc to the Doctor in July 1977 was a striking indication of this. Finally, the expansion of the State, at the expense of private wealth placed a very heavy premium on its appropriate manipulation. We have studied three instances in Bluville, the construction of Beach Way, the estate takeover and the management of the Co-operatives, where the sitting MP actually lost support through an inappropriate handling of the instruments at his command.

But, even with appropriate handling, the local politician's ability to succeed is constrained by external (national and international) factors. In Bluville, such factors, as they affect local matters, have come to play an increasing role in successive elections. In July 1977, the national shortages of consumer durables (distributed through the Co-operatives) lost the SLFP support. In October 1982 the replacement of the ration system by the open market had the same consequences for the UNP in the paddy-growing areas of the electorate. Several local projects continue to rely on a suitable foreign aid and trade climate for their success. This external environment will therefore always have to be considered in assessing future patterns of political allegiance in Bluville.

5

Greenville: the patronage networks of the Mou/Nous and the Pou/Kous (1947–1959)

Introduction

Greenville is a constituency with many similarities to Bluville: both constituencies are in the Low Country; both are largely rural; in both over nine-tenths of the population is Sinhala Buddhist; and both have a very similar history, geography and socio-economic and administrative structure. The major difference lies in the economic and social positions of the castes. In Greenville the *Goigama* community is economically and socially dominant at both the village and the electoral levels. By and large, all other castes bear a client-type relationship to it. There has to date been no caste like the *Karave* in Bluville to challenge this dominance, and the two major political factions have both been led by members of this community. We shall try to show that the support these leaders drew during this early period (1947–59) rested on the same bases as in Bluville: namely through ties of economic and social dependence (via the land, the *Mudaliyar* system and local government), rather than via any caste identity with the voters, who were overwhelmingly *Goigama*.

In 1946 the electorate covered an area of about 120 square miles and consisted of three constituent parts: first Groville *Korale* containing over half the electorate's population; secondly, a part of Kross *Korale* North accounting for another third or so, and finally sections of Yap *Korale* (East and West) with the remainder.[1] In 1959 the electoral boundaries were redrawn to exclude Kross *Korale* North and include only a part of Groville *Korale*, and a reduced extent of Yap *Korale* (East and West).[2] As the so called lower castes (*Batgam, Vahumpura, Hunu* and *Pannama*) were concentrated in Kross *Korale* North and the northern parts of Yap *Korale*, this change meant that these groups accounted for a slightly smaller proportion of the total electoral strength after 1959 (about 33 per cent), than before (say 40 per cent). The potential for a left-wing candidate to exploit the oppression of these groups for electoral advantage, as

[1] GOC (1946).   [2] GOC (1959).

had been done in 1947, was thereby diminished. The Left has therefore tended to avoid this seat since then. Further, Yap *Korale* (where the Pous and the Kous continued to exercise considerable influence until the early 1970s) accounting for a larger proportion of the constituency after 1959 than before (about 26 per cent compared to 17 per cent), the electoral success of these families was more marked here during the later period than during the early. Although the share of Groville *Korale* also rose (from 55 per cent to about 75 per cent), the electoral success of the Mous and the Nous, who were dominant here, did not increase proportionately. This was due to family feuds, the atrophying of their patronage networks in the area and the role of a rival State based network initiated by the Pou/Kous after 1956. These factors are more fully examined in Chapter 6.

The main economic activity of the people of Greenville in 1947 was agriculture. Coconut was, by far, the chief crop grown, accounting for over nine-tenths of the cultivated area.[3] Most of this was concentrated in the form of large estates owned by two sets of families: the Mou/Nous and the Pou/Kous.[4] But many of the middle-rung *Goigama* families, from whom the village headmen tended to be drawn and through whom the big patrons operated, owned smallholdings of coconut. Such headmen almost always owned less than fifty and generally below twenty-five acres,[5] but this was sufficient to provide them with a surplus above their subsistence needs. They were therefore in a position to employ others, have a clientele of landless or near landless villagers indebted to them, and thus act as smaller scale patrons in their own right.

This power was enhanced by the way the cottage industries of the area functioned.[6] Many of the poorer families from the depressed castes would weave baskets, make pottery and cultivate cashew nuts to supplement their income. They depended on the richer families, generally of the *Goigama* community, for credit and the working capital to conduct their businesses; kilns in the case of potters, cane in that of weavers. The richer families by providing these items, purchasing back the finished products at prearranged prices, and then transporting the goods to Colombo, where they sold well, made the poor groups highly dependent upon them. A type of patron–client tie therefore developed between many of these (often *Goigama*) families and those of the depressed castes.

---

[3] Reading of Ordnance Survey Maps (Survey Department, Sri Lanka, published periodically).
[4] Ibid. and Ferguson's (1941–56).
[5] See SLNA Lot 33.
[6] Ibid. for the basis for this paragraph and the next.

However, the nature of this tie, and so the basis on which political support was rendered, was different to that in the fishing villages of Bluville, being more oppressive and less paternalistic. This provided the basis for the emergence of a socially discontented, depressed caste group, which was to vote 'left' in 1947 and succeeding elections.

Meanwhile, since Greenville was not a deltaic area, paddy was not a significant crop in the way it was in Bluville. In both electorates the scope for owners as patrons to exert influence over more than say ten (non-family) clients had been limited. This was because paddy was a small-holder's crop, and there were few, if any, cultivators owning more than about ten acres. In Greenville, as in Bluville, many small owners failed to produce even their subsistence needs and depended on other sources to supplement their income. In some cases, those who leased out their land to tenants also worked as tenants themselves, though labour sharing was a more common means of augmenting personal requirements. So, to sum up, in both electorates a paddy land owner tended not to exert the sort of influence over others that a tea, rubber or to a lesser extent coconut, estate owner did.

However, in Bluville the scale of paddy cultivation was far greater than in Greenville, nearly 5,000 acres being devoted to the crop.[7] In Greenville, with no river delta, less than 500 acres came under paddy.[8] Consequently, the scope for patronage by the *Mudaliyars* of the *Vel-Vidanes*, when it came to *Huwandiram* auctions and grain tax collection, was far less in Greenville then in Bluville. Indeed in many parts of Yap *Korale Huwandirams* were unheard of. Moreover, there had been no separate *Vel-Vidane* to maintain the *yaya* and supervise grain tax collection, this latter function being performed by the headmen in the few paddy growing localities of the district.[9] The net result was that Greenville did not have the large class of favoured *Vel-Vidanes* that Bluville did. True, there was some scope for the *Mudaliyar* to favour the ordinary cultivator and village headmen, as will be seen later.[10] But, quantitatively, connivance in grain tax irregularities by the *Mudaliyar* was not as significant a means of earning goodwill amongst lesser headmen and cultivators in Greenville as it was in Bluville.

Rubber cultivation, as a means of underpinning patron–client relationships, was also not as important in Greenville as in Bluville. The climate being less wet, it was grown on a far lesser scale, most landowners

---

[7] Reading of Ordnance Survey Maps.   [8] Ibid.   [9] SLNA 33/62.
[10] Ibid. When the Government attempted to introduce *Vel-Vidanes* many headmen resisted the move fiercely, and the plan had to be dropped. The headmen were getting a share of the crop as commission, which presumably they felt they would lose to the new *Vel-Vidanes*.

preferring to devote their resources to coconut. For instance, the largest landowner in the district owned only 425 acres of rubber (as against 3,147 acres of coconut) in 1941.[11]

Most rubber was concentrated in Groville *Korale* and coconut in Yap *Korale*. The different agro-ecological structures in the two *korales* were to be important in explaining differences in the nature of the patron–client relationships both within Greenville and as compared to those in Bluville.

From the early part of this century we can distinguish two major patronage networks in the Greenville area. The first, that of the Pous and the Kous, was based on the ownership of extensive coconut lands and a near monopoly of *Mudaliyarships* and lesser posts within the Provincial Administration. It was most marked in Yap *Korale* or the southern part of the electorate, for it was here that the family lands tended to be concentrated and *Mudaliyarships* monopolized. The second, that of the Mous and the Nous, was more marked in Groville *Korale* or the northern part of the electorate. It was based on land ownership, services, and the appropriate use of State institutions from 1931. The influence of the Pous and the Kous has, however, traditionally been greater in Greenville electorate, and we shall begin by focussing on this network first.

The Pous and the Kous: family background

The Pous and the Kous are a part of a set of closely interrelated *Goigama* families which had, since the eighteenth century, monopolized *Mudaliyarships* and other posts within the Provincial Administration in much of this area. These families were to throw up many political leaders during the twentieth century.

However, they:

originated low in the Portuguese administration – their duties centering on the recruitment of labour, revenue collection, and the maintenance of local control. They served in ranked competitive offices as interpreters, book keepers, translators, tax-collectors, foremen, legal advisers to the rulers, scouts and commanders of the local militia.[12]

It was education which gave them their positions and power.[13] And this power was wielded by virtue of their positions in the bureaucracy rather than through land.[14] As Peebles has emphasized 'the *Mudaliyars* were

---

[11] Ferguson's (1941) and Ordnance Survey Maps form the basis for this sentence and the next.

[12] Peebles (1973), p. 24.   [13] Ibid., pp. 24–7.   [14] Ibid.

not independent chieftains, but subordinate members of the colonial bureaucracy.[15] Their accomodesans (*badavädili*) were not fiefs, but small non-transferable grants of land revenue from one or more villages awarded to office holders in lieu of salary.'[16] 'In late Dutch times the largest [such] accomodesan [was] only twenty *amunams* (about forty acres), awarded to [the] highest ranking *Mudaliyar*, the *Maha-Mudaliyar*.[17] Obviously neither the aggregate extent of such grants nor the economic return to the grantee was comparable to European fiefs.'[18] They bore no special relationship to the Crown. These *Mudaliyars* then were not 'feudal lords' (as some have loosely described them), and were certainly no more aristocratic than, say, the Coos or the Bees (described earlier).

The accomodesan or right to revenue from a particular piece of land was only awarded to a given *Mudaliyar* during his period in office.[19] However, the Dutch tended to grant the same fields (and offices) to heirs of the previous holders.[20] Thus, by the time of the British conquest the land, and to a lesser extent the offices, had a *de facto* hereditary character.[21] Even so, large-scale landholding was not to be found at this stage in low-country Sri Lanka.[22]

It was during the nineteenth century that the major change occurred. The power and social position of the *Mudaliyars* was enhanced by two important reforms the British introduced. First, Governor Brownrigg, anxious for a large coolie workforce with which to reconquer and retain Kandy, introduced regulations (in 1818) authorizing the *Mudaliyars* to 'seize, take, arrest, send and employ in the service of Government all and every person or persons who by his or their castes, tenure of land or other custom of these settlements, is or are found to serve Government as coolies or otherwise'.[23] This regulation created a vital role for the *Mudaliyars* in administration, especially those in this area where the main invasion effort was being organized and labour recruitment most widespread. They were now given the legal sanction to formulate a caste hierarchy and press-gang those landless or near landless individuals in their areas into the army under the guise of their being 'low-caste' and 'destined to serve as coolies'. Many of these unfortunates were later used as personal servants and labourers on the *Mudaliyar* estates.[24]

Secondly, during the early nineteenth century, the British embarked on a policy of vesting uncultivated waste land in the Crown and granting it to those most likely to cultivate it. During the late nineteenth century, the vested land began to be auctioned to the highest bidder. The

---

[15] Ibid., p. 28.   [16] Ibid., pp. 28–9.   [17] Ibid., p. 29.
[18] Ibid., p. 29.   [19] Ibid.   [20] Ibid.   [21] Ibid.
[22] Ibid.   [23] Ibid., p. 90   [24] Ibid., pp. 90–1, 94–5 and 127.

Mudaliyars in the Greenville region (with their close proximity to the centre of Government) were best placed to convince the British that they could most easily recruit agricultural labour and develop the land.[25] Not surprisingly, these families were thus able to emerge as large landed proprietors in the early nineteenth century on a scale not known in Ceylon earlier.[26] With the sale of Crown lands after 1840, the *Mudaliyars* were able to augment their holdings further. According to Peebles:

(they) and their families had a distinct advantage in land sales. Not only did they know the lands better, they knew when lands were sold, and were regularly present. They were accused of not advertising sales, which was one of their duties, in order to reduce competition and gain land cheaply for themselves at the upset price.[27]

By the end of the nineteenth century, the set of *Mudaliyar* families from the Greenville region had emerged as one of the leading elites in low-country Ceylon. Several factors can be advanced for their economic and administrative success *vis-à-vis* other elites. First, their proximity to the capital and centre of administration enabled them to secure cheap land and high offices such as the *Maha-Mudaliyarship*, which leading families elsewhere were not so well placed to gain. They also tended to be favoured more than the provincial elites because their district lay between the capital and the still rebellious Kandy and the British found their co-operation indispensable (in a way they did not find that of other leading families). Secondly, the district was also one of the most populous, with many landless families in the country. Press-ganging for land development and the construction of roads was easier and legal sanction was also more readily available as it was here that resources were being raised for the invasion of Kandy and construction of roads to that town. Politically, then, the oppression of a patron over a client tended to be more marked here than in Bluville and the *Mudaliyars* of the Greenville region exerted stronger local influence than those of other areas. Financially too they benefited, by getting officially paid labourers to work on their private estates. Thirdly, the *Mudaliyars* of the Greenville region were able to emerge as richer than those of other districts because their area was one of the most fertile in the country, coconut yields per acre being higher than in most other areas. Fourthly, roads and communications developed here before they did elsewhere. The British built a major road through the area in the nineteenth century. The *Mudaliyars* were the first to reap the financial rewards from this. They were able to transport their rubber, coconut and perishable products more cheaply

[25] Ibid., pp. 98–100.   [26] Ibid., p. 99.   [27] Ibid., pp. 151–2.

and more easily than other provincial families. In the case of perishables, bananas, papaws, vegetables and the like, these could be sold in Colombo at prices above those prevailing in other provincial towns where the same products of other local elites were sold. The Greenville region *Mudaliyar* families were therefore able to reap financial rewards by virtue of their geographical position which leading families of, say, Purville *Korale* were unable to. Finally, with the capital urbanizing rapidly at the turn of the century, the *Mudaliyar* families of the district, with their administrative connections, and by now considerable financial resources, were the best placed to acquire prime properties there and take advantage of the rapidly appreciating land values.

For these reasons the Greenville region *Mudaliyar* families emerged as an economically and administratively dominant bloc by the turn of the century in a way other *Mudaliyar* families did not. Members of this group were to secure a number of parliamentary seats and ministerial posts after Independence and to become nationally prominent. This rise to prominence was not due to any caste identity with the majority community of the Sinhalese electorate, as many writers have fallaciously supposed. Rather, it was due to the factors sketched above, which enabled them to become administratively and economically powerful *vis-à-vis* other provincial elites.

Their local influence as patrons was also probably greater than that of *Mudaliyar* families in other areas. This was because, unlike other provincial elites, the *Mudaliyars* of the Greenville region monopolized both the administration and the land in their area. The power of the one reinforced that of the other in a way not to be found in, say, Bluville. We shall seek to illustrate these contentions by focussing on one branch of the family, that of the Pous and the Kous, operating in one (of the several) electorates within the district, Greenville. We shall look at their role as patrons via the *Mudaliyar* system, before examining the influence they wielded through land-ownership.

The Pous and the Kous: patrons as *Mudaliyars*

By the early twentieth century many *Mudaliyarships* had a *de facto* quasi-hereditary character. In Groville *Korale*, which was later to form a part of Greenville electorate, three generations of Nees held the post in succession before its abolition. A. B. Nee (1875–96) was succeeded by his son B. C. Nee (1896–1926), who was in turn succeeded by his son, Z. A. Nee (1926–1953).[28] In Yap *Korale* East, a part of which went to form the electorate, Christo Pou (1849–87) was succeeded by his son Monti

---

[28] GOC *Blue Books* and *Civil Lists* (1849–1954).

(1887–95).[29] Monti Pou was succeeded by a kinsman Arti Yoo (1895–1914), a son of a former *Maha-Mudaliyar*, Erni Yoo (d. 1879).[30] Arti Yoo was in turn succeeded by Adi Kou (1914–27), a nephew of Monti Pou's (sister's son), and father of the future MP of Greenville.[31] When Adi Kou retired in 1927 to succeed his uncle as the *Maha-Mudaliyar*, his post was taken by Kit Yoo (1927–38), a nephew (brother's son) of the previous *Mudaliyar* of the *Korale*, Arti Yoo.[32] The power of these families was compounded by their also holding positions in the civil service, police and judiciary.[33] In this way they intruded into the everyday life of many villagers.

Meanwhile, their monopoly of *Mudaliyarships* and *Muhandiramships* enabled them to establish very powerful patron–client relationships with the middle-rung landowning headmen of their localities. Certain families in certain localities formed an influential small-scale landowing stratum, which was traditionally favoured with headmanships by the *Mudaliyar* families.[34]

As in Purville *Korale*, such headmen had used their positions to favour their friends and allies, and bully their enemies. In Groville *Korale*, for instance, we find numerous cases of *Police-Vidanes* being accused of stealing cattle, coconuts, fruits and vegetables belonging to individuals antipathetic to them.[35] In another case a *Police-Vidane*, on bad terms with a villager, had, allegedly, destroyed the house belonging to his two orphaned minor nieces and appropriated the timber thereof. In this instance the *Police-Vidane* had apparently borne a grudge against the petitioner for his not having sold him a paddy field he had desired.[36] Sometimes the *Police-Vidane* would turn the entire village against the man he disliked merely by encouraging others to harass him in the knowledge that if he retaliated, he, and not they, would be prosecuted.[37] Again, in any third party dispute, the *Police-Vidane* could work against the man who had antagonized him and could fail to appear in court on the latter's behalf if this were needed. Meanwhile he could favour friends and allies by overlooking their misdeeds; encroachment on Crown land, illicit felling of timber, illicit distilling of arrack, the operation of gambling dens and such activities. Thus, as in Bluville, the headman built up a clientele for himself in his locality.

And, as in Bluville, the *Mudaliyars* of the Greenville area *Korales* supported their headmen in these activities, dismissing petitions against them as 'malicious and pseudonymous', 'unsubstantiated due to lack of

---

[29] Ibid.   [30] Ibid.   [31] Ibid.   [32] Ibid.
[33] Statement based on a study of the *Blue Books* and *Civil Lists*.
[34] Statement based on a study of SLNA Lot 33.
[35] SLNA 33/3619–33/3633 inclusive.   [36] SLNA 33/3619.   [37] Ibid.

witnesses', or whatever. Indeed our study of the evidence between 1880 and 1940 suggests that the abuses in this part of the region were far greater than those in Purville *Korale*.[38] Not merely were the village headmen more high-handed, but the *Mudaliyars* seem to have supported them to a greater extent than in the Bluville region.

In many instances the British Superintendent of Police for the province had to communicate directly with the British GA to complain about the high crime rate in the area and the failure of headmen to take action. The latter were presumed to connive in these crimes and even to encourage their friends and relations to harass their opponents by indulging in such activities.[39] In such cases the *Mudaliyars* tried to gloss over the faults of their subordinates. One *Mudaliyar* of a *korale*, when asked to explain the high incidence of crime in a *peruwa*, tried to defend his men by pointing out the cases in which they had charged individuals and secured convictions.[40] He said that the only fault he could find with them was their failure to note the dates on which they patrolled their areas in their diaries.[41] On hearing this, the GA instructed that each *Police-Vidane* who had failed to make such entries be given a bad mark, and that such note-taking be enforced more sternly in future.[42] After a second complaint from the Superintendent of Police in August 1920, the GA had to order the lesser headmen to report directly to him with their Report Books and Diaries, bypassing the *Mudaliyar*.[43] A harsher policy was followed with more checks, warnings and dismissals.[44]

The initiative in punishing lesser headmen tended to come from the (British) Superintendent of Police. The *Mudaliyar* was often not informed, let alone consulted. When one VA tried to shield his nephew from prosecution (on a charge of manure theft), by stating that he was not to be found in the village, the Superintendent of Police wrote directly to the GA.[45] In this case, as in others, the GA himself sanctioned punishment, without recourse to the *Mudaliyar*'s advice.[46] Similarly, when the Superintendent of Police wrote to the GA requesting an Inquiry into the conduct of a *Police-Vidane* (regarding the theft of a cow), the GA reprimanded the *Police-Vidane* without informing the *Mudaliyar*.[47] And when the Assistant Superintendent of Police complained that one *Police-Vidane* had manufactured evidence in court to suit the accused, thus

---

[38] SLNA 33/3619–33/3633 inclusive; 33/3677–33/3678 inclusive; 33/3681–33/3703 inclusive; 33/3717; 33/3719; 33/3726; 33/3790–33/3811 inclusive; 33/3821; 33/3822; 33/3830; 33/3593–33/3596 inclusive; 33/3600–33/3609 inclusive; 33/3611–33/3618 inclusive; Diaries of the GA (WP) (1910–40), SLNA 33/33–33/51 inclusive; Diaries of the AGA (Colombo and Negombo) (1910–40). SLNA 33/52–33/64 inclusive.
[39] SLNA 33/3798; 33/3799; 33/33.
[40] SLNA 33/3798.   [41] Ibid.   [42] Ibid.   [43] Ibid.   [44] Ibid.
[45] SLNA 33/3799.   [46] Ibid.   [47] SLNA 33/3800.

spoiling a good case, he was warned and discharged by the GA, without the *Mudaliyar*'s knowledge.[48]

Meanwhile various other Government institutions were forced to complain directly to the GA (bypassing the *Mudaliyar*) when they encountered errors of omission or commission on the part of lesser headmen. In such cases, the GA was often forced to reprimand the *Mudaliyar*, as well as the subordinate officer concerned. In one case of 1919, for instance, a *Vidane-Arachchi* (and a fairly influential small-scale landowner) was supposed to have failed to render assistance to the Sanitary Inspector when asked to do so. The *Mudaliyar* had attempted to defend his officer.[49] The GA, disbelieving the excuse offered, was forced to write to the *Mudaliyar*, asking that the *Vidane-Arachchi* concerned be censured for his neglect of duty. The GA added that 'any neglect on the part of your headmen to co-operate cordially with this (Sanitary) Dept., reflects no credit on you'.[50] On another occasion, when a *Mudaliyar* tried to defend a headman accused of conniving in coconut thefts, the GA had to overrule the *Mudaliyar* and instruct that the official concerned 'be severely censured and fined Rs 2–50'.[51] In one *korale* the GA had to start dismissing *Police-Vidanes* on his own initiative (following complaints from outside Government bodies), often against the advice of the *Mudaliyar*.[52]

Such action was necessary because the *Mudaliyars* of this area were known to be particularly indulgent of the misdeeds of their subordinates. Indeed, this feeling was so widespread that numerous petitioners specifically requested that Inquiries be held by the GA and not the *Mudaliyar*.[53] The GA's tendency to act in concert with the police, bypassing the *Mudaliyar* (a phenomenon not seen in Bluville), may have detracted slightly from the latter's role as the chief native law enforcing officer in the area. But it in no way detracted from his ability to inspire awe and fear in the hearts of his subordinates. Indeed, the *Mudaliyar*'s control of land in the area (on a scale not seen in Bluville) enhanced both his real and potential power to cow his subordinates. His leniency in administration, then, was seen more as charity than necessity. This was very different to the situation in Bluville, where *Mudaliyar* Foo often had to appoint headmen (who were clients of the Coos), by virtue of their own local standing and influence. Such appointments were dictated by the social structure and the need to have prominent local influentials as headmen for smooth administration, rather than by the *Mudaliyar*'s personal fancy.

---

[48] SLNA 33/54; entry of 27 October 1937. [49] SLNA 33/3799.
[50] Ibid.   [51] Ibid.   [52] Ibid.   [53] SLNA 33/3682; 33/3800.

We have examined the general protection the *Mudaliyars* of the Greenville area afforded their headmen and the way in which they connived in
their harassment of the villagers. We have found that this harassment
was both sharper and more widespread than in Bluville, and also that the
Mudaliyar's indulgence of these misdeeds was greater. We shall now look
at the economic patronage the *Mudaliyars* of this area gave their headmen; namely the ways in which they helped the latter to become, and
remain, the village elite.

Economic patronage was disbursed through three main channels.
First, the *Mudaliyars* would connive in their headmen's charging of illicit
fees. One *Police-Vidane*, for instance, was accused of having collected the
Riot Compensation dues of his area without giving the villagers their
receipts.[54] The Police Magistrate, writing to the GA said that, although
forced to re-collect these dues, he believed the villagers' charge that the
Police-Vidane had misappropriated the funds.[55] Significantly, the *Mudaliyar* of the area had done nothing to check the *Vidane*.[56]

This was not surprising, for as the Headmen's Commission of 1935
reported, the appropriation of illict fees and benefits was practised right
up the hierarchy.[57] The *Police-Vidane* was conventionally, but not
legally, allowed a certain fee for certain of his services, the *Vidane-
Arachchi* a larger one, and the *Mudaliyar*, the largest of all.

The evidence suggests that this practice was far more widespread in
the district within which Greenville fell than within the district of which
Purville *Korale* was a part. Indeed, many *Mudaliyars* of the Greenville
area had lost their posts after having been discovered to be corrupt. One
Mudaliyar was dismissed in 1904 after having been found guilty of an
irregularity in the granting of pistol licences.[58] It seems that another
Muhandiram[59] and an *Atapattu-Mudaliyar* of the region,[60] had vacated
their posts (in 1890 and 1892 respectively) in questionable circumstances. And in 1931 a *Korale-Muhandiram* was accused of having misappropriated money collected by him through the sale of cattle voucher
receipts. In this case, the GA, believing that there was sufficient evidence
to charge him, had to hold the Inquiry into the matter himself, bypassing
the *Mudaliyar*.[61] Corruption, then, permeated the whole system. And
the *Mudaliyars*, being parties to the vices of their subordinates, by
allowing and indeed encouraging them in these activities, built up a very
strong personal bond with the latter.

The second channel through which the *Mudaliyars* patronized
their lesser headmen economically was in the collection of grain taxes.

54 SLNA 33/3799.   55 Ibid.   56 Ibid.
57 GOC (1935).   58 SLNA 33/3717.   59 SLNA 33/3821.
60 SLNA 33/3719.   61 SLNA 33/53, entries of 9 and 10 March.

Quantitatively, paddy not being such a widely grown crop in the area, this was less significant as a means of enriching the headmen than in Purville *Korale*. Moreover, most areas did not have *Vel-Vidanes*, and *Huwandirams* were not auctioned. The tax was assessed and collected by the *Vidane-Arachchi*. However, there was some scope for the under-estimation of the yield, the sharing of the proceeds between the headmen and cultivators and the payment of a low tax to Government. In this the *Mudaliyars* seem to have connived. In 1891 the GA had to write to the *Mudaliyars* of four *korales* saying that he was 'highly dissatisfied with the work of the grain tax collectors in these areas'.[62] In many districts the *Vidane-Arachchis* had failed to seize the properties of tax defaulters. One *Mudaliyar* wrote to the GA saying that he was 'satisfied after due inquiry that [their fields] did not yield three-fold of the quantity sown' (the tax threshold), thus exonerating the defaulters as well as his own headmen.[63] By such means the *Mudaliyar* could allow the *Vidane-Arachchis* to underestimate yield, deprive the Government of revenue and share the proceeds with the cultivators, thus creating goodwill between himself, his headmen and, to a lesser extent, the villagers.[64]

The third major means by which the *Mudaliyar* could favour the headmen and families of the village elite lay in the distribution of Crown land. The early twentieth century saw a fairly widespread sale of small blocks of Crown land.[65] These were generally less than ten acres in extent, and often below five. Whereas during the previous century land had been auctioned, now tenders were being invited for their purchase. Only if two or more prospective purchasers tendered for the same amount was the land auctioned. The *Mudaliyars* were in charge of appraising the land. They could therefore collude with prospective tenderers and advise them of the 'correct' price to offer, thus favouring them. In the event of an auction, they were instrumental in advertising the venue, and could thus ensure that their favourites were present. Finally, in the event of a village headman or relation desiring a portion of Crown land lying close to some other property of his, the *Mudaliyar* could value this at a low price, and secure it for him. By such means the

---

[62] SLNA 33/3596. [63] Ibid.

[64] The fact that yields were underestimated can be seen by comparing the *Huwandiram-Rent* Records in SLNA Lot 33 during the *Mudaliyar* period with those after. In the period before 1940/50, when the *Mudaliyars* began to retire, yields were estimated at seldom more than two to three times the quantity sown; after this, at seldom less than five times. This was so despite there being no improvement in field layout, climate or technology after 1940/50. The only inference is that the *Mudaliyars* were far more partial to their headmen than the DROs who succeeded them.

[65] SLNA 33/3620–33/3632 inclusive form the basis for this paragraph and the next.

Mudaliyars could channel small areas of Crown property into the hands of their nominees.

These nominees and favourites were generally already small-scale landowners coming from the village elite, from which headmen tended to be drawn. They were generally of the *Goigama* caste, reflecting the community's dominance in landholding at the village level. There was no other group to challenge this dominance like the *Karave* in Bluville. Their being favoured was the result of this dominance and the consequent use they were to the *Mudaliyars* in administration. It was not the result of any caste identity they had with their *Mudaliyar* patrons.

Such groups were also favoured when it came to encroachments upon Crown land. One petition for instance refers to a small-scale landowner having encroached upon and cultivated six acres of Crown property with the connivance and help of the village headmen and *Mudaliyar*.[66] In this case, because of the GA's persistence and several notes, the *Mudaliyar* was forced to look into the matter and fine the offender.[67] But generally such encroachments were widespread and facilitated by the leniency of administrative officials at all levels.

Such lenience was not to be seen in the case of landless villagers from the depressed communities. This was because favouring them through land grants would have broken their dependence upon the *Goigama* village elite (by giving them an independent source of income). It was precisely because they were landless that they were dependent on these families for periodic work in coconut lands (at nominal wages), service at social functions and the operation of cottage industries. Indeed it was this dependence which underlay the economic wealth, political influence and social prestige of the richer families (and through them of the *Mudaliyars*). It was therefore not in the latter's interests to destroy these ties of dependence, which formed the bases of their power. Thus, whereas it was the rule for the so-called lower caste encroachers to be driven out of Crown property (by the local headmen and *Mudaliyar*), the richer *Goigama* was allowed to expand. And the *Mudaliyars* encouraged such discrimination. In one case, when a family of the *Batgam* community claimed (with documentary evidence) that a portion of Crown land had been gifted to them by the Dutch, and complained that the local headman had intruded upon this, the *Mudaliyar* summarily dismissed their plea.[68] And this was the same *Mudaliyar* who had adopted such an indulgent attitude towards the richer *Goigama* encroacher of the previous paragraph. Numerous other such cases can be cited.

---

[66] SLNA 33/3631.   [67] Ibid.   [68] Ibid.

By these means the *Mudaliyar* families came to be the traditional patrons of the village elite. Long after they had lost office they (and their relations) would be sought after by the elite in times of trouble. In 1932, when a certain *Vidane-Arachchi* was dismissed for having failed to distrain tax defaulters he appealed to a member of a *Mudaliyar* family from the Greenville area, and then a State Councillor. The latter pleaded with the GA on the headman's behalf (but in this case, to no avail).[69] Similarly, when another *Vidane-Arachchi* was dismissed, he tried to present his case through the son of a former *Maha-Mudaliyar*, who saw the GA on his behalf.[70] Canvassing on behalf of favourites was not uncommon. When a Deputy Registrar for a Division had to be appointed, the GA was favoured with personal visits from a Minister and an ex-*Maha-Mudaliyar*.[71]

Later, members of the *Mudaliyar* families would use their contacts with the administration to advance the interests of particular families of the village elite in the hope of thereby strengthening their political base. One member of these *Mudaliyar* families, when a Minister, would sometimes personally call on the GA or AGA to canvass on behalf of particular applicants for headmanships in his constitutency.[72] Similarly he 'tried to interfere in the allotment of land under the Peasant Proprietorship Scheme' in December 1935, with a view to favouring his clients.[73] The AGA, writing about this, said:

This is the very thing which Government has desired to guard against. Life for the Allotting Officer will be quite impossible, if the local (State-Council) member follows him around, trying to get grants of land for his nominees and supporters. Already in one constituency (not in this district), it is said that the villagers will not vote through fear, whilst in others it is said that people will vote for the sitting member on the principle of backing the winning horse.[74]

By such means the *Mudaliyar* families favoured a certain section of the village elite. This section had been given headmanships, allowed to charge illicit fees, defraud the Government of grain taxes, accumulate land on a small scale, and generally oppress the ordinary villagers, especially those of the depressed communities. The *Mudaliyars* encouraged these activities and thus sustained the position of these richer villagers as the local elite. Consequently, a bond was established between the two; a bond which was not purely commercial in nature.

---

69 SLNA 33/43, entry of 20 July 1932.
70 Ibid., entry of 22 August 1932.
71 SLNA 33/46, entry of 16 November 1938.
72 Ibid., entry of 2 December 1937.
73 SLNA 33/45, entry of 13 December 1935.   74 Ibid.

Thus, even today, the watcher at the Pous' Colombo residence serves not merely for financial renumeration, but partly as a token of his family's obligation to the Pous. His family had been allowed to acquire medium-sized landholdings during the tenure of various Pous as *Mudaliyars* of the Yap *Korales*. He himself owns twenty-five acres of coconut, which generates a very handsome income of Rs 3,000–5,000 a month; more than sufficient to make him independent enough not to work in a household. However, his family having been tied to the Pous by traditional bonds of obligation for generations, his service today is an acknowledgment of this. It is a source of pride to him that he has this special connection with the leading family of the area, and that he is able to serve in a responsible position in their household. Materially, it reinforces his ability to act as an intermediary between the leading family and the ordinary villagers. This gives him added status and power in his locality. And the Pous for their part prefer to have as watcher a man from a trusted family (known to them for generations) and with some degree of local influence than a rank outsider.

In such cases the considerations of status and power-broking, inherent in the patron–client bond, are more important than financial remuneration alone. Of these two considerations the access to present (or possible future) political leaders, and the potential for power-broking this gives, is probably the more fundamental reason for service of the above kind. This can be seen by the fact that there tend to be more clients serving political leaders (on a non-financial or partly financial basis) than are serving the relations of these same leaders. Thus, Tani Kou (a past MP and Deputy Minister) and his wife, who are still active in politics, tend to have a larger clientele of the village elite serving in their households than their first cousins do. Again, in Bluville, the Doctor tends to have more such clients than either his brother or sister do. The implication is that it is not the pure bond of obligation or consideration of status that motivates such service. Rather, the potential for access to jobs and the prospects for tangible material benefits seem to be the reasons for such loyalty. The local public's perception of particular village level families' ties to a particular patron tends to encourage the former to persist in traditional loyalties and not to desert their mentor when the latter is temporarily out of office. Desertion is also discouraged by the fact that a rival patron will always favour his traditional clients before he does newcomers.

Patron–client bonds then were very strong. In Greenville, as in Bluville, long after the *Mudaliyars* had lost their positions, their progeny when contesting elections could count on their families' traditional clients, the village headmen, to deliver them whole blocs of votes. Indeed, at Independence, the power of the Pou–Kou family nexus was probably greater than that of any *Mudaliyar* group elsewhere in the Low Country. This was because first, they had sought and secured elections to the legislature and Government as early as 1931. So by 1947 they had been able to use these offices to build a small State based patronage network augmenting their private contacts in a way that, say, the Foos of Bluville had been unable to. Secondly, and more significantly, they owned very extensive landholdings in their districts; landholdings which reinforced their power as *Mudaliyars*, landholdings which *Mudaliyar* families of other areas did not possess. In Purville *Korale*, for instance, *Mudaliyar* Kit Foo owned only fifty-three acres, a negligible holding compared to that of the Bees and the Coos. The *Mudaliyar* families of the Greenville region were powerful precisely because they were not challenged as landowners in their area in a way that, say, the Foos were in Bluville. The Pous and the Kous were *both* the dominant landowners *and* the *Mudaliyars* of their district. Their holdings were retained until the early 1970s, and proved to be a more potent and enduring means of sustaining the patronage networks of the area than the *Mudaliyar* system itself. The next section deals with the power the *Mudaliyar* families wielded through land.

The Pous and the Kous: patrons as landowners

As we have seen, the *Mudaliyars* had used their official positions to secure vast extents of Crown land during the nineteenth century. By the twentieth century their families had risen from their earlier low and humble origins to be landowners on a scale not witnessed earlier. Monti Pou owned 3,749 acres largely devoted to coconut in the Greenville area.[75] His sister, mother of a *Maha-Mudaliyar* and grandmother of the future MP of the area, had left 1,270 acres of undivided land in the area to her heirs, apart from various smaller holdings.[76] Of all these holdings, Monti Pou's two largest holdings of 775 acres and 541 acres and his sister's 700 acres were some of the largest single estates in the area.[77]

Other kinsmen were also substantial landowners in the district. One Pou had left 1,668 acres, of which 658 acres were in the Greenville region.[78] Monti Kou's son Fritz, a one-time State Councillor, had been left 678 acres in the area and his sister, Mrs Kit Foo (mother of Dee), another 400.[79] Apart from Fritz's estates, 580 acres of which were in Groville *Korale*, the bulk of the Pou and Kou lands were concentrated in Yap *Korale*, the area where they had traditionally monopolized *Mudaliyarships* and which was to form the southern part of Greenville electorate.

[75] Ferguson's (1946).   [76] Ibid.
[77] Ibid.   [78] Ibid.   [79] Ibid.

These families, then, were the dominant large-scale landowners in the area, in much the same way that the four *Karave* families (described in Chapter 2) were in their area. Seven of the ten estates of over 500 acres, and twelve of the nineteen estates of over 300 acres, belonged to one of their members.[80] Of these members, the most prominent were Monti Pou and his sister. The other large estates were chiefly held by non-Sinhalese, so that there were no locally based groups to challenge the power of these families. All three of the other estates of over 500 acres were so held, one by a Tamil, one by a Moor, and one by a Burgher.[81] And of the seven estates of over 300 acres not held by these *Mudaliyar* families, only one belonged to a rival Sinhalese family, a 325-acre estate belonging to Mrs Dip.[82]

The dual monopoly of large estates and *Mudaliyarships* by the families of this area was a phenomenon not to be found in other parts of Sri Lanka. It meant that the power they wielded in their district, both as landowners and *Mudaliyars*, was greater than that of other Sinhalese provincial elites. And this power could almost be one of life and death over the ordinary villager. It has been alleged for instance that Monti Pou used to take his pick of concubines from the village girls in his area. Again, legend has it that another relative (1823–73), one of whose daughters Monti Kou married, and whose granddaughter married Monti Pou, committed such a misdeed that all his descendants have a curse upon them.

There can be little doubt that these families did use their positions to amass wealth and oppress the ordinary villager. Generally, it was the landless or depressed caste groups which suffered most. A petition of 16 September 1909, sent by some members of the *Vahumpura* caste, refers to a *Mudaliyar* leading a number of village headmen and others into their land, assaulting them, and appropriating a part thereof.[83] The *Mudaliyar*, in his report of 20 September 1909, asserted that the land was his and that the petitioners had encroached upon it.[84] But, whomever the land belonged to, the fact remains that the *Mudaliyar* had been able to use his position to enforce his will without recourse to Court.

Other landowners could not secure their pleasure in such a high-handed way and with such complete impunity. When some wealthy individuals invaded some small-holdings, maltreated the squatters, and burnt a hut and felled the timber in 1910, the police and *Mudaliyar* held an Inquiry, and the GA was also informed.[85] And similar action was taken in the case of vandalism at another estate in the region.[86]

---

[80] Ibid.   [81] Ibid.   [82] Ibid.   [83] SLNA 33/3682.   [84] Ibid.
[85] SLNA 33/33, entries of 7/8 February 1910.
[86] SLNA 33/54, entry of 9 October 1937.

As a general rule, then, the *Mudaliyar*'s office augmented his powers as a landowner. The villagers were kept in a state of fear. And what they did for these families was largely through such fear.

It does not seem that the Pou/Kou families were benevolent landowners in the way that the Coos and the Bees were in Bluville. This was partly the result of the nature of the crops grown. Whereas the Bluville families owned tea and rubber, the Pous and the Kous had coconut. Tea and rubber require permanent resident labour forces. Such labour would receive fringe benefits denied to the casual labourers periodically required to pluck coconuts. Moreover, as they were employed on a casual basis, the *Mudaliyar* landowners did not feel that they had a legal or moral obligation to hire them during difficult times. Many were unemployed during the Great Depression.[87] Further, these labourers were not patronized in times of need with gifts in cash and kind, in the way that the village elite were. As a result, these groups seem to have had no affection for the *Mudaliyar* landowners in the way that the labourers on the Coo and Bee estates did for their employers.

Indeed, what power the *Mudaliyars* wielded over the people was through the families of the village headmen. And the influence the village headmen had over these landless groups was based on ties of oppressive, rather than paternalistic, dependence; ties very different to those prevailing in the fishing villages of Bluville; ties which will be more fully examined on pp. 105–7. Suffice it to say here that, in so far as the *Mudaliyar* landowners were able to secure the votes of these landless depressed caste groups it was through the fear they inspired rather than through any genuine affection inculcated.

The second reason for coconut land ownership not being conducive to bonds of affection lay in their inviting intrusions and thefts, in a way tea and rubber estates did not (see Chapter 2, pp. 28–9). Consequently, a coconut estate had to be guarded, in a way a tea or rubber estate did not.

For this reason, it seems that the Pous and the Kous were very selfish with the use of their land, in a manner the Coos and the Bees were not. They tended not to allow ordinary villagers the right of passage through their properties, let alone the facilities to under-crop or graze cattle. For instance, in 1913, the *Mudaliyar* of Yap *Korale* East had blocked a path from a certain village to a burial ground at the point it crossed his estates, on the grounds that the passers-by plucked his coconuts. The villagers had petitioned the GA, and the AGA in his Diary noted that he 'believed the grievances genuine'.[88] He went on to say

[87] SLNA 33/53.   [88] SLNA 33/60, entry of 13 August 1913.

I think [the *Mudaliyar*] is interfering with an established right of way which is furthermore a way of necessity to the villagers in question. However, as the road [is not one] that has been taken over or improved either by Government or the VC I do not see that the GA has any *locus standi* in the matter, or that we can do anything more than advise the *Mudaliyar* to desist from his illiberal attitude as squire of the village and protector of the people. He ought to be less selfish.[89]

Similarly, in 1928, when the residents of another village requested a road from their village to the highway through an estate, the owner (who was a brother of the *Maha-Mudaliyar* and uncle of the future MP) refused.[90] He was only prevailed upon to do so after the GA had made repeated entreaties, and then too, only on condition that the path was fenced on either side.[91]

Numerous other instances of such behaviour can be cited.[92] The general conclusion is that the *Mudaliyar* families were very selfish with their land, especially as regards the poorer depressed caste groups.[93] The only individuals who benefited to a limited extent were those drawn from the village elite. These traditional clients were allowed easier access to the land, and, where they worked as conductors or watchers, to plant subsidiary food crops, graze cattle, pluck jak fruit, use timber and palms for building, thatch and firewood, and take periodic rations of nuts.

The Kous had donated small plots of land for the construction of schools. Again, these benefited only the families of the traditional clients, the village elite. Apart from the financial costs of text-books, uniforms, sandals and the like, which depressed caste villagers could not bear, there were social and administrative obstacles to their sending their children to these institutions. The schools were far from depressed caste areas. Where children of these communities attended they were generally beaten by the others, with the connivance of teachers, and warned not to return. We have not come across any instance of a Pou or a Kou intervening to prevent such action as *Mudaliyar* Coo had done in Bluville (see Chapter 2).

The value of donations of land and access to it lay not in its quantitative financial magnitude, which was slight. Rather, it lay in the qualitative manner in which it helped sustain the village hierarchy. Access to land for cultivation meant access to income and wealth. And access to education meant access to prestigious city jobs and again enhanced income, wealth and status. (And, as seen, only the traditional clients of the village

89 Ibid.   90 SLNA 33/64, entry of 6 November 1928.
91 SLNA 33/43, entry of 3 April 1930.
92 See for instance SLNA 33/59, entry of 11 March 1912, and SLNA 33/53, entry of 18 December 1931 amongst others.
93 SLNA Lot 33 forms the basis for this paragraph and the next three.

elites enjoyed such access.) Moreover, the discrimination against the depressed castes in land allocation (see pp. 93–4) helped maintain a large surplus labour force of landless villagers. And such a force, being highly dependent on the village elite for employment and income, became clients of the latter (see pp. 105–7). In these ways the *Mudaliyars* helped sustain a very inegalitarian social hierarchy with the *(Goigama)* families of the landed village headmen at its apex.

And naturally this village elite of Yap *Korale*, which owed its economic and social position to the Pous and the Kous, supported them at elections. In Greenville, in 1947, when the Pous and Kous were in the UNP, they worked for Marti Mou, the party nominee, whose own base was in Groville *Korale*. In 1952 (and 1977) they supported Tani Kou, the son of a *Mudaliyar*, and in 1965 and 1970 his wife. We shall now turn to the main rival faction in Greenville politics: that of the Mous and the Nous.

The Mous and the Nous

The influence of the Mou and Nou families in Greenville has not been as substantial or enduring as that of the Pous and the Kous. This has been so for two major reasons. First, they have not held *Korale-Mudaliyarships* in the way the Pous and the Kous have. Secondly, they have not owned land on the same scale.

Although both sets of families were from the *Goigama* community, there was a clear distinction of status between them, a distinction almost as marked as that between certain castes. *Mudaliyar* Mou (d. 1910) had been an *arrack-renter* and it was in this business that the family fortunes had been founded.[94] The family did not start acquiring land until the late nineteenth and early twentieth centuries.[95] For this reason many Pous and Kous regarded them as 'upstarts' and *'nouveau riche'*. This attitude has persisted up to the present. When I asked one Kou about the relationship between the two families, he disdainfully replied, 'We do not associate with the Mous. We regard them as middle-class, *nouveau riche* upstarts.' Thus, although there was one notable case of intermarriage, the two sets of families have generally kept a distance.

The relationship between the Mous and the Nous was, however, far more substantial.[96] *Muhandiram* Nou (d. 1935), who founded the family fortunes, had been a close friend of *Mudaliyar* Mou. They had much in common. Both had risen (from relatively humble origins) through

---

[94] Roberts (1979b).
[95] Ibid. and SLNA Lot 33 regarding Crown Land purchases.
[96] See Roberts (1979b), for some details on the social background of these families.

business, and both had become fairly substantial landowners in Groville *Korale* by the early twentieth century. Both had been generous philanthropists and Buddhists, and both had received honorary titles in recognition of this. *Mudaliyar* Mou's granddaughter had married *Muhandiram* Nou's younger son, Noni Nou. The elder brother Nerti Nou was to be employed as a close confidant, adviser and later Private Secretary of *Mudaliyar* Mou's son, Marti. And when Marti died in 1951, Nerti Nou was to succeed him as the UNP candidate for the seat. Later, in 1965, Marti Mou's son, Moni, was to help Nerti Nou's younger brother, Noni (married to his first cousin) secure an important State office.

The influence of these two families was concentrated in the northern part of the electorate, Groville *Korale*, where they owned coconut and rubber estates and plumbago mines, and had established various service-based patronage networks. The Mous owned 778 acres in the Greenville area in 1946, most of which was coconut and about a third (259 acres) rubber.[97] Noni Nou, the future MP's younger brother, owned a 340-acre estate on the northern boundary of the electorate, and a 39-acre block of rubber, near Greenville town.[98] In 1946 most of the former estate was devoted to coconut cultivation, only twenty-five acres being cropped with rubber.[99] But the Mous (with a not inconsiderable amount of rubber) had some scope for extending fringe benefits and patronage on the lines of the Coos and the Bees in Bluville.

More significantly, however, *Muhandiram* Nou had developed a vast coconut transport and hulling business. He used to buy coconut from both large and small landowners within a range of about ten or twelve miles of his home town, and transport this to various desiccating coconut mills in the area. Many of these were owned by a large Colombo-based firm and some by him. This business enabled the *Muhandiram* to build very close personal contacts at the grass-roots level; contacts which some of the larger Pou and Kou landowners tended not to have.

A patron–client type bond of interdependence and trust therefore developed between the *Muhandiram* and many small landowners. For instance, the Nous had a decorated travelling cart, which they lent for hundreds of weddings in the locality. Again, having a large number of carts for their business, they were in a position to provide free transport to sick villagers. And whenever floods, epidemics or other calamities struck, the family traditionally provided gifts in cash and kind to needy residents. In return, these people would work on the Nou paddy fields, or help in the construction and maintenance of their buildings at nominal wages.

---

[97] Ferguson's (1946).   [98] Ibid.   [99] Ibid.

There was more affection and mutual obligation and less fear and oppression than in the sort of patron–client bonds prevalent in Yap *Korale*.

The Nous were also prominent as the major patrons of the local Buddhist temples and associated schools or *pirivenas*. There were four in particular with which the family had very close ties. All four lay within a radius of about four miles of the *Muhandiram*'s residence and, so, enjoyed regular personal contact with family members. Moreover, the latter two of these temples were of the *Ramayana Nikaya*. This sect had seceded from the main *Siam Nikaya* on the grounds that it discriminated against the non-*Goigama*, refusing them entry into the priesthood. As a result it had considerable support amongst the depressed communities, and in Groville *Korale* the two temples of the sect were the ones patronized by these communities. The fact that the Nous, a leading *Goigama* family of the area, were the major benefactors of their two temples earned them the goodwill of the depressed groups. So when Marti Mou contested in 1947, he carried their votes. Significantly, this was the only area where he got the support of these communities. In Yap *Korale* they voted en bloc for Mervi Fip, the left candidate, where administrative circumstances permitted. (This will be more closely examined in the next section.)

As a result of their activities the Nou family seems to have enjoyed a genuine measure of popular support in the district. *Muhandiram* Nou was elected to the ward of the local Village Council and then, in July 1934, the Chairman of that body.[100] When he died, in 1935, his elder son, Nerti Nou, was elected uncontested to fill his positions. He was able to use these offices (and his access to Government) to help the rural people in various ways. Roads and schools were constructed, piped water and electricity introduced and land allocated under the Peasant Proprietorship Scheme. More significantly, when he was appointed President of the Greenville Co-operative Retail Depot in 1941, and of the wider-ranging Groville Multi-Purpose Co-operative Society the following year, his honesty and dedication earned him much approbation. Consumer durables and government-subsidized fertilizer and agricultural imports were distributed fairly at the official prices and there were no attempts to siphon off goods and sell them at black-market prices for private gain (as in some Co-operatives). In 1950, Nerti Nou was appointed President of a major co-operative bank. Greenville was one of many constituencies which fell within his sphere now. He used his position to introduce easy credit for small landowners in the area and for agricultural societies which sought to diversify into high-yielding cash

[100] SLNA 33/54, entry of 5 July 1934.

crops (such as cashew nut). However, the sort of groups which benefited from these measures (as well as the roads, schools and public works embarked upon) still tended to come from the small-scale landowning village elite.

Indeed, it seems that paddy was not purchased at the guaranteed Government prices in the area for fear of offending this group. Members of this group used to purchase paddy from smallholders at nominal prices (below the Government-guaranteed rates) and sell in the black market for a larger profit. If the Co-operative had embarked on a policy of purchasing paddy at the official rate, these groups would have been forced out of business. Their social power was such that they were able to prevent this. Even if such a scheme had been implemented, their control over personnel may have enabled them to forcibly prevent its success. And in some paddy growing areas inhabited by members of the depressed communities such as Wun (about one and a half miles south-west of Greenville railway station), this may just have been accepted. It seems, therefore, that Nerti Nou accepted that innovations of this type would have lost him support at the village elite level, and that any extra popularity gained amongst the depressed groups may not have been sufficiently well organized to assist him. He may also have seen the potential for social conflict in such a move. He therefore did not embark on the type of strategy of breaking the power of the middle groups described in chapter 2, p. 23. In Groville *Korale* it was these individuals who proved the organizational backbone of his support. So, again, when they objected to a scheme of his to bring fresh vegetables cheaply from up country for sale in Greenville, on the grounds that it would destroy their own market, he dropped the idea.

The Mous too seem to have favoured this group, the village elite, over others. It was these families in Groville *Korale* which had received gifts in cash and kind during times of need. And Marti Mou, son of the honorary *Mudaliyar*, had been able to use his position as a senior official in the sixteen years preceding Independence to favour them. A Land Development Ordinance (initiated by him) enabled small extents of uncultivated Crown property to be distributed amongst needy villagers. It was the families of the village headmen which benefited first.[101] They secured the best plots of land in Groville *Korale*. And they were even able to use the Ordinance as a pretext to eject landless depressed caste villagers from the locality, after giving them the paper title to bare land in the barren North-Central Province.[102]

---

[101] See SLNA Lot 33 for a general substantiation of this statement.   [102] Ibid.

However, the depressed castes in many parts of Groville *Korale* do not seem to have viewed the Mous and the Nous as oppressors, to the same extent that they did the Pou and Kou *Mudaliyars* of Yap *Korale*. This was partially due to the different agro-ecological and economic conditions in the different parts of the electorate. The Mous and the Nous owned rubber, which gave greater scope for patronage disbursement, and offered less room for intrusion, thefts and friction, which the coconut holdings of the Pous and the Kous invited. Moreover, they had not monopolized *Mudaliyarships* and tyrannized the ordinary villagers in quite the same way that these latter families had done. Finally, in Greenville, where the depressed castes lived in close proximity to their home base, the Nous had cultivated a personal and familial rapport with them. They patronized their temples, assisted them in times of need, and visited them with gifts during weddings and such social functions.

Nevertheless, the traditional intermediaries of the Nous as of the Mous, Pous and Kous were drawn chiefly from the ranks of the *Goigama* village elites. These elites had a vested interest in oppressing and subjugating poorer *Goigama* and depressed caste clients. As such, the Nous, like the Mous, Pous and Kous were (sometimes involuntarily) involved in such oppression, albeit less directly, on a smaller scale, and over a shorter historical period than the latter two families.

Conclusion: caste and the left in Greenville

As we have seen, both family factions in Greenville had a certain section of the village elite under forms of obligation to them: the Pous and the Kous through their control of the *Mudaliyar* system and land, the Mous and the Nous through business, estates and governmental connections. They both operated in very similar ways, counting on the village headmen to deliver them blocs of votes at election times. They both tended to favour these groups at the expense of others and, with the exception of the Nous in the case of *Ramayana Nikaya* temples, they both allowed close favourites to tyrannize the landless villagers (especially those of the depressed castes) to varying degrees. The major difference between the two factions lay not in the nature of the patronage networks utilized, but in their geographical locus of influence. The Mou/Nou power was largely restricted to Groville *Korale* where they tended to get nine out of every ten votes cast, that of the Pous and the Kous to Yap *Korale*, where they tended to draw about two out of every three votes cast at elections during this early period.

Unlike in much of Bluville, these families, except for the Nous, seem to have commanded little genuine affection amongst the landless and depressed communities.[103] This was partially due to their connivance in the village headmen's oppression of these groups, and partially to the nature of the crops grown. Moreover, the depressed communities tended to be economically and socially ostracized and not treated with the paternalistic care shown to the village elites. The Pous, Kous and Mous never gave them the gifts in cash and kind during time of need that they would give to the village headmen. Still less did they patronize their weddings and other social functions, in the way they would those of the local *Vidane-Arachchi*. Indeed, it seems that they would sometimes connive in the headmen's disruption of these functions, if these were deemed to be too lavish in relation to the participants' social standing. So the depressed communities felt outcastes in the most general sense of the term. They saw the *Mudaliyars* and large-scale landowners as their oppressors. And they saw this 'oppression' as being implemented through the headmen and richer villagers.

The richer villager had the depressed communities completely dependent upon him. He would have them work in his coconut plots and produce baskets, pots, mats and whatever with the working capital he lent them. He would buy back the finished products at prearranged low prices, and then transport them to Colombo, where he could sell them for a huge profit. Each family of the village elite had a certain set of clients bonded to it in this way. And each family had a tacit understanding with the others not to poach upon the clients of another. In this way the monopsonistic power of the group was not broken. The business proved lucrative, and the economic and social position of the elite was maintained.

The tie which bound such a member of the elite to his depressed caste clients was more exploitative and less paternalistic than that between the fish *mudalali* and fishermen of Bluville and not reinforced by ties of kin, as sometimes was the case in the latter area. For instance, there was no convention by which the village patron in Greenville helped his depressed caste client during times of need. This was very different to Bluville where a fish *mudalali* traditionally supported the families of client fishermen who had died in his service.

Consequently, there was a widespread feeling amongst the depressed groups of Greenville of being exploited by the *Goigama* village elite. It was believed that landed *Goigama* headmen would block schools being established in their areas in order to maintain their servile bondage. It was alleged that even if an entire village of the depressed castes (including the lower-caste headman or *Police Duraya*) petitioned for such a school,

---

[103] Ibid. forms the basis for this paragraph and the next three.

the higher-ranking *(Goigama) Vidane-Arachchi*, or even *Mudaliyar*, would have blocked it. [104] And again it was said that although there were national schemes to assist rural arts and crafts, these were blocked at the local level by the village elite; this, because the latter wished to maintain its monopsony in the field, and its control over the lucrative marketing and distribution of products. There seems then to have been a strong conviction amongst the depressed groups that the village elite was consciously seeking to deny them opportunity, and thus maintain its stranglehold over them for its own selfish ends. This conviction fuelled a sense of caste and class consciousness.

In this context, the Trotskyist LSSP's promise to dismantle every facet of the village headmen's system, and allow the depressed group greater access to land, opportunity and resources, struck a welcome chord. Mervi Fip, the party candidate in 1947, came from a recognized *Goigama* family connected to the Mous. His brother had married Marti Mou's niece. Mervi's paternal uncle had been *Mudaliyar* of Kross *Korale* from 1912 to 1930. This background was an indirect asset to him. On two occasions, when depressed caste supporters of his had been harassed by local notables, he threatened severe reprisals. He warned that the repetition of such acts would force him to see his relation Marti Mou (his opponent in the election) and that the latter would probably have the officials dismissed for partiality. In both cases the officers concerned backed down with profuse apologies. One headman went so far as to prostrate himself before the LSSP candidate and beg forgiveness. Mervi Fip would probably have been unable to influence such men and afford his supporters protection if he had not come from a recognized, landowning *Mudaliyar* family of the area and possessed the family connections he did. Fip's personal presence was however needed in such instances. His election agents could not secure the same degree of respect and inspire similar fear. Many were beaten up on polling day and prevented from overseeing his interests.

But this was the only extent to which these kin connections were useful to him. He asserts that his support was not drawn from the traditional clients but from the lower castes, and that the issue was one of social and economic exploitation along the lines described earlier. He estimates that about 95 per cent of his votes were drawn from the depressed communities for the sort of reasons detailed earlier. He recalls that those villages which were totally depressed caste, and so had headmen from these communities, voted solidly for him. In some villages in Yap *Korale*, for instance, Marti Mou (the only other candidate) failed to secure a single

[104] Ibid. and Rees (1955/6).

vote, this despite Fip having no personal contacts in the area. Such a vote was possible only because the headmen, also being of the depressed community, did not attempt to fraudulently, or forcibly, distort the result. Fip suspects that in *Goigama* villages with *Goigama* headmen (where there were pockets of the depressed groups) the lower castes may have been forced to vote against their wishes and against him.

He asserts that there were serious instances of harassment, intimidation and fraud on election day. As noted, many of his agents were driven out of the polling stations. The village headmen responsible for checking voter identity are then supposed to have connived in double voting by known Mou supporters. Other forms of deception were perpetrated. In one instance, when a troop of Fip's supporters had turned up at the polling booth, they had been brusquely asked whether they were going to vote for the lamp (the LSSP symbol) or the elephant (of the UNP). When they declared their intention of voting for the lamp, they were told that this was to be in the evening. They were instructed to vote for the 'elephant' in the morning and to return later to vote for the 'lamp'. The villagers dutifully voted for the elephant and, needless to say, when they returned in the evening, found that they could not vote again.

Such incidents were largely the result of the overwhelming organizational superiority Mou had over his rival. Control over the administration, the village elites and transport proved decisive. The supervising staff at the polling booths were almost entirely his supporters, Fip's having been driven away. Again, Mou had a whole fleet of cars to take his supporters to the polling booths. Fip had only a dilapidated vehicle for the entire campaign and often it had to be pushed.

Moreover, he was not a landowner on the scale of the Mous or Pou/Kous. He owned only about fifty acres in the electorate and his elder brother, the richest in the family, owned 170 acres about four miles north of Greenville town. Moreover, his supporters were highly vulnerable to intimidation. One man (who wished to give his garden for an LSSP meeting) found that coconuts had been dumped on it the previous night, thus wrecking his plans. Party supporters (in the rare cases when they possessed land) were reluctant to give this for meetings for fear of such reprisals. Only two large-scale landowners, both LSSP stalwarts, were willing to risk this. And in both cases the estates concerned were confiscated after the election, ostensibly for 'village expansion'.

Thus ended the left challenge in Greenville. Following the birth of the SLFP in 1951, elections tended to be fought largely between the Kous (with their support coming from Yap *Korale*) and the Mous and the Nous. In 1952, Nerti Nou, elder son of the *Muhandiram*, defeated Tani

Kou, the son of a *Mudaliyar*, and in 1956 another candidate, with the support of the Kou family, recaptured the seat for them.

It was the patronage network of these families, as modified by the agro-ecological surroundings of the area, which proved the basis of their political support. As in Bluville, caste *per se* played little, if any, role in elections. Depressed caste candidates failed to capture their community's vote (as in the case of Gip *Mudalali* in 1965, referred to in the next chapter). Only when a candidate (offering tangible economic benefits to a community) appealed to it on a class basis, as Fip did in 1947, was he successful. And even then, support was translated into votes only in so far as the economic power of the major (rival) patron, Mou, permitted it. So, in the last analysis, it was these patron–client networks which were decisive in political success. And caste cannot be said to have been important, except in so far as it was congruent with class.

6

Greenville: the growth of the State
(1956–1982)

Introduction

In 1952, Nerti Nou had won Greenville by a sizeable majority, securing over 60 per cent of all votes cast. However, in 1956, he lost by an equally sizeable majority to Mrs Rou who was contesting on the SLFP ticket. He attributes the large swing against him to two factors. First, it represented a part of the national swing. Nou believes that the vast majority of new voters, especially those outside Groville *Korale*, were likely to have voted against him, as they did against most sitting UNP MPs. Secondly, polling in Greenville being on the third and last day of the election when his party had secured only eight seats to the MEP coalition's forty-two, a vote for him would have been a vote for a candidate of the defeated party; a candidate unlikely to be able to reward supporters with any form of State patronage over the next five years. In this context, marginalistic, opportunistic groups are likely to have turned against him, as they had against the Doctor in Bluville three days earlier.

Given this, what is surprising is not that Nou lost, but that he managed to secure as much as a quarter of the total polled; this, when the Opposition seemed certain to form the next Government and his rival to hold a senior position in it. Nou regards these votes as having come from his hard-core support of family clients. This hard-core support was largely from the northern part of Groville *Korale*, where his family and that of the Mous controlled land and temples and had village headmen under obligation to them.

Elsewhere in the electorate, the UNP vote fell off significantly. This was especially so in the western and southern parts of the electorate, where sizeable concentrations of the depressed castes were to be found. Nou attributes this phenomenon largely to his having neglected these particular regions during his tenure as Government MP from 1952 to 1956. No major State schemes had been launched to assist the people in these regions, and Nou himself had been unable to visit these villagers and participate in their social functions as much as he may have liked. In addition, the SLFP's general socialist message, and in particular its promise to abolish the oppressive village headmens' system, are likely to have earned votes for it in these areas. Finally, Nou's rival had an electoral organization far better than that of previous Opposition candidates. This enabled her to translate her support in the depressed caste areas into votes, on a scale Mervi Fip had been unable to in 1947.

Mrs Rou herself cannot be regarded as having been a strong candidate. She had married Bimi Rou, whose family had helped found the UNP and continued to be identified with that party. Bimi Rou himself was the maternal uncle of Don Dip, MP for Red Town and a prominent Minister in the outgoing Cabinet. His nephew was to marry the granddaughter of Marti Mou, MP for Greenville in 1947 and a prominent UNP leader. Yet, despite these ties of blood, a split had emerged in the ranks of these UNP founding families; a split which is examined more closely in the next two chapters. This split had meant that Bimi Rou and his wife had chosen to associate themselves with the Pous and the Kous, rather than with their own kinsmen. Not being substantial landowners or philanthropists in the area, the support they drew was therefore more on the basis of the patronage networks of these allies, the Pous and the Kous, than on their own personal resources.

It has been said that the High Priest of the Red Town Temple (founded and substantially maintained by the Rous) played a major role in encouraging the priests of Greenville to switch to Mrs Rou and the SLFP. However, the extent of his influence has probably been grossly overestimated. First, the financial resources he would have brought to bear are unlikely to have been significant in relation to those the major UNP landowners of the area could raise. Secondly, his own personal conduct is likely to have robbed him of any moral influence he may otherwise have enjoyed. Mrs Rou's victory can be attributed to three sources: first, the hard-core support she drew from the Pou/Kou dominated Yap *Korale*; secondly, the national swing to the SLFP, especially amongst new voters; and thirdly, associated with this, the switch by marginal opportunistic groups, which chose to ally themselves on the final day of the poll with the victorious party.

The nine years following this victory were to see a rapid turnover of candidates contesting the seat in both the UNP and SLFP. But both sets of candidates were to continue to draw a solid core of support from the two patronage networks established in the preceding decades, and described in the previous chapter. These networks were however, to a limited extent, modified by the expansion of the State witnessed during these years. It is to this that we shall now turn.

The expansion of the State in Greenville (1956–65)

Agriculture

Agriculture being the major economic activity in Greenville, it was here that the impact of State reforms were first felt. The Paddy Lands Act of 1958 sought to increase the security of tenure of tenants (or *ande* cultivators), and regulate the rents they paid.[1] The Act provided for the creation of Cultivation Committees, covering about twenty-five to thirty acres, to be elected by the farmers of the areas. These Committees were entrusted with the maintenance of a Paddy Lands Register covering the areas of their jurisdiction. Cultivators were required to register themselves in this. Those so registering as tenants were then legally insured against eviction. A ceiling on the rent they paid of a quarter of the produce or five bushels per acre, whichever was less, was also imposed, on paper.

However, a number of loopholes existed in the law. The Courts interpreted the term eviction to mean 'the forcible and physical ejection of tenants from the paddy fields'. The landowners, realizing the legal implications of this, desisted from forcible and physical ejection, but secured eviction by giving the land to another cultivator and informing the tenant of this. By rotating each *ande* cultivator rapidly around different plots, the landowner could preclude him from laying tenancy claims to any particular field, and thus registering himself as a tenant under the terms of the Act (and benefiting from its provisions). Another popular practice was that of *kootu ande*, whereby the landowner worked alongside his tenant, classing him as an 'agricultural labourer'. Both means could be used to deny the *ande* cultivator tenancy status under the terms of the Act, thus effectively circumventing its provisions.

Meanwhile many Cultivation Committees, entrusted with the maintenance of the Register and implementation of the Act at the grass-roots level were dysfunctional. The Act stipulated that a quarter of each Committee be composed of landlords, those not having this proportion being deemed inoperative. Many landlords were therefore able to sabotage the Committees simply by failing to attend election meetings. An amendment to the Act, made in 1964, partially solved the problem by removing non-cultivating owners of paddy land from the eligibility to vote or be represented on the Committee. However, many landlords were able to maintain their control of these bodies by manipulating the dependent relationship their tenants had with them.

More important than this retention of control, however, was the scope for friction which the Act engendered. Paddy had always been very much

[1] ARTI (1975) forms the basis for this paragraph and the next two.

a smallholder's crop in this area. The largest holder would not have owned more than twenty-five acres at the most, and there would have been no more than three such men in the entire electorate. Most 'wealthy' paddy landowners would have had five to ten acres, at the very most. Such men tended to be from the 'village elite' (or the families providing the headmen through whom the nationally prominent Pous, Kous and Mous operated). Their influence stemmed not from their economic wealth (which was slight), or the direct control which they exercised over their tenants (who would generally not have numbered more than ten at the very most). Rather, it stemmed from the goodwill they could generate by offering fringe benefits to their tenants and from the type of patron–client relationship they could establish with these families. This influence was substantially reinforced by their control over lesser headmanships and their role as the intermediaries between the poorer villager and the larger landowners cum *Mudaliyars* of the district.

The Paddy Lands Act represented the first blow to these families. By substantially increasing the scope for friction with their clients it broke the traditional bond of goodwill they had with these groups. We have already seen how, in many areas, landowners sought to circumvent the Act by preventing tenants from registering and the Cultivation Committees from functioning, thus engendering ill-will. In the areas where *ande* cultivators were allowed to register as tenants they began to flout the authority of their lessors.

The case of Tip, a former headmaster of the Greenville *Maha Vidyalaya*, and the present MP for a neighbouring seat, provides a good example. Tip hailed from a family of the traditional village elite. His father had been a *Vidane Arachchi* for forty years with jurisdiction over the eastern half of Groville *Korale*, an area of about thirty to thirty-five square miles with a population of about 25,000 in 1946.[2] Tip himself had inherited six acres of paddy in his native village. He was the largest paddy landowner there. He enjoyed considerable social prestige in the village by virtue of this, his father's background and his family's contacts with members of the national elite. He used to lease his land out on an *ande* basis to nine individuals from families which had been traditional clients of his. These tenants had always been very deferential towards him, never daring to oppose him in public. With the advent of the Paddy Lands Act, all this changed. Tip (unlike some landlords) valuing the goodwill he enjoyed amongst his tenants, had allowed them to register under the terms of the Act. He then found them adopting a more forward attitude towards him. Subsidiary inputs, such as seed and fertilizer,

[2] GOC (1946).

which had previously been donated as a favour, now began to be demanded as a right. Tip was told that if these were not given regularly, the tenant cultivators would refuse to pay more than the stipulated one fourth share of the crop as rent. In most areas landowners continued to draw more than their stipulated rent, about three quarters of all tenants in the district paying the customary half share.[3] With such threats and counter-threats, friction with his tenants increased. Ultimately, Tip found three of them actively opposing him politically and canvassing for the SLFP; a phenomenon beyond the realms of possibility in the pre-1956 era.

Many other local patrons found themselves facing similar problems. This was especially so amongst those who had tried to maintain political goodwill, at the expense of economic security, by allowing tenants to register under the terms of the Act.

The power of these local patrons was more decisively undermined by two other important developments during this period. First, they began to gradually lose their headmanships after 1957, those retiring not being replaced by new ones. However, many headmen continued in office until 1962, for it was only then that their period of service was compulsorily terminated. Secondly, those that remained until 1962 found their ability to deliver blocs of votes at elections considerably circumscribed by the electoral reforms introduced after 1956. These reforms and their effects on the scope of local notables to deliver support at elections have been examined on pp. 53–9, so we shall not elaborate on them further here.

To conclude this section then, the Paddy Lands Act did not decisively curtail the power of the village elite. In many areas landowners retained control until the 1970s by circumventing the Act. In other areas, where landowners tried to maintain goodwill by allowing their tenants the freedom to register under the Act, this freedom seems generally to have been abused. In both cases, the scope for friction between the local patrons and their clients was increased as a result of the Act. Thus, the Paddy Lands Act went some way towards reducing the goodwill the village elite could command in their areas. However, the loss of village headmanships and the electoral reforms of 1956–65 were probably more important in reducing their actual coercive powers.

The schools takeover

The next major impact of State policy during this period (1956–65) was seen in the field of education. There had been several small assisted schools in the electorate patronized by locally prominent families and

[3] ARTI (1975), p. 23.

receiving State grants in addition. They all provided only a primary education and none had more than 200 students or about ten teachers. Thus, their resources could not be, and were not, used in electoral campaigns in the same way that those of Augusta College had been in Bluville. However, patronizing families could reward traditional clients with posts in these institutions, and also influence the choice of teachers and curricula, thereby moulding the social values of fairly young children. This influence was lost with the takeover of these schools by the State in 1957.

Thereafter the Department of Education appointed the teachers from a national pool of graduates. These appointments were made without any reference to the teachers' past histories, political backgrounds or whatever. By the 1960s these teachers tended to be graduates from poor backgrounds, the products of the free education initiated in 1944. Many had unemployed brothers and sisters, and found great difficulty in making ends meet. Most were dissatisfied with their social and financial positions, having expected far more prestigious and well-paid jobs after the education they had enjoyed. In this context, they began to profess very left-wing ideas, even in the classroom.

Two factors conduced to their influencing their pupils to a greater extent, and producing a larger proportion of JVP activists, than in Bluville. First, as noted, the locally dominant patrons had never exerted the same degree of control over these schools that the Doctor had done in Bluville. Not only had the two largest schools in the electorate been State run since their inception in 1944, but the schools the Pous, Kous and Mous had assisted had been small, few, and far between. In Bluville, on the other hand, the largest school, Augusta College, had been founded by the Doctor's grandfather, *Mudaliyar* Coo, in 1883, and managed by the family ever since. Moreover, the family also controlled the leading girls' school in Okerville, the second largest town in the electorate, and their in-laws, the Bees, managed another thirty-eight smaller schools spread throughout the province.

Even after the takeover of these institutions in 1957, the Doctor continued to take a paternal interest in their welfare. In February 1982, the JVP and Communist parties organized a protest against the Government White Paper on Education. They infiltrated thirteen of the fifty-four schools in the electorate, effecting demonstrations. Amongst those apprehended as having been involved in this was one Dou, a pupil at Augusta College who came from a family traditionally bound to the Doctor's. His father had been a principal of the school, and his uncle, a village headman. The Doctor spoke to the boy, and then got him unconditionally released by the police. Dou and most others involved do not seem to have understood the issues at stake. For instance, children in Hamville had been found shouting 'Davala Patarete Jayawewa' (Cheers for the White Paper) when they had really been meant to protest against it. Realizing this, the Doctor had got several others released. By this act of clemency he reinforced bonds with traditional clients (which had been fast eroding) whilst simultaneously asserting his authority, thus earning both respect and goodwill. Of course, since the takeover, such influence has been really effective only when the Doctor has held Government office. Nevertheless, it has not been seen on the part of the families of the Yap and Groville *Korales*, even when their members have been in the Cabinet. Thus the Pous, Kous and Mous never did wield the same sort of influence via the schools as the Doctor had and continued to, when possible.

The second factor in Greenville providing a larger base for JVP recruits than Bluville probably lay in its less egalitarian socio-economic structure. One found far greater differences in the economic and social status of castes in Greenville than in Bluville. Moreover, as argued in Chapter 5, the patron–client bonds prevailing in Greenville tended to be far less benevolent and more oppressive than those prevailing in Bluville. As a result, one found a far larger section of socially oppressed, disgruntled and bitter individuals in the Greenville area than in the Bluville.

To conclude this section, then, the schools takeover did not undermine the power of the leading families of the area to the same extent as in Bluville. First, schools in Greenville had never been as important a means of control. (This and the less egalitarian social structure explain the easier spread of JVP ideas here than in Bluville.) Secondly, the control the leading families exercised via the land remained intact until the 1970s. When, for instance, the UNP Government attempted to take over a section of a Kou estate for 'village expansion' in the late 1960s, the family was able to manipulate the village leaders to secure a mass petition protesting against the move. The petition succeeded and the proposed takeover was shelved. The fact that the family could still exert influence of this nature, in spite of its being in the Opposition, is indicative of how little the State reforms of 1956–65 had eroded its base, and of the power it still wielded (by virtue of its landholdings) at this late stage. It was not until the Land Reform of the 1970s that this power was to be undermined.

Meanwhile, as noted earlier, the period saw a rapid turnover of candidates of both parties. The next section deals with the different individuals involved, their personal, social and economic bases for support, and their linkages with the national administration and chain of events.

The candidates and their campaigns (1956–70)[4]

Mrs Rou had won Greenville in 1956 by virtue of the patronage networks of the Pous and the Kous in the Yap *Korale* and the nationwide swing to the SLFP. Although appointed to an influential post in Government, she does not seem to have used this to try to create a strong personal support base in Greenville. She did not contest the March 1960 General Election.

Instead, it was a relatively unknown man named Teri Tee who secured the SLFP ticket. Tee hailed from what may be termed the *petit bourgeoisie*, rather than the more nationally prominent and wealthier Mou–Pou–Kou nexus. He owned about twenty-five to thirty acres of coconut land in his native hamlet, about three miles south west of Greenville town. His main source of income, however, was a business he operated, purchasing, processing and transporting plumbago, for sale in Colombo. But neither this, nor his land, yielded a sufficiently large income for him to be termed 'rich' by electoral standards. He could not therefore have been termed a major patron on the scale of say Tani Kou, Marti Mou or Nerti Nou.

However, a *Goigama*, he had married from one of the depressed castes, the *Batgam*. Having been oppressed by the leading *Goigama* families for generations, these groups had a community of economic interests and what may be tentatively termed a very rudimentary 'class consciousness'. Tee, therefore, was able to draw support on this basis, especially as he had helped various families of his wife's community living in his area. However, the SLFP ticket was probably a more important asset, Bandaranaike having identified his party ideologically with the oppressed classes, given key Cabinet posts to members of these communities in his administration of 1956–9 and, at the grass-roots level, initiated the dismantling of the village headmen's system. In this context, Tee was able to draw almost all the depressed caste votes in March 1960, accounting for nearly 90 per cent of his total vote. But, as noted, these votes were drawn more on a party than a personal basis, for, at the July 1960 elections, when he contested as an Independent, he secured less than 400 votes, the bulk of his former support going to the new SLFP candidate, Ree.

Tee's rival, Verni Mou, was a nephew of Marti Mou, MP for Greenville in the Parliament of 1947–52. Verni was related to Marti's son Moni, twice over, being a double first cousin. Not only were Verni and Moni's fathers brothers, but their mothers were sisters. As a result Verni enjoyed a very close relationship with Moni, a key figure in the UNP.

[4] *CDN* (1956), *CDN* (1960), *CDN* (1965), *CDN* (1970) and GOSL (1972b) form the basis for this section.

Thus, in addition to the traditional Mou vote, Verni may have drawn some support from those who saw him as a confidant of Moni and a possible rising star.

However, as against these factors, many regarded Verni as too aloof and a poor campaigner. He refused, for instance, to speak in Sinhala at public meetings, getting his wife to deliver his messages. Indeed, he would merely say (in English) that there were too many talkers in Sri Lanka and that he would therefore not deliver a speech, have this translated into the vernacular, sit down, and hand the meeting over to his wife. Campaigning was conducted in a very half-hearted manner with little in the way of house-to-house visits. Verni himself declares that the party ticket was foisted upon him, much against his will, and another politician of the area and former MP has confirmed this.

In the event, Verni still came within just over a hundred votes of securing the seat. This was indicative of the power his family still wielded in the area despite the gradual retirement of the village headmen, which was proceeding apace at the time. One index of the influence these men still enjoyed at the March 1960 election can be seen by the way polling proceeded. It was the practice for individual candidates to maintain their own ballot box, with their personal or party colours, at each polling station. Voters voting for a particular candidate generally cast their ballot paper in that candidate's box. Villagers knowing the loyalties or preferences of their local headmen for a particular candidate tended to cast their papers in that candidate's box. The headmen hung around the polling station, supervising this operation, and often openly declaring their loyalties (through posters, loudspeakers and the like). There had even been cases (before 1956) of their examining ballot papers prior to their casting, or of their casting them on behalf of voters. By March 1960 most such practices had been legally curbed, but the headmen still maintained a presence at these stations. They could not directly check the way individuals voted, but they could still note the ballot boxes in which these votes were cast, and thus, supposedly, have an idea of the candidate who was receiving the most support. It was indicative of the Mou power at this stage that three quarters or more of those voting cast their papers in the family candidate's box. Of course, a third or more of these were not votes for Verni Mou himself. However, the fact that such votes were cast in his box reveals the implicit intimidation that his intermediary support bloc of village headmen could still exert by their presence at the poll. Villagers, knowing their local headman's preference for Mou, seem to have pretended to vote for him, by casting their papers in his box.

As noted, however, Teri Tee scraped through as MP by a slim majority. He was not to retain the post for long. The March 1960 election had produced a hung Parliament. The UNP, as the largest single party (with 50 seats to the SLFP's 46 in a house of 151) formed a minority Government. However, this Government was defeated on its Vote of Thanks on the Throne Speech in April 1960. Parliament was then dissolved and new elections set for 20 July 1960.

Teri Tee, even though he was the sitting MP, failed to secure SLFP renomination for this (July) election. It seems that he did not have the personal connections with the new party leadership that he had enjoyed with the old.

Indeed, the SLFP ticket went to Jo Jip, a planter and company director. Jip may be termed as having been from the upper middle class and of a higher social status than Teri Tee. However, he did not have the social standing or vast estates that the Mous, Pous and Kous did. His father had begun life fairly humbly as a notary public (or solicitor), emigrating to Greenville, and amassing wealth through his practice there. He had been able to acquire about 200 acres of land in the area and educate his sons at prestigious Colombo schools. The family, therefore, had some social standing and personally based clientele in the area, but it was nothing like on the scale of that enjoyed by the Mous, Pous and Kous.

The votes Jip secured then (in July 1960) would have been largely on a party basis from the depressed castes and the personal bloc support from the (*Goigama*) Kou clients in the Yap *Korale*. He is also likely to have got the bloc support of those casting their vote for the first time. This was because, unlike in March 1960, the left parties were united by a no-contest pact in July, and could appeal to the youth on a common anti-UNP platform. Thus, whereas in March 1960 this (left) vote had been split between the SLFP and the MEP, in July, it went en-bloc to Jip, the sole 'left' candidate, ensuring his victory. (The pattern was repeated nationally, enabling the SLFP to secure a majority, with 75 of the 151 elected seats in the House.)

However, Jip himself cannot be termed as ever having been left wing. As with the leading SLFP families, his involvement with the party had been dictated more by personal contacts and friendships and a certain degree of Sinhalese Buddhist fervour than by any ideological commitment to socialism. A fundamental contradiction was now to arise between such individuals, who had allied with the left for pure electoral gain and seizure of power, and those who saw it as a step towards a more socialist administration. In 1963–4 several LSSP-led strikes disrupted industry and administration in Colombo. Mrs Bandaranaike decided that the most appropriate means of containing the crisis was to form a coalition with the LSSP and allow its leaders into her Cabinet. In June 1964 she reshuffled her Ministers and gave three key portfolios to LSSP stalwarts. The party leader, Dr N. M. Perera, was given the Ministry of Finance, Cholomondely Goonewardene, the Ministry of Public Works, and Anil Moonesinghe, that of Communications. This move alarmed some of the rightists in her own party.

The crisis climaxed in December 1964 over the proposed takeover of an important group of newspapers. This group was controlled by a family closely connected to the UNP leadership. Thus, the group followed a very conservative, and generally pro-UNP editorial policy.

Mrs Bandaranaike had always regarded it as a threat to her. In December 1964 she proposed its takeover in the Throne Speech. Fourteen SLFP MPs, led by C. P. de Silva, Leader of the House and Minister of Land, Irrigation and Power, opposed the move, crossed the floor and voted against the Government. Most of these men declared the proposed takeover as a further step towards leftist totalitarianism. Their defection led to the Government's defeat by one vote on the Address of Thanks. Parliament was dissolved on 17 December 1964 and elections set for 22 March 1965.

Jip had been one of the fourteen who had crossed the floor of the House. He now became a member of the new party formed by the leader of the breakaway faction, C. P. de Silva, the Sri Lanka Freedom (Socialist) Party. Despite its name, this party was to the right of the sitting SLFP. It entered into an electoral no-contest pact with the Opposition UNP. So, in Greenville, Jip faced only one major opponent, the SLFP's Zela Kou.

It is indicative of the way in which party (as opposed to personal) politics had been established by the 1960s that Jip, who had previously got the depressed caste vote as the SLFP candidate, was now to lose it to the new SLFP candidate, Zela Kou, when he stood on the UNP/SLFSP ticket. Instead, Jip secured the traditional Mou votes from the Groville *Korale*, which had previously been cast against him.

In the event, Jip failed by a narrow margin to secure re-election. He would have got the bulk of the youth vote, which on this occasion went to the UNP, but it was insufficient to give him victory. The electoral redemarcation of 1959 had weighted the seat against any prospective UNP candidate. Not only did the Yap *Korale*'s population of Kou clients account for a greater proportion of the electorate than previously (about 26 per cent as opposed to 17 per cent), but so did that of the so-called depressed castes. These factors meant that the core of traditional SLFP support was greater in the post-1959 era than previously. So, even with the national swing to the UNP in 1965, Jip was unable to recapture the seat for his party.

The new MP, Mrs Zela Kou was the wife of Tani Kou, the son of a former *Mudaliyar*. It was the clientage of her husband's family, as well as depressed-caste support, which had secured her victory. During this, her first period in Parliament, from 1965 to 1970, little of note occurred in Greenville. As an Opposition MP, she was not in a position to initiate major social or economic schemes in the area. Moreover, the UNP Government of 1965–70 itself did not embark on any policies which were fundamentally to alter the socio-economic structures underlying the patronage networks of the area. It did not attempt to denationalize the schools, or revoke the Paddy Lands Act, or fundamentally reverse the extension of the State initiated by the SLFP between 1956 and 1965. Rather, it accepted the status quo, so that the social structures prevailing in March 1965 continued to prevail unaltered in May 1970 (when the next election was called).

The UNP was to find great difficulty in selecting a suitable candidate for Greenville at this election. Jo Jip had died, and the party leadership tried to persuade a certain local influential owning coconut lands and a desiccating mill to stand on its ticket. This influential was known as a philanthropist and would have had some measure of local support, in addition to the party vote, in any election. However, he refused nomination.

Eventually, after much searching, the party ticket was given to one Keri Kip. Kip, although not from the area, had married the daughter of an influential notary living in Greenville town. In addition, he was nationally famous as a highly learned man, and one of the most eloquent of speakers in Sinhala. These factors, it was believed, would help him to draw some personal support, especially from the youth.

However, although married to a *Goigama*, Kip is supposed to have been from one of the depressed castes. This is a highly sensitive matter and most individuals involved in the campaign have been overly reticent and reluctant to talk about it. Nevertheless, it seems that many of the ex-headmen and members of the *Goigama* village elite, the traditional intermediaries of the Mous and the UNP in the Groville *Korale*, did not offer Kip as whole-hearted a measure of support as they might have done.

In addition, Kip's association with the rightist UNP and his personal style of campaigning lost him support amongst sections of the depressed classes and youth (which he might otherwise have conceivably gained). He began to be regarded as aloof and arrogant. On election platforms he would refer to his wife as *Mathini*, a term normally used only for the spouses of feudal aristocrats. Moreover, he did not campaign intensively from house to house. Doubtless, the lack of support he got from the party's and Mous' traditional intermediaries was the major factor in this. Nevertheless, it was not seen as such by locals, and Kip, perhaps unjustly, earned the reputation of being a vain, haughty man.

In the event, he polled just over 40 per cent of the total vote cast (largely from the Mous' Groville *Korale* area), and Zela Kou, the balance. The majority was the largest any SLFP candidate had enjoyed since the delimitation of 1959. It was undoubtedly largely attributable to the national swing against the UNP and the fact that over nine-tenths of the youth in this electorate, as elsewhere, had voted against the party. Nevertheless, the personal limitations with which Kip had had to contend were certainly another factor.

In this section, then, we have seen how the party became increasingly important in determining a candidate's electoral prospects. Men such as Teri Tee, Jo Jip and Keri Kip had little in the way of the large family clienteles of the Pous, Kous and Mous. The support they drew was largely on the basis of their association with these families, which in turn had come to be associated with certain parties and ideologies. Thus, when Tee contested as an Independent in July 1960 he lost the traditional SLFP Kou and depressed-caste votes he had secured in March and secured a paltry total of less than 400 votes. Similarly, when Jo Jip crossed over from the SLFP into an alliance with the UNP in March 1965, he lost these votes (but gained those of the Mous from the Groville *Korale*). And again, Keri Kip was able to draw these votes in May 1970, but not those of his own depressed *Batgam* community. Meanwhile, Independent candidates could draw little more than a few hundred personal votes, and these too largely from the areas they lived in and patronized.

It was the party ticket, then, which came to determine one's electoral prospects; a trend which we have examined in Bluville. It was to become even more apparent nationally in 1970 when large-scale patrons, such as R. G. Senanayake in Dambadeniya, contesting as Independents, actually lost their seats. The major factor underlying this trend was the growing importance of the State, the party being seen as the chief vehicle by which State power could be captured, and patronage disbursed. This extension of State patronage was to become even more marked in Greenville during the United Front's seven year tenure of office from 1970 to 1977, with land reform and the growth of the Co-operative network. It is to this period, and these two facets of Government policy, that we shall now turn.

The United Front Administration (1970–7)[5]

The United Front, elected in May 1970, and led by Mrs Bandaranaike, represented a coalition of three parties: her own SLFP, which had secured ninety-one seats, the Trotskyist LSSP with nineteen seats, and the Communist Party (Moscow Wing) with six. It was the first Government to enjoy a two-thirds majority in Parliament, and the SLFP alone had sufficient seats to command an overall majority in the 151 member elected House.

The electoral victory was so decisive that many senior members of Mrs Bandaranaike's own party, including several of her relatives, believed that the leftist coalition partners could be discarded. Indeed, one relative (who was to hold a senior position in the incoming Administration) is supposed to have advised the Prime Minister to drop the idea of LSSP or CP participation in the Government. However, Mrs Bandaranaike kept to her pre-election arrangement, giving the key portfolios of Finance, Communications, Plantation Industries (and later Constitutional Affairs) to leaders of the LSSP, and that of Housing and Construction to the Communist Party leader.

Nevertheless, from its very inception the alliance was a shaky one. The problem was compounded by a Kandyan–Low Country cleavage within the Administration. Since the nineteenth century, large sections of Kandyan society had come to feel increasingly ostracized from the mainstream of nationalist politics and government. The so-called Kandyan aristocrats were dissatisfied with their losses of feudal privileges and rights to revenue from land and to services from the so-called 'lower castes'. They were particularly peeved when large tracts of land over which they had once held sway began to be auctioned off to low-country *Goigama* and *Karave* families, as well as to British planters. Meanwhile, the better-off Kandyan (*Goigama*) peasantry, forming the village elites, began also to feel disgruntled as they were displaced to less fertile areas by the new tea plantations which were being opened up in this area. The result was a growing community of interests between these different social classes on the basis of a common Kandyan identity.

This identity had never been able to manifest itself, politically, in Government. The leading protagonists in the quest for Independence had been from the wealthy low-country *Goigama* and *Karave* families, and it was these individuals who had formed successive Administrations in the country. Mrs Bandaranaike, although a Kandyan by birth, had achieved power chiefly on the basis of her husband's political heritage

---

[5] GOSL (1972b) forms the basis for part of this section, unless otherwise stated.

and wealth. And, even after her advent to power, the old guard of the SLFP continued to dominate until 1964. It was only after the exit of this group that she began to fill top posts in the party with her own Kandyan relations and associates. And it was only after her victory in 1970 that these men were able to hold positions of power and authority.

Chief amongst these was Ando, who held an important Ministry. Like so many other so-called Kandyan aristocrats, he claimed a good pedigree but had little wealth to substantiate this; a mere 108 acres, compared to the thousands owned by the more prominent low-country families.

In this context, Ando pressed for a radical policy of land reform. Not merely would his personal grudges against what he regarded as 'up-start' low-country aristocrats have been settled, but he believed the measure would be electorally popular in his home seat. Mrs Bandaranaike is supposed to have been personally unhappy over the proposal, standing to lose much. However, the JVP insurrection of April 1971 lent added urgency to the need for such a move, and, in August 1972, legislation was enacted setting a ceiling on the private ownership of agricultural property.[6] This ceiling was fixed at twenty-five acres in the case of paddy, and fifty acres in the case of other land.[7] Provisions were made for landowners to transfer properties in excess of the ceiling to children over the age of eighteen, subject, of course, to no child or married couple exceeding the ceiling.[8] Medium-scale landowners (owning say 200 to 300 acres) were thereby able to maintain control of family estates and, to a very limited extent, the patronage that went with it. However, the large-scale patrons, especially those in the UNP, who had no access to alternative State-based sources of patronage, saw their power decisively curtailed. In the next section we shall examine this phenomenon as it manifested itself in Greenville.

Land Reform in Greenville

The Kous, for obvious reasons, had opposed the Land Reform proposals, when first mooted in the SLFP inner circle. When interviewed, several members of the family spoke disparagingly of Ando, and some asserted that Mrs Bandaranaike tended to favour him (and her Kandyan clique) at their expense. However, Zela Kou, being close to Government, was able to mitigate the impact of land reform on her husband's family's powers of patronage disbursement.

---

[6] Estates (Control of Transfer and Acquisition) Act, No. 2 of 1972.
[7] Land Reform Law, No. 1 of 1972.   [8] Ibid.

In Greenville, a total of 630 acres, drawn from twelve estates, were appropriated and allocated to the Estate Management Services.[9] This body, operating under the auspices of the Land Reform Commission (LRC), was supposed to utilize the properties for employment generating projects. Needless to say, prospective job applicants had to be recommended by the local SLFP Branch President before being considered, and any posts given were subject to confirmation by the local MP. By these means, Zela Kou was able to reward the younger members of families traditionally loyal to her.

Meanwhile, just over eighty-five acres were redistributed in half acre or one acre blocks to landless villagers as an initial step.[10] Such redistribution was facilitated by the agro-ecological conditions of the electorate. Greenville had a large extent of coconut land, which could be subdivided and run by smallholders more easily than the tea and rubber in Bluville could. Significantly, it was the traditional clients of the Pous and the Kous who were favoured. Thus blocs in Groville *Korale* were not redistributed to the local Mou clients or their followers but to the Pou/Kou loyalists from the Yap *Korale*, five to ten miles away.[11]

Many of the small landowning *Goigama* intermediaries (through whom the Kous operated) saw Land Reform as a threat to their positions. They were particularly alarmed that the depressed castes would use it to gain economic and, perhaps, social, parity with them. They therefore used all possible means to prevent such an eventuality.

It was the members of the *Goigama* village elite who sat on the three Agricultural Productivity Committees (APCs) covering the Greenville electorate. These Committees, created under the Agricultural Productivity Law, No. 2 of 1972, were responsible for the planning and implementation of the agricultural programmes in their areas of authority. They had powers regarding the promotion, co-ordination and development of agriculture, the formation and implementation of programmes and targets, the maintenance of a register of all agricultural lands and, most important, the acquisition and disposal of property. (They could order any person having an interest in land or carrying out any agricultural operation to provide information, and, on paper, were charged with the more vigorous implementation of the Paddy Lands Act of 1958.)

Each Agricultural Productivity Committee consisted of ten members, appointed by the Minister of Agriculture and Lands on the recommendation of the local MP (or, in the case of an Opposition seat, the SLFP

---

[9] LRC (1972–9).   [10] Ibid.
[11] Ibid. and Wanigaratne and Shanmugaratnam (1979) forms the basis for the next sentence and the next five paragraphs.

organizer of the area). In Greenville the three APCs were dominated by the traditional clients of the Kous. The Woville APC, which encompassed the north-western part of the electorate, was one such Committee. Its members were totally insensitive to the requests of the so-called depressed castes, even when these had proved to be long-standing SLFP loyalists. When the depressed *Panna* members of the Wun Cultivation Committee, who had always been SLFP supporters, pleaded that they be given small blocks of land from the confiscated portions of the three estates surrounding their village they were ignored. Instead, this land was given to *Goigama* relations and associates of those on the APC, almost all of whom were richer than the Wun inhabitants. Indeed, some blocks were reserved for Kou clients from the Yap *Korale*, living five to six miles away!

Again, it was these already relatively 'privileged' groups which secured jobs on the Government inter-cropping projects launched in the area. The Wun inhabitants were hardly considered. And when they pleaded for a five acre block from a nearby estate for a housing project, so that the congestion in their village could be eased, they were again ignored.

Finally, the Wun villagers, like so many others elsewhere, lost the fringe benefits they had enjoyed under the regime of private land-ownership. The State did not allow them to acquire palm leaves for thatch and firewood, or jak fruit and other such items, from its recently acquired properties. And of course it did not distribute gifts in cash and kind during times of need, as so many private patrons had done.

Not surprisingly, Wun, which had been a traditional SLFP strong-hold, switched over to the UNP at the July 1977 General Election. The new (UNP) MP, Napi Nip, has attempted to assuage some of the more pressing grievances of the villagers. Most significantly, he has launched a housing project in the area as well as giving job opportunities and small blocks of land to the youth from the village. Thus, he has gone some way towards consolidating the new found UNP support in the area.

Meanwhile, at a more general level, land reform earned much ill-will. It is true that a greater proportion of local inhabitants would have benefited from the scheme in Greenville than in Bluville. This was because the coconut properties in the former area could be subdivided and redistributed to villagers to be run as smallholdings more easily than the tea and rubber properties in Bluville could. Moreover, with their greater filtration of sunlight, coconut land offered a potential for inter-cropping which tea and rubber did not. Thus, a number of employment-creating projects emerged in Greenville, which could never be considered in Bluville.

Nevertheless, in both areas, mismanagement was rife, and only a small section of the favoured clientele benefited over and above the mass. On many estates, where the yield was low, trees were felled and sold for firewood or cheap timber. In certain areas, a food crop, manioc, was cultivated, thus ruining the fertility of the soil, and making it totally unsuitable for replanting with coconut; this, in one of the best coconut growing areas of the country. And of course on properties owned by prominent supporters of the UNP, all moveable assets, comprising cattle, carts, bungalow fittings, furniture, linen and the like, were appropriated and sold. With such asset stripping and disinvestment, the estates became less viable as commercial propositions, and unable to provide the seasonal employment they had done in the past. This, the non-provision of fringe benefits which villagers had become accustomed to, and the enrichment of a select few at the general expense, earned much ill-will. These were certainly factors in the UNP's sweeping victory of July 1977.

To sum up, then, land reform in Greenville, as in Bluville, proved a measure which lost public support. True, it represented a major extension of the State, and true the local MP was able to reward supporters with the increased patronage at her disposal. However, such rewards were confined to a select few: the traditional clients of the Kous. These clients enjoyed a privileged economic and social position at the village level by virtue of their control over certain depressed and landless groups. They were determined to protect this position and ensure that land reform did not impair the ties of obligation and dependence which bound the poorer villagers to them. Consequently, they strove to withhold the patronage at their disposal from these sections, even when the latter had been long-standing SLFP loyalists. As a result, many depressed communities, resentful at the treatment they had received, switched support to the UNP at the July 1977 General Election. So, as in Bluville, land reform proved a classic case of an 'inappropriate' manipulation of State patronage with a consequent loss of electoral support. The other sphere in which this was manifest was in the handling of the Co-operative network. It is to this that we shall now turn.

The Co-operatives in Greenville (1970–7)

As noted in Chapter 4, by the early 1970s, the Co-operatives had become near monopolists in the distribution of scarce consumer goods, agricultural credit and products, as well as monopsonists in the purchase of various agricultural goods. Thus, their activities intruded into the daily lives of almost every inhabitant of Sri Lanka. Following the UF victory in May 1970, Government control over this institution was extended, the MP (or District Political Authority) being empowered to nominate nine of the fifteen directors of the Board of the Local Co-operative.[12]

In Greenville, as in Bluville, it was the traditional loyalists of the sitting MP who were rewarded with these coveted posts.[13] And, as in Bluville, it was these groups which filled the managerial (and other) offices in the local branches. And again, as in Bluville, these groups used these offices to enrich themselves, their relatives and their associates, at the public expense. Four senior officers were charged with having misappropriated a total of Rs 6,470.91. A further sum of Rs 74,354.65 was found due from eighteen branch managers, and Rs 10,463 from another twenty-three officers. In another case three senior officers are supposed to have misappropriated Rs 2,828.30 in connection with the transport of some chillies in 1976.

There were also cases of fraud perpetrated against members of the public, either directly or indirectly. In one such instance, three senior officers are supposed to have accepted a cheque for Rs 1,000 which was later dishonoured. In another case, two officers had arranged a loan of Rs 2,452.80 for a certain lady, drawn the money from the Society coffers, but not passed it on to her. The Investigating Officers concluded that the two had appropriated the money themselves. In another case, this time of indirect fraud, a senior officer was found to have misappropriated some Lakspray worth Rs 435.61. It was presumed that this was used either for personal consumption or sale in the black market.

Meanwhile, there seem to have been numerous cases of misappropriation connected to favouritism. Co-operative resources were used as a means of enriching one's friends and associates. For instance, on five occasions in 1976, gunny bags and sarongs had been purchased from favourites at prices in excess of their market values and sold at cheaper rates, forcing a loss upon the Society amounting to Rs 12,101.79. Large stocks of rice are believed to have been misappropriated from a depot (between 11 September 1975 and 30 September 1977), and later sold on the black market. Naturally, the shortages engendered by such activities and the hardships caused to the ordinary consumer did not earn those in office much goodwill.

This was especially so as only a very small circle of Co-operative Society officers and their friends, relations and associates benefited. Even in the matters of employment and pay such personal connections,

---

[12] Asiriwatham (1981).
[13] Commissioner of Co-operative Development (Investigations Department), Confidential Files of Inquiry into the Greenville MPCS (1970–7) form the basis for the rest of this paragraph and the next eight.

rather than ability or merit, proved the criterion of selection. One officer was found to have overpaid some favoured staff to the tune of Rs 267.97. In another case an unqualified man was chosen to fill a relatively responsible position. His fraudulent certificates had been accepted, and he had been overpaid to the tune of Rs 5,927.

There seems to have been an utter disregard for public welfare on the part of those controlling these State bodies, that is, if they had any notion of such a concept in the first instance. The use of funds had never been carefully monitored. One officer, for instance, had sold sweep tickets, forcing the Society to incur a loss of Rs 2,246.50. Meanwhile, none of the local branches had been insured against fire or burglary. Thus, when two outlets were burgled to the tune of Rs 4,427.39 and Rs 2,060.52, no claim could be secured in recompense. Moreover, no maximum limit had been set on the stores kept at the different branches (as required by law), so that insurance companies had refused to accept liability for the losses suffered at five other stores.

Meanwhile, funds had been misappropriated and spent recklessly. A sum of Rs 20,621.50 had been withdrawn from a section and expended on the construction of a new office for the senior staff of the Society. The Investigating Officers in their Report on this noted that protocol had not been followed in this matter. Money from this section had been wrongly appropriated whereas a bank loan should have been secured for the project.

Finally, some Co-operative Society officers were found to have used their positions and access to funds explicitly to further the SLFP cause. At the July 1977 election, some officers are supposed to have drawn Rs 195 from the Society funds for the publication of party leaflets and literature. And, of course, vehicles, furniture, and other assets belonging to the institution are said to have been used (on behalf of the party) during the campaign.

Meanwhile, a powerful local personality is supposed to have been involved in some allegedly unauthorized dealings. This personality is accused of having sanctioned payment of Rs 1,500 without having secured prior Board approval. The personality is also said to have withdrawn Rs 2,776.56 from Society coffers for the repair of a dispensary without having followed the proper administrative procedure in the matter. The Government was contemplating preferring charges against this individual on these two counts.

It may well be that these acts were more a reflection of the personality's high-handed impatience and desire to circumvent tedious protocol than premeditated attempts to defraud the Society. But, be that as it may, they were part of a more general abuse of State patronage. The

Co-operatives were used to benefit only a select few and, certainly at the lower levels, embezzlement and misappropriation of funds were widespread. As a result, many essential commodities came to be in short supply. In other instances, they were available only on the black market, sold by traders known to have acquired them illicitly through the Co-operative. In both cases, the institution, its officers and the Government which had appointed them earned the reputation of corruption. And, in both cases, great hardship was caused to the ordinary consumer. Not surprisingly, this hardship earned the Government which encouraged it much ill-will. And again, not surprisingly, this ill-will was translated into a massive swing of votes against the SLFP at the July 1977 General Election.

In this section then we have seen how the extension of governmental control of the Co-operatives was used to benefit only a select few who then utilized their positions for self-aggrandizement at the public expense, with a consequent loss of political goodwill and support. It was yet another instance of an inappropriate manipulation of the State, and an almost exact replication of what occurred in the Purville *Korale* MPCS over the same period (1970–7).

The consolidation of State power in Greenville (1977–81)

The July 1977 election saw a landslide win for the UNP. In Greenville, the party's candidate, Napi Nip secured about 60 per cent of the total vote polled. The SLFP lost almost the entire youth vote and a large section of the depressed caste and poorer *Goigama* support, which it had enjoyed in the past.

The new MP was a first cousin of Nerti Nou's and secured the traditional Nou/Mou/UNP support in the Groville *Korale*. However, as in Bluville and most other electorates that year, national issues and the party ticket were the prime factors in his victory.

Not holding a senior Cabinet position, as the Doctor does, Nip has been unable to patronize the area to the same extent. However, he has been able to establish three coconut mills, producing oil, poonac and charcoal, and seven fibre mills. All are highly labour intensive, the coconut mills providing about 450 jobs between them, and the fibre mills about 350. They were confined to the Groville *Korale* which has historically supported the Mous and the Nous.

The traditional (Mou/Nou/UNP) client-families of this area had failed to benefit by the Land Reform programme initiated under the previous regime. Their grievances were now redressed to a limited degree by the dismantling of the old APC-CC structure and the establishment of a new organization, the Agrarian Services Committee (ASC), to which they have been appointed.[14] So one set of village elites has been replaced by another. These former members of the village elite are, however, to occupy no more than six of the fourteen seats on each ASC.[15] The remaining eight seats are reserved for certain State officers, including a new cadre of personnel termed Cultivation Officers (or COs) who are supposed to be technically conversant with the latest agricultural techniques.[16]

Meanwhile, other sections, especially amongst the depressed groups which failed to benefit during the SLFP's tenure in office, have not been forgotten. Twenty sawmills, most concentrated in their areas, and providing employment for about 300 individuals in all, have been established. A tile factory employing about fifty people has been founded on the Colombo–Kandy Road as well as a concrete-block producing complex. A number of small-scale self-employment textile schemes have also been initiated, though the liberalized import policy has militated against their success.

Most important, perhaps, are the three housing schemes launched in the electorate as part of the National Programme. These schemes are specifically designed for the poorest groups in each electorate. In Greenville, these groups are from the depressed castes. By providing each family from selected depressed villages with a house, and sufficient land and infrastructure for self-supporting cultivation, their dependence upon the *Goigama* village elite has been broken to a certain extent. However, only two to three such schemes have been launched in each electorate, so that quantitatively their social impact has been minimal.

We have examined the case of Wun. Another such instance is that of Tau, a depressed-caste village in the Yap *Korale* where the inhabitants used to cultivate cashew nut, and sell it to richer *Goigama* villagers who transported it to Colombo and sold it there at a huge profit. The Tau villagers were kept in a state of abject and servile dependence, hardly daring to question the authority of the local elite. In the pre-1956 era, they had often been coerced into voting as this elite demanded, and even after that had exercised little genuine free-will at elections. The village had enjoyed a reputation for providing the mistresses of some of the *walauwe* owners in the vicinity, notably Monti Pou.

Following the UNP's 1977 election victory, Tau had been chosen as one of the villages in the Greenville electorate most deserving of a

---

14 See the Agrarian Services Act, No. 58 of 1979, and Wanigaratne and Shanmugaratnam (1979).
15 Ibid.   16 Ibid.

housing scheme. Half acre blocks had been reserved for each family and additional land granted for the cultivation of cashew nut. Electricity, water, tools and other infrastructural facilities had also been provided. Most important, retail outlets for the sale of cashew had been established in the vicinity. These, bordering a major highway, were to enjoy good custom with the boom in tourist traffic. The net result is that the dependence of these villagers upon the *Goigama* elite has been broken. Tau is one of several such villages in the district where the national housing schemes have undermined these ties of dependence and obligation.

Meanwhile, members of the village elite, especially those in the Yap *Korale* affiliated to the Pous and the Kous, have become increasingly disgruntled. Many have threatened to assault the Tau villagers (as well as those from other new housing schemes in the area). They assert that the peace and harmony of their region is being destroyed by these schemes. However, there is almost certainly an element of pique, if not jealousy, in these claims.

In the neighbouring electorate, 2,000 houses are being built on 200 acres of agricultural land bordering two villages. A forest in the area (at present a sanctuary) is being destroyed for the purpose. According to the village elites, the result will be the destruction of the water sources (originating in the sanctuary) that feed 700 acres of paddy in Greenville and the neighbouring electorate. Earth has already blocked up many of their paddy channels. They claim that all this is part of a plot to ruin them economically. Whether this can be believed or not is a moot point. The fact remains that the housing schemes have polarized the richer *Goigama* patrons and their former depressed caste clients into two distinct groups, exposing the conflict of class interests inherent in the tie.

The hold of these intermediating lesser patrons upon their clients has thereby been undermined, if not destroyed. That of the large scale patrons upon their intermediaries has also atrophied, especially since Land Reform. The Kous still try to maintain what links they can, but theirs is a dying power. Recently, Tani Kou heard that one of his traditional clients had had a daughter married. Kou had not been invited to the wedding; a lapse beyond the realm of belief two decades ago. On meeting the client, Kou had given him a handsome cash present, chiding him for not having invited him to the function, and patronizingly warning him never to err in that manner again.

By such means, Kou and other one-time large-scale patrons still attempt to retain the loyalty of these groups. But, increasingly, this loyalty is coming to be based on a shrewder perception of self-interest; a perception which sees loyalty to those controlling, or likely to control, the State, as yielding greater material dividends than an allegiance to impoverished landowners unable to offer the material largesse they had done in the past. In Greenville, for instance, several *mudalali* traders who had formerly supported the Kous switched over to the UNP soon after the 1977 election, in return for Government contracts for housing (and other 'development') projects.

As in Bluville, then, the political following that these families can maintain is largely on the basis of their being alternative candidates for Government and control of State bodies. And again, as in Bluville, once in office, it is the appropriate manipulation of these bodies, subject to external constraints, which determines a politician's likely success. We have described the extension of the State in Greenville in the period 1970–7, and seen how abuse of the Co-operative and Land Reform Programmes actually lost much goodwill. Since then, the new MP has attempted to use the institutions at his command judiciously, largely to consolidate his support base. But, as in Bluville, his success is, to a certain extent, being hampered by the recession and by protectionist policies followed in the West. Indeed the textile industry, here accounting for more employment than in the Bluville region (the two largest factories near Greenville employing 1,200 individuals from the electorate and 7,000 altogether), employment and political goodwill is threatened to a greater extent than in Bluville.

The Elections of 1982[17]

Presidential Elections were called suddenly in October 1982. In Greenville a new SLFP organizer with poor roots in the area had been appointed. The Kous, although antipathetic to him and the SLFP presidential candidate, remained on the sidelines, not taking an active part in the campaign. Internal party differences therefore were not as apparent as in Bluville and Red Town.

Nevertheless, the UNP won the seat comfortably, with over half the votes cast. This represented a drop in the UNP's 1977 share, but a rise in the SLFP's 1977 share. A significant proportion of depressed caste votes (about 5 per cent of the total), especially that of their youth, seems to have been garnered by the JVP on this occasion.

It seems that although there have been a number of State projects in depressed-caste areas, these have not generated as much political goodwill as they might have done. This has been due to three factors. First,

---

[17] GOSL (1983), GOSL (1987) and personal observations (rechecked with election results published in the *CDN* and *Island* newspapers) form the basis for this section.

the *Goigama* village elites, by virtue of their better educational qualifications (and perhaps personal links with the local MP), have been able to fill key positions in the supra-village level consultative, advisory, and decision making, bodies. Amongst these were the Agrarian Services Committees, and various rural development societies represented on the *Gramodaya Mandalayas*. As such they have been able to favour their own kith and kin in disbursing agricultural inputs, credit, and (via their powers of recommendation) employment. The depressed groups have not benefited as much as they might have. This is so even in their own areas where projects have been launched.

Secondly, even where they have benefited, the quantitative impact on their income and employment levels and housing conditions has been small. The total number of houses built in Greenville to date would number no more than about 200, directly benefiting about 600 voters at the most in an electorate of over 70,000. This is because local resource constraints (coupled with the adverse international trade and aid climate) have limited the size of projects launched. Thus, for every party supporter gaining a job or house, there have been several more disappointed in their expectations. These disappointed groups, especially when they have come from the depressed castes, seem to have lost faith in the Government.

Thirdly, the post-1977 price inflation seems to have exacerbated the caste and class tensions characterizing Greenville particularly markedly. The prices of coconuts, vegetables and fruit-crops escalated, making subsistence more difficult for the landless villager, and also increasing the incentive to steal from the richer small-scale landowner. Such thefts led to reprisals, further increasing the existing tensions between the groups. The depressed castes, which had traditionally not enjoyed the same warm relationship with the *Goigama* village elites that the client groups in the fishing villages of Bluville had with the fish *mudalalis*, were particularly bitter. They felt that they had failed to benefit under both the SLFP and the UNP. It was these feelings which seem to have been translated into a vote for the JVP in October 1982.

In the event, the Government, although winning comfortably, failed to make major gains in the electorate at the Presidential Poll. Its performance in Greenville was very characteristic of its performance in the district and in the nation at large. Its share of the valid vote in the electorate was just under its average share in the district, and just over its share nationally. It represented a median performance for the UNP in the district. As such, it could be classed as a very mediocre one.

In this context it was important that the results of the Referendum be an improvement. MPs faring poorly faced the threat of being expelled by the party. Consequently, a fairly vigorous campaign was launched.

The Opposition, which was totally disorganized in the area (as elsewhere), was ineffectual. In many polling booths it did not even have polling agents who knew the area to supervise its interests. The regularity of the poll in many parts of the country was questioned by the Commissioner of Elections in his Report on the first Referendum in Sri Lanka.

In the event, two-thirds in Greenville voted for the Government in December 1982. This proportion was almost the highest in the district. It was well above the district and national averages. Nip was thus able to remain as the MP of the area for another six-year term.

Conclusion

In this chapter we have traced the growth of the State in Greenville. A fairly similar pattern to that in Bluville can be discerned. In both electorates the chief political actors had been from landowning and/or *Mudaliyar* families. In both areas they had exercised control over intermediaries through their landed wealth and the *Mudaliyar* system. These intermediaries, in turn, had controlled the ordinary villagers through their monopoly of lesser headmanships, land and credit. With the extension of the State during the periods 1960–5 and 1970–7, the power of both the large-scale patrons and their intermediaries was undermined. The former, in particular, had to rely increasingly on their role as the most likely candidates for State office to maintain a position as patrons. This was best achieved through identification with a party, the party being seen as the most likely vehicle through which State power could be captured and retained at the national level. (The greater importance of the party was perhaps more apparent in Greenville than in Bluville as so many large-scale patrons there desisted from active politics after 1956, their votes going to the candidates of the parties they were identified with.) Once State power had been achieved, a patron had to appropriately manipulate the institutions at his command to consolidate, maintain and extend his political following. We have seen how, in both electorates, patrons lost support by an inappropriate manipulation of the institutions at their command.

But, even with appropriate manipulation, success is constrained by local, national and international factors. In Greenville the prevailing social structure, and the way this is reflected in local political institutions, has prevented State benefits from percolating down to all sections.

The *Goigama* village elites have monopolized key local posts under both SLFP and UNP regimes, excluding the depressed groups. They have thereby been able to secure the plums of political patronage, in terms of employment and assets, for themselves. In the process the depressed groups have been forced to the margin, although this has been contrary to the declared aims of successive governments. The efforts of both the UNP and the SLFP to garner their support has therefore been frustrated by the way in which the patronage system (reflecting the local social structure) operates. The depressed groups have, since 1970, followed a pattern of voting against the sitting Government. In 1982 a significant part of their support went to the JVP.

Nationally, Napi Nip's position as a mere MP limited his ability to secure benefits for his electorate, in a way not seen in Bluville. Internationally, the unfavourable trade and aid climate have, as in Bluville, harmed the local textile industry, and limited the scope for employment generation and the maintenance of political goodwill. (Its social impact in Greenville has however been greater than in Bluville due to the greater quantitative importance of the textile industry there.)

The major differences in the histories of Bluville and Greenville can be traced to their different power structures, dictated largely by their different agro-ecological and socio-economic circumstances. In Bluville the local bus magnates and schools having been more important than in Greenville, the takeovers during the period 1956–65 undermined the Doctor's base to a greater extent than that of the Pous, Kous and Mous in their areas. In Greenville, on the other hand, the primary impact of State policy had to wait till the Land Reform of the 1970s. The Pous, Kous and Mous, therefore, continued to maintain their powers of private patronage disbursement intact for perhaps a longer period than the Doctor and his allies managed to do in Bluville. However, the sharper caste/class differences and less benevolent village level patronage networks in Greenville constrained their ability, and later that of Napi Nip, to broaden their support base in a way they did not in Bluville.

7

Red Town: the urban setting (1947–1959)

Introduction

Red Town, an urban constituency, lies on the outskirts of Colombo.[1] In 1946 the electorate covered an area of approximately fifty-five square miles stretching from two highly urbanized and rapidly industrializing *peruwas* in the west to a less urban *peruwa* in the east, and three much more rural and agrarian *peruwas* in the north-east. Thus, under the first delimitation (1946–59), just over a third of the electorate's population fell within a highly urbanized frame of reference and about a half within a largely agrarian setting.

Unlike the Bluville and Greenville electorates of this time, in both of which Buddhists represented over 90 per cent of the electoral strength, and no other religious community accounted for over 5 per cent of the total, in Red Town, the Christians formed a numerically important minority. In 1946 they accounted for about one sixth of the electorate's population. They were concentrated in the more urbanized western part of the electorate. The majority were Sinhalese, and a large proportion hailed from non-*Goigama* castes, particularly the *Vahumpura*.

With regard to caste, in the electorate as a whole, about 50 per cent of the constituents would have been *Goigama* at this time, about 25 per cent *Batgam*, and about 20 per cent *Vahumpura*, the remainder being from other minor communities. The *Goigama* were spread fairly evenly throughout the electorate. Most of the *Batgam* and about half the *Vahumpura* were concentrated in the agricultural eastern part of the electorate. Here, they were bound to the *Goigama* village elite by ties of obligations and dependence, very similar to those operating in Greenville. About half of the electorate's *Vahumpura* population would have been concentrated in the urbanized western part where they were free of such ties and more exposed to trade union and industrial influence.

In 1959 the electorate was redrawn.[2] This meant that the new Red Town electorate had about two-thirds of its population in the two highly

---

[1] GOC (1946) forms the basis for this paragraph and the next.
[2] GOC (1959) forms the basis for this paragraph.

urbanized *peruwas*, and so contained a far higher proportion of individuals exposed to urban influences than previously. Even the eastern *peruwa*, accounting for most of the remaining third of the electorate's population, was urbanizing and industrializing rapidly during this time.

With the delimitation of 1976 this process was carried one step further.[3] Red Town was once again redrawn and confined to a land area of approximately seven square miles in the western part of the former electorate. Thus, the electorate of 1976 was more than seven times as densely populated as that of 1946, and completely 'urbanized'. This change meant that the constituents were now drawn largely from what may be termed the lower middle and working classes. They were employed in factories in the electorate itself, or as port, railway or clerical staff in Colombo, commuting there daily. The sort of influences they were subject to, therefore, were very different to those that the constituents in the eastern agricultural part of the electorate of 1946 were.

The delimitations of 1959 and 1976 also meant a gradual reduction of the proportion of Buddhists in the electorate from over four-fifths in 1946,[4] to just below this in 1959[5] and less than three-quarters in 1976.[6] This was because the chief Buddhist concentrations were in the agricultural eastern part of the electorate, which was gradually whittled away. At the same time the proportion of Muslims and Hindus rose, from below one twentieth in 1946[7] to just over this in 1959[8] and then about one sixth in 1976.[9] This largely represented the increased role of the western urbanized part of the electorate, bordering Colombo (where these minorities were concentrated), with the successive delimitations. The proportion of Christians however remained fairly constant at about one sixth throughout this period.[10]

As regards caste the successive delimitations and greater role of the urban sector meant that the proportion of *Vahumpura* in the electorate is also likely to have risen at the expense of the *Goigama* and the *Batgam*. By 1976 the *Vahumpura* would have accounted for at least 30 to 40 per cent of the electorate's strength.

To conclude then, Red Town, like Bluville and Greenville, was a low-country electorate with very similar historical antecedents. Socially, economically and geographically during this early period (1947–56), the north-eastern agricultural part of Red Town bore many similarities to Greenville. Indeed, in 1946, the northernmost part of the electorate was only five to six miles from the southernmost part of Greenville, though

---

[3] GOSL (1976) forms the basis for this paragraph.
[4] GOC (1946). [5] GOC (1959). [6] GOSL (1976).
[7] GOC (1946). [8] GOC (1959). [9] GOSL (1976).
[10] GOC (1946); GOC (1959); GOSL (1976).

with the 1959 delimitation this difference had increased to between twelve and fifteen miles, and by 1976 to about sixteen miles.[11] However, it had a large urban sector, which by 1959 came to account for a greater proportion of its population.

In 1946 we could distinguish three important patronage networks in Red Town. The first was based on control of land and, more significantly, influence over the village headmen, especially in the agricultural north-eastern *peruwas*. This network was instrumental in securing Don Dip's election to the Red Town State Council seat before Independence, and underpinning his support at the General Elections of 1947 and 1952. The second source of influence is popularly, although in our view mistakenly, believed to be the Red Town temple (and its associated Red Town *Pirivena* or training school for monks). The third group comprised the trade unions and LSSP-based worker groups, concentrated in the industrial and urbanized western part of the electorate. This network provided the core of the left vote in the General Elections of 1947 and 1952. We shall begin by focussing on the networks operating in the agricultural north-east, however, which provided the main base for Don Dip's support.

The landowners, *Mudaliyars* and lesser headmen of Red Town

Unlike in Greenville, large-scale landholdings were not a characteristic of Red Town. This was so even in the agricultural north-eastern part of the electorate. True, there were two large coconut estates on the northern border of the constituency: one 640-acre estate and another 602-acre property.[12] True, both owners were a part of the influential Pou–Kou nexus described in Chapter 5. Nevertheless, the main holdings of these families were concentrated elsewhere.[13]

Moreover, although their members had held *Mudaliyarships* in the vicinity of Red Town, they had not monopolized these to anything like the same extent that they had in the Yap *Korale*, within which Greenville fell. The monopoly of *Mudaliyarships* in the Greenville region is described on pp. 88–9.

In the *korale* within which the Red Town electorate fell, the pattern was very different. Here the succession of *Mudaliyars* came from very different families.[14] Although some of the *Mudaliyars* were distantly connected to one another, they did not bear the close interlocking ties that those in the Greenville region *korales* did. It was certainly not a case

11 Ordnance Survey Map (Survey Department, Sri Lanka, published periodically).
12 Ferguson's (1941).   13 Ibid.
14 *Blue Books* (1877–1947) and *Civil Lists* (1877–1947).

of son succeeding father, as had occurred sometimes over three generations in Groville *Korale*, or over several generations (from at least the eighteenth century onwards) in Purville *Korale*. *Mudaliyarships* in the Red Town region did not have this quasi-hereditary character.

The result was that no one family or set of families was able to build up a close working relationship with the lesser headmen of Red Town, as the Pous and the Kous had in Greenville, and the Foos in Bluville. This was to make it much easier for a relative 'outsider' (with no *Mudaliyar* family background) to penetrate their ranks than elsewhere. Such penetration could be effected through other institutions, such as the temples, which we shall examine later.

Another factor facilitating this penetration was the structure of land distribution in the electorate. As noted, even the agricultural part of Red Town was not characterized by large estates. There were only two estates of over 500 acres in the electorate, and another two of over 100.[15] Most holdings were less than 100 acres in extent, and even the elite families of the area did not own large blocks. Don Dip's maternal uncle owned only forty-five acres in Red Town, and his wife another forty-five acres.[16] Of course, these nationally prominent families had very extensive holdings in other parts of the country. But, in their home base of Red Town proper, they exercised little influence through land *per se*; and certainly land was nothing like as important a means of control as the rubber estates of Bluville, or even the coconut estates of Greenville, were. (This was, of course, a reflection of Red Town's greater proximity to Colombo, and the greater degree of urbanization than in the other two electorates; this, even in the 'agricultural north-east'.)

Meanwhile, some of the richer *Vidane-Arachchis* themselves would have owned anything from twenty-five to fifty acres, spread over many blocks.[17] The *Vidane-Arachchi* of one north-eastern *peruwa* may have even owned from 100 to 200 acres in the electorate, and the Registrar of Marriages in a hamlet in the vicinity (brother of the local *Police-Vidane* and father of the present MP for a neighbouring electorate), also had sizeable extents, totalling about fifty to a hundred acres altogether. This structure of land-ownership meant that, at the local level, some of these richer families of the village elite were relatively independent of the large nationally prominent landed families of the area, such as the Dips and the Rous, in a way that their brethren in Bluville and Greenville were not.

This was especially so in many of the *peruwas*. *Vidane-Arachchi* families dominated in much the same way that the *Mudaliyars* did in their *korales*. There was a quasi-hereditary aspect to the *Vidane-Arachchiship*

[15] Ferguson's (1941).   [16] Ibid.
[17] See in particular SLNA 33/3600 regarding the basis for this paragraph and the next.

of Red Town and a near monopoly of posts by a few families. For instance, in one particular *peruwa*, successive generations of a certain family held the *Vidane-Arachchiship*, as the Tips had done in an eastern *peruwa* of Groville *Korale*. Posts within a particular *peruwa* were confined to a few families. For instance, of the eleven *Police-Vidaneships* of a certain Red Town *peruwa* at the turn of the century, two were held by the *Vidane-Arachchi*'s brothers, one by him in an acting capacity, and another two shared between two closely related families.

Thus, a few families of the village elites maintained influence over villagers via control of the land and headmanships, the last often on a quasi-hereditary basis. This influence was accentuated by the fact that these village elites were relatively independent of the nationally prominent families of the area, the latter not having monopolized either land or *Mudaliyarships*, as in Greenville and Bluville.

To conclude then, the more egalitarian structure of land ownership at the higher levels, coupled with the absence of a monopoly of *Mudaliyarships* through time, meant that no one family or set of families was able to establish control over village elites (as in Greenville and Bluville). Yet, in the State Council election and the subsequent General Elections, Don Dip carried these headmen, and so the agricultural east and north-east of the electorate, en bloc. How did he manage this? To answer this question we have to focus on the Red Town temple, which forms the subject of our next section.

The Red Town temple

There is a popular belief that temples were influential in swaying public opinion at elections.[18] Such a belief presupposes that temples had a certain degree of moral influence over laymen. Its protagonists point to the political activism of the priests at elections, as recounted in various newspapers, with special reference to the literature they produced, public meetings addressed, door-to-door campaigning and the like.[19] The pursuit of such activities is certainly an indication of the fervour of the priests. It is not, however, an index of their actual success in swaying laymen around to their particular viewpoints. It is significant, in this context, that although the Red Town temple (and associated Red Town *Pirivena*) campaigned against Don Dip in 1947 and 1952 they made little impact on his success. Moreover, the largely urban area surrounding their temple voted solidly for the left candidate at this election, and not for their nominee, Mrs Rou. Indeed, it is likely that the political

18 See Phadnis (1976), pp. 188, 202–3 and 251–2 and Smith (1966), pp. 490–5.
19 Smith (1966), p. 489.

campaigning of the Red Town temple backfired, bringing an already disreputable institution to even lower levels of public esteem.

It is our contention that, as early as the late nineteenth century, Buddhist temples, including the one at Red Town, carried very little moral influence, if any, and certainly not enough to sway elections by the 1940s. This is a controversial proposition, so we shall go to some lengths to substantiate it.

The Portuguese and Dutch periods had seen a large-scale desecration of the low-country temples. For instance, the Temple Lands Commission of 1956 noted that the largest Vishnu *Devale* in the Maritime Provinces owned only 1.75 acres of land and the Tissamaharama *Vihare*, 9.75 acres of highland and paddy.[20] Such small temple-holdings were attributed to large scale alienation of these lands by the Colonial Administrations.[21]

This was very different to the experience of the Kandyan temples. These had not been subject to the desecrations of the Portuguese and Dutch, in the way the low-country temples had. When the British assumed the mantle of power, they did so under terms of the Kandyan Convention of 1815, which guaranteed the protection of Buddhism and its institutions. In succeeding years the Colonial Administration continued to scrupulously observe the terms of this convention, leaving the temple lands of the region intact, and the priests and lay trustees free to appropriate the massive revenues therefrom without having to pay tax.

To give an idea of the scale of their holdings, in Sabaragamuwa, the Maha Saman *Devale* owned just over 1,126 *amunams* of paddy and 2,667 *amunams* of highland, whilst the Alutnuwara Kataragama *Devale* owned 453 *amunams* of paddy and 623 *amunams* of highland.[22] The Kandy Maha *Devale* and Nata *Devale* owned 578 *amunams* each, the Pattini *Devale*, 25 *amunams*, the Kataragama *Devale*, 77 *amunams*, and the *Dalada Maligawa*, 41 *amunams*.[23] Whole villages were owned, and the inhabitants bound by service tenures to these institutions.[24] The Kiriella *Vihare* in Kuruwita *Korale*, Sabaragamuwa, owned one whole village, Dumbura, with a surveyed extent of 8,305 acres and the next richest *Vihare* in the Province, Potgul, owned another village, Galature, with a surveyed extent of 5,765 acres.[25]

In some instances subsidiary sources of income were available. The Dumbura village owned by the Kiriella *Vihare*, for instance, was rich in plumbago, the mining of which gave the temple additional revenue.[26] Finally, all these incomes accruing to the temples were free of tax (as required by terms of the Kandyan Convention of 1815).[27]

---

[20] GOC (1956), p. 78.   [21] Ibid.   [22] SLNA 33/4010.   [23] Ibid.
[24] Evers (1972).   [25] SLNA 33/4010.   [26] Ibid.   [27] Ibid.

These huge incomes were misappropriated by the incumbents and lay trustees of the temples. The incomes were, in the words of one *Rate-mahatmaya*, 'exacted not for the benefit of the *Vihare* ... [but for the incumbents' and trustees'] ... personal and unlawful purposes ... [and the enriching of relations]'.[28] The AGA of Ratnapura noted that he had never heard of a *Basnayake-Nilame* rendering any account of his recoveries.[29] He said that, on his election, each *Basnayake-Nilame* could be considered to have added to his yearly private income the average annual value of the *devale*.[30] He went on to describe their administration as a 'fraudulent misappropriation of trust money'.[31]

To compound the problem, the priests led a dissolute life. Many had 'given up their *Pansalas* (temples) ... openly living like laymen in houses with women and children'.[32]

Misappropriation, especially for such dissolute purposes, aroused great public ill-will. This was particularly so amongst temple tenants. There were several appeals by such tenants, ordinary villagers and various local officials, for Government intervention to reduce the burden of temple dues and ensure their use for public purposes.[33] There were even appeals for the secularization of all ecclesiastical land.[34] Such requests came from a wide cross-section of Sinhala-Buddhist society, and they came as early as the nineteenth century.

In the Low Country, the temples were not as rich as in the Kandyan areas. The largest temple in the western part of Yap *Korale*, within which Red Town fell, owned only just over fifty-seven acres.[35] The second largest, the Red Town *Vihare* owned thirty-five acres[36] and the third largest, thirty and a half acres.[37] Some temples owned as little as forty perches.[38] Moreover, the land owned and leased to tenants did not have service obligations (or *rajakariya* duties) attached to them, in the way the Kandyan temple lands did.

Nevertheless, the priests were as corrupt, and generated as much contempt, if not ill-will, as in the Kandyan areas. Misappropriation of temple revenues was widespread. One *Mudaliyar* reported that in the eastern part of Yap *Korale*:

the income [of the temples] as well as the offerings [made] are appropriated by the priests in the very worst manner. Buddhist priests in general at present put on their yellow robes, not for the sake of their religion and the doctrines of the Buddha, but to fill up their bellies with the fat of the soil, and to enrich their

---

[28] Ibid., letter to the AGA Ratnapura, 30 July 1885.
[29] Ibid., report to the GA (WP), 5 June 1885.   [30] Ibid.   [31] Ibid.
[32] SLNA 33/4010, Ellawella *Ratemahatmaya*'s letter to the AGA Ratnapura, 30 July 1885.
[33] SLNA 33/4010.   [34] Ibid.
[35] Ibid., List of Temple Lands.   [36] Ibid.   [37] Ibid.   [38] Ibid.

relations and their disguised families and give bad advice to the inhabitants, and to screen the offenders by the yellow robes.[39]

In a further letter, the *Mudaliyar* charged that several priests bought properties in their own names out of the offerings made to the temples and the incomes from the ecclesiastical lands.[40] This practice seems to have been widespread in the Low Country, the *Mudaliyar* of the *korale* within which Red Town fell, confirming it in two despatches to the GA of the province.[41] Of the forty-three plots of land owned by the Red Town *Vihare* in 1885, for example, no less than sixteen covering a total of twelve acres, or a third of the temple's entire holdings, were registered in the names of three senior priests.[42]

The British, recognizing the widespread prevalence of these mal-practices, had provided for the election of district committees of laymen to supervise the temple lands.[43] The district committees were empowered to check the accounts of temples within their area of jurisdiction, and remove any lay trustees or priests deemed guilty of misappropriation or malpractices.

However, the system did not work as smoothly as planned. For a start, there were rigorous property qualifications restricting the electorate. An individual had to be possessed either of property to the value of at least Rs 750 or an annual income of at least Rs 300, and also have been the occupier of a house within the subdistrict for at least a year prior to the date of the election.[44] Moreover, a (*paravenu* or *maravenu*) tenant of a temple was expressly debarred from voting.[45] The result was that the electorate was restricted to a very narrow and economically privileged section of the local community; a section which was relatively unaffected by, and so unconcerned with, the widespread abuses prevalent in the temples.

Consequently, there was relatively little interest shown in the elections to the district committees. At least three of the eight members of the district committee within which Red Town fell were returned unopposed at the election of 1908, the first following the amended ordinance of 1905.[46] One of these three (who was later to be President of the district committee) was elected by five individuals, one of whom acted as his proposer and another as his seconder.[47] The proposer and seconder

---

[39] SLNA 33/4010, letter to the GA (WP), 19 June 1885.
[40] SLNA 33/4010, letter to the GA (WP), 26 June 1885.
[41] SLNA 33/4010, despatches 27 June and 13 July, 1885.
[42] SLNA 33/4010, List of Temple Lands.
[43] Ordinance 3, 1889, as amended by Ordinance 8, 1905, following the recommendations of the Buddhist Temporalities Commission, 1876.
[44] Ibid.   [45] Ibid.   [46] SLNA 33/4002.   [47] Ibid.

were lay friends, the other three individuals turning up to vote being priests.[48] So the interest these elections aroused seems to have been minimal.

This may have been partially because those eligible to vote were those least affected by, and concerned about, the temple abuses. It may also have been the result of a feeling on the part of the electorate that their vote would do little to curtail the prevailing malpractices.

Such a feeling was justified by subsequent events. The Chief Incumbent of the Red Town *Vihare*, for instance, refused to hand over charge of the institution's properties to the local district committee, as he should have.[49] The GA suspected the Incumbent of trying to keep the temple income for himself.[50] He suggested that Police Courts have jurisdiction in such matters and not Village Tribunals (which were dominated by members of the rural elite, who had close links with the monks).[51] Moreover Police Courts would have afforded summary trial and punishment, bypassing the need for expensive and protracted litigation, which generally had to be borne by the trustee personally.[52] In this particular intance, the trustees of the Red Town *Vihare*, finding that it would be necessary to prosecute the Incumbent and bear the cost of the litigation themselves, had resigned.[53] No one could thereafter be persuaded to come forward to fill the post of the temple trustee.[54] Significantly, the recalcitrant priest had given trouble before. Two previous trustees had resigned in similar circumstances.[55]

In succeeding years no trustee could be found for the Red Town temple. Eleven years later, in 1921, the president of the local district committee was forced to write to the GA about this. He said, 'we failed to get a trustee for the Red Town temple though several attempts were made, as the first trustee found it difficult to enforce the law against an obstructing Priest . . .'[56] As a result, several gifts of land by laymen to this (and similar) temples could not be sanctioned by the Governor, the Ordinance of 1905 having specified that only temples with trustees be eligible to receive such gifts.[57]

Meanwhile, the district committees lapsed into apathy and inaction. By 1921, for instance, fully four of the seven places on the district committee (within which the Red Town temple fell) had been rendered

[48] Ibid.
[49] SLNA 33/4005, GA (WP), letter to the Colonial Secretary, 8 March 1911.
[50] SLNA 33/4005, GA (WP), note to the Colonial Secretary, 7 March 1911.
[51] Ibid. [52] Ibid.
[53] SLNA 33/4005, GA (WP), letter to the Colonial Secretary, 8 March 1911.
[54] Ibid.
[55] SLNA 33/4005, President of the Buddhist Temporalities Ordinance, letters to the GA (WP), 28 January and 5 and 9 February and 22 March 1910.
[56] SLNA 33/4004.   [57] SLNA 33/4005.

vacant and remained unfilled for want of candidates.[58] When the Government proposed to amend the Ordinance of 1905, so as to have GAs and AGAs as chairmen of their local district committees, the move was met with howls of protest. Several GAs wrote complaining that they were Christians, and also that this added responsibility would involve them in more work.[59] The proposal had to be dropped.[60] Thus the district committees continued inactive. They failed to prevent radically, or even moderate, the widespread corruption rampant in many of the Buddhist temples.

This corruption earned the temples of the district within which Red Town fell, as elsewhere, widespread ill-will. Although the scale of corruption (and especially the oppression over tenants) was not as great as in the Kandyan areas, many of the Red Town region temples had close connections with the latter. Traditionally, the High Priest of the Red Town *Vihare*, for instance, was chosen by the *Maha-Nayakaya* of a *nikaya*, based in Kandy. Such links did not add to Red Town's repute. Instead, like so many of the other larger and richer low-country temples, Red Town was seen as just an appendage of a large, corrupt, decadent institution, oppressing the ordinary villager. Successive High Priests of Red Town were known to have paramours, and in some cases illegitimate children.

Thus, it is not surprising to find several cases of disrespect shown to the temple's incumbents. At the turn of the century, we find cases of children molesting pilgrims and throwing stones into the temple compound, with the priests totally unable to restrain them. Indeed, one of the priests had to ask the GA to assign an additional *Police-Vidane* to the area, to protect temple property. The GA commenting on this noted: 'it is a striking comment on the influence of the Priests that they cannot induce the villagers at the temple door to restrain their children'.[61] There were cases in other temples of priests being assaulted for supposedly having mistresses, or indulging in such activities, and having to ask the GA for police protection.[62] Finally, when the High Priest of Red Town tried to interfere in the election of the Red Town Village Council Chairman in 1956, he was told to mind his own business by all concerned. In such instances the priests can be said to have had little 'moral influence', if any.

Meanwhile, the Red Town temple itself did not enjoy the status and position regionally *vis-à-vis* other temples that was attributed to it in later years. As noted, at the turn of the century, it was not the richest temple in

[58] SLNA 33/4004, President of the CDC; letter to the GA (WP), 16 February 1921.
[59] SLNA 33/4004.   [60] Ibid.
[61] SLNA 33/33; entry of 18 January 1910.   [62] SLNA 33/4003.

the *korale*, this position being enjoyed by another *vihare*. Moreover, there had been several schisms in the clergy, and continuous competition between the High Priests of the different temples of the district for offices. Red Town was not accepted by the other *vihares* as the premier temple of the area.[63] The High Priesthood of the district, within which Red Town fell, had traditionally been the prerogative of the Zoni Raja *Maha-Vihare*, and not of the Red Town temple. In 1853, Reverend Heyho, who held this office, had disassociated himself from the *Malwatte Chapter* of the *Siam Nikaya* (which claimed to exercise suzerainty over several low-country temples). Thereafter, the *Malwatte Vihare* had appointed two Chief Priests to administer the *korales* of the district. Significantly, neither of them had been from Red Town. On Heyho's death, in 1872, the division had surfaced once again, his successor at Zoni, Reverend Geyho, being challenged for the High Priesthood of the district by the *Malwatte Chapter*'s new nominee, Reverend Pejay. In the conflict, both candidates depended heavily on the Colonial Government's backing to secure any sort of recognition amongst the clergy and laity. One, Geyho, petitioning the GA, said, 'I cannot exercise control over (the priests) and direct the rites pertaining to religious matters without the aid of Government.'[64] This was hardly indicative of widespread moral influence of the priests, by virtue of their office *per se*. In the event, neither candidate secured any form of Government recognition. The incident reveals the divisions within the temples of the district, and their seeming inability to provide any sort of moral leadership to the people of the area. It also underlines the relative unimportance of Red Town, which did not even figure in this major conflict.

How then did Red Town acquire the aura of being a leading Buddhist temple of the district by the mid twentieth century? This, in our view, was closely linked to an important economic development in the area, notably a major construction boom and the rise of the Rou family towards the end of the nineteenth century.

Zolti Rou had begun life humbly as a timber merchant in Tayville, a hamlet about a mile from Red Town.[65] With the construction boom in the late nineteenth century demand for timber rose. Tayville, on the border of the Red Town River, was strategically placed to benefit most from this construction boom. Logs felled in the interior could be floated down the river, collected at Tayville, and then handled, the whole operation not incurring major road or rail transport costs. Zolti Rou's business flourished, and by the early part of the twentieth century, his family had emerged as one of the richest in the area.

63 SLNA 33/3996 and 33/3997 form the basis for the rest of this paragraph.
64 SLNA 33/3997, Petition to the GA (WP), 15 September 1890.
65 Some biographical data on Zolti Rou forms the basis for this paragraph and the next.

Zolti Rou died early, but his widow began to patronize heavily the nearest temple in her area. This temple happened to be the Red Town *Vihare*. She built and renovated several parts of it, including the *vihare stupa* itself, at the turn of the century and the family instituted a *perahera*.[66] This ritualistic procession is supposed to have involved about a thousand men and fifty elephants. The Rous, attired in elaborate clothes and playing a prominent part in the parade, carrying a sacred relic, may have believed that their status as aristocratic patrons would be boosted by their participation in it. A *Dayakaya-Sabha* or council of lay trustees for the temple, was also formed. All these developments may have strengthened the Rous' control over the temple, and perhaps given them a more aristocratic image than they had previously enjoyed. Nevertheless, they are unlikely to have added to the moral influence of the priests, if this existed at all, or the actual political influence they wielded.

This may be seen by the Red Town–Yoplace *Pirivena* episode. The Red Town *Pirivena*, or training centre for monks, was founded in the late nineteenth century. It is supposed to have started turning left in the 1940s with the return to Sri Lanka of several of its members, who had been to India and come under the influence of the semi-socialist nationalist movement there. These priests saw the Ceylon National Congress leadership of the time as conniving with the Imperial authorities, and not as nationalistic and patriotic as the Trotskyist LSSP. They involved themselves in journalism, pamphleteering and, during the 1952 and 1956 elections, active political campaigning.

In the 1940s, the *Dayakaya-Sabha* was relatively united against this sort of leftism and acted in concert to curtail the influence of the priests. Funds were restricted. When, in 1941, the *Pirivena* priests founded a school, Yoplace *Vidyalaya*, through which they began to propagate their ideas, the *Sabha* reacted quickly. The school was closed and shifted to new premises and a new set of teachers appointed. One of the chief *dayakayas* living in the vicinity acted in a supervisory capacity, overseeing the conduct of the new appointees and ensuring that political propaganda was not disseminated through the institution. Such an effective clamp-down was possible because the *Sabha* members were united on this occasion and issue, and acted in concert. In future years disunity in the *Sabha* was to preclude such action, and give the Red Town priests greater scope for political campaigning (as will be seen in the next chapter). However, even then, their moral influence was so limited that they were unlikely to have significantly swayed the electorate.

[66] See Seneviratne (1978) for an account of how families use *peraheras* and religious functions to boost their claims to aristocratic status.

So, to sum up, the Buddhist church generally was regarded as a corrupt, degenerate institution as early as the nineteenth century. Priests were, by and large, viewed as oppressive parasites. Thus, even in the Low Country, where the temples were not large landowners, they generated ill-will. They could not be said to have wielded any moral influence over the lay populace. Successive attempts on the part of the Colonial Government to reform the institution failed by the early twentieth century and the Buddhist church remained as decadent and corrupt as before. Red Town was no exception to this rule, her priests earning little respect amongst local inhabitants. Relatively unimportant at the time, the temple only rose to some prominence in the 1930s with the patronage of the Rous; patronage which may have been motivated at least partially by a desire to add an aristocratic aura to the family's new-found wealth. But even this recent prominence was more a sheen than an index of the priests' political influence. The priests were unlikely to have significantly swayed the electorate, due to the low esteem in which they were held by the public. Moreover, so long as the *Dayakaya-Sabha* remained united it could circumscribe the activities of the priests, as it did so effectively in the case of the Yoplace *Vidayalaya*.

Despite the limited moral influence of the priests, the Red Town temple proved politically important in one respect. Its *Dayakaya-Sabha* contained a number of members of the village (and urban) elite who could, to a limited extent, deliver blocs of votes.

Two of the five *Vidane Arachchis* of the electorate acted as Vice Presidents of the *Sabha* in 1946. One *Police-Vidane* was on the *Perahera* Committee, and another three sat on the General Committee of the *Sabha*. The *Vidane-Arachchi* of one *peruwa* acted as the Treasurer. Such men wielded influence over the village elites directly, through their lesser headmanships (and land), or indirectly, through their connections with these headmen. The way in which such influence was exercised in rural Red Town was similar to the way it was exercised in Bluville and Greenville, and as it has been described in Chapters 3 and 5, we shall not elaborate on it further here.

There were other men with patronage networks in the urban part of Red Town, who also sat on the *Dayakaya-Sabha*. The headmaster of a Government school in the area was the Secretary, and Zip, a fish *mudalali* from Colombo and Chairman of the Red Town UC, the auditor. (Zip's patronage network is described more fully in Chapter 8.) A bakery owner, and a publisher, sat on the *Perahera* Committee, and on the General Committee were a hotel owner, a furniture magnate, a jeweller, a small-scale landed proprietor, two proctors, an *ayurvedic* physician, and a social worker.

These urban patrons had a clientele of individuals whom they assisted in cash and kind during times of need. The lawyers and doctors, for instance, would offer their legal and medical services free, if necessary, and the richer of the businessmen would offer cash loans and gifts. However, with the exception perhaps of Zip, none of these urban patrons had quite the same degree of control over their clients that, say, the fish *mudalalis* in Bluville, or even some of the village headmen in rural Red Town, did. They also had far fewer clients, sometimes less than twenty or thirty. This was because the urban patrons faced more competition in disbursing patronage, their clients often having alternative sources of assistance. Moreover, the socio-economic structure of urban Red Town was such that class differences were more pronounced than in the rural areas, thereby undermining the patron–client tie. In explaining the basis for Don Dip's (and later Mrs Rou's and Herbi Mou's) political support, then, the urban patrons were less important than the rural.

The urban patrons came from a wide variety of castes, the *Vahumpura*, *Navandanna* and *Goigama*. Their patronage networks also, though highly localized and limited, cut across caste ties.

The patrons who sat on the *Dayakaya-Sabha*, and especially those from the rural part of Red Town, were to prove the core of Don Dip's support. They knew him as a relation of Mrs Zolti Rou's and a senior official of the *Sabha*. This acquaintance was strengthened by the lavish gifts Don Dip bestowed on them just prior to his first election, the acts of assistance he rendered, and the public works he instituted thereafter. The absence of any strong rival from a *Mudaliyar* family background with connections amongst the village (and urban) elite, and Don Dip's prospects of holding a senior Government post, also facilitated his election. At the State Council and 1947 elections Don Dip polled an impressive two-thirds or so of all valid votes cast. His support was chiefly drawn from the rural areas, in the east and north-east of the electorate. He was able to operate through the village headmen in a manner similar to that of the leading families in Bluville, Greenville, and so many other electorates. The largely *Goigama* village headmen delivered blocs of votes from groups which cut across caste ties. So, as there were large concentrations of the *Batgam* and *Vahumpura* communities in the rural areas, Don Dip got significant support from them too. This was especially so in 1947.

By 1952, however, the Rou nexus had split. Mrs Rou, the wife of the President of the *Sabha*, stood on the SLFP ticket. She was able to utilize some of the village elite members of the *Sabha*, as well as certain contacts with VC chairmen, to break into much of Don Dip's traditional base.

In particular, she garnered support in parts of the agricultural *peruwas*. The areas which remained quite firmly with Don Dip were those in which he had long-standing links, cemented by public works benefiting the local elite. In particular, his housing scheme and road and irrigation measures assured him of support; this, even in 1956, when the national swing went so markedly against his party. Finally, the Red Town election being held on the fourth and final day of the poll, when it was clear that the UNP was heading for a landslide victory, and certain to form another Administration, with Don Dip himself holding a senior position in it, he is likely to have got some marginal opportunistic support. In the event, he secured the seat comfortably (with about 60 per cent of the valid votes cast).

To sum up then, both Mrs Rou and Don Dip operated through the village headmen, drawing their support largely from the rural areas. Contacts were established and strengthened via the *Dayakaya-Sabha* of the Red Town temple, and not through the *Mudaliyar* system or control of the land, as in Bluville and Greenville. Thus, the ties binding these two candidates to the village elites were probably less substantial and enduring than in the case of the land-based ties of Bluville and Greenville. The village elites delivered blocs of client votes on a basis which cut across caste. Meanwhile, in the urbanized west, a different set of social relationships prevailed. This set of relationships provided the basis for the leftist vote, and it is to this that we shall now turn.

The urban-industrial sector

In 1946 the urban-industrial sector, largely confined to two *peruwas*, accounted for about a third of the electorate's entire population. Whereas the agricultural *peruwas* enjoyed a population density of about 1,400 to 1,500 individuals per square mile, the two more urban-industrial *peruwas* had a density of 5,300 to 5,400 per square mile. In other words, this section was about three to four times as congested as the agricultural part of the electorate. This congestion was especially marked in the extreme west of the electorate.

In this area there existed a large concentration of dock workers. They were hired largely on a contract basis in the Colombo port, and would commute the two and a half to three miles to their work place daily. There was also a group of railway workers in this area comprising mechanics, blacksmiths, carpenters, boilermakers, fitters and unskilled labourers. They worked either at the Main Railway Depot or the repair sheds.

Both these groups had long histories of militancy behind them. The railway workers had struck in 1912,[67] 1915,[68] and again in 1920,[69] when strikes were still illegal under the Labour Ordinance of 1865.[70] They had unionized as early as 1919, though this group disintegrated within two years, apparently for want of funds.[71] The port workers, of whom there may have been about four to five thousand at the turn of the century, had also struck in 1901, 1920 and 1923, again when such strikes were still illegal.[72] It was the railway workers who had initiated the General Strike of 1923, and the port workers who had joined it soon after.[73] And, finally, it was the port workers who had secured the first major strike victory in 1927.[74]

Often there seems to have been a tendency for these workers to have struck on their own initiative, only later appealing to enlightened upper-class supporters for backing. This had happened in 1912, when the railway workers had struck and only later approached a number of prominent and wealthy individuals for financial, legal and political assist-ance,[75] and again in 1923, when they had consulted the Ceylon Workers' Federation only after going on strike.[76] Similarly, the port workers had sought help from A. E. Goonesinghe only after the first of their members had struck in 1920,[77] as had the railway workers in 1923. Thus, these particular sets of workers seem to have been prepared impulsively to take direct action on their own initiative without leadership from above, but were forced later to appeal for help by financial, legal and other, con-straints. This points to a certain degree of resolution and independent militancy on their part.

Such militancy was encouraged by three factors.[78] First, living in a small, congested geographical area and sharing the same poor living conditions (exposed to periodic flooding), both groups of workers de-veloped a community of economic interests. Secondly, this was strength-ened by their poor common working conditions. Insecurity of employment (especially in the port with its contract-labour system), and more important, the inequity in wage rates (when contrasted with that of British workers doing the equivalent jobs in Ceylon) earned ill-will, and engendered a feeling of common solidarity. Thus, the poor living

---

[67] Jayawardene (1972), Introduction and p. 155.
[68] Ibid., Chapter 7.   [69] Ibid., pp. 221–3.
[70] Ibid., Introduction. Strikes remained a criminal offence until the Ordinance of 1865 was repealed in 1922.
[71] Ibid., p. 217.
[72] Ibid., pp. 222–3.   [73] Ibid., Chapter 9.   [74] Ibid., pp. 286–8.
[75] Ibid., Chapter 6.   [76] Ibid., pp. 221–2.   [77] Ibid., pp. 222–3.
[78] See for instance Jayawardene (1972) and Kearney (1971) regarding the basis for this paragraph and the next nine.

conditions both groups shared were matched by the poor working conditions they had to labour under. Thirdly, both groups performed absolutely essential transport functions in the commodity export economy of the time. Many were skilled labourers, and could not easily be replaced. Therefore employers were often forced to submit to at least some of their demands. With every success, the confidence of these groups seems to have further increased.

This helped foster community consciousness in the area. With the Depression of 1929–33, and the reverses Goonesinghe's union suffered over this period, the way was left open for the LSSP to cultivate support amongst these sections of labour. The party in the 1930s and early 1940s, insisted that all office holders participate in some form of trade-union activity. Classes and discussion groups were conducted in the evenings. These were facilitated by the concentration of the workers in a small area. In this way, the community consciousness of the workers was translated into a rudimentary form of class consciousness.

Meanwhile, many LSSP leaders also benefited from the nationalist aura which their stints in jail gave them. Politically, this was particularly useful in an urban area like Red Town, for many workers here believed they suffered from a form of racist discrimination; discrimination which rural inhabitants were not exposed to. For instance, local engine drivers did not receive the same pay or increments as British engine drivers in the colony doing the same work. Local drivers and such workers, therefore, harboured much resentment against the Administration. The CNC's participation in this Colonial Administration did not earn it the goodwill of these worker groups. The LSSP's more strident anti-British tone, its much publicized *Suriyamal* campaign in Sabaragamuwa, and the imprisonment several of its leaders had to undergo during the War contrasted with this. It earned the party much goodwill in the urban-industrial sector of Red Town, and other such localities. This, coupled with activism in an environment conducive to the spread of its ideology, enabled the LSSP to establish a strong base in western Red Town by 1947.

Meanwhile, there were several hundred workers employed in three important factories in the electorate. These were the Dinosaur Brand Match Company, Zeeb and Company, and the Top Works, the last two both producing fertilizer. Each factory employed about 300 to 400 workers, who were organized mainly by the LSSP, though in the Top Works there existed a Communist Party presence. As elsewhere in Sri Lanka, each factory had its own trade union, in some cases several. The trade union in the Dinosaur Brand Match Factory was the best organized and strongest. It had taken part in the General Strikes of 1946 and 1947, and won several benefits for its members thereafter.

The reasons for this relative success are revealing of some of the factors determining labour's organized strength in Ceylon at the time. First, we shall deal with management cohesion. Dinosaur Brand was locally owned and managed, unlike Zeeb and Top, which were British-controlled. This meant that its management could not count on State backing at the time to quite the same extent that the latter two institutions could. Moreover, Dinosaur Brand followed a far more 'open' labour policy than Zeeb and Top did. When, for instance, two leftist leaders had attempted to enter the Top Works, just before the 1947 General Election, they were charged with trespass by the management. The Dinosaur Brand factory's management, however, allowed such leaders easier access to its workers. So management's more enlightened policy in the Dinosaur Brand factory allowed labour a better chance to coalesce than in the Zeeb and Top Works.

The second set of factors explaining the relative strength of labour in the Dinosaur Brand factory *vis-à-vis* that of labour in the other two institutions lay in its greater facilities for worker organization. The workers at the Dinosaur Brand factory all lived in close proximity to their workplace. They could, and did, meet easily at a private house close by of an evening, after the day's routine. At Top and Zeeb, on the other hand, many employees lived some distance away and were only too anxious to return home straight after work. They could therefore not be organized for political classes and discussions as easily as those of the Dinosaur Brand factory could. Moreover, living in close proximity to one another, the Dinosaur Brand workers seem to have formed a very close-knit community, rather like the fishermen of some coastal villages in Bluville, or coal-miners in England. This was not always synonymous with a class consciousness however. In some labour disputes, for instance, Dinosaur Brand workers had demanded that preference in the allocation of jobs be given to their own kith and kin, over and above labourers from outside the area. Nevertheless, the close-knit nature of the group made it easier to organize them at a grass-roots level.

The final set of factors explaining the organizational strength of labour in the Dinosaur Brand factory can be found in the nature of its production process. Unlike Zeeb and Top, the Dinosaur Brand factory employed a large proportion of skilled workers: machine operators, welders, trained foremen and so on. Such men could not easily be replaced, and so management was forced, to a certain extent, to pursue a more liberal line towards the labour force. In Zeeb and Top, on the other hand, where the main activities consisted of mixing the fertilizer and loading and unloading it, the labour employed was unskilled, and could more easily be dispensed with. (Indeed, many workers were hired on a casual basis, and few stayed for long periods.) Management could, and did, therefore, pursue a harsher line when encountering wage (or other) demands.

The other important economic activity in this part of the electorate in 1946/47 centred around the bus transport network. This was dominated by a single, private bus magnate, a staunch UNP supporter. He operated a bus company, with up to 300 employees and several dozen buses. He was supposed to be one of the largest fleet owners in the country. However, his labour force was divided. Some of the employees were favoured with fringe benefits and used as thugs to coerce the rest. Moreover, the failure of the 1947 and 1949 transport strikes had demoralized the workers in this sector. The LSSP never penetrated their ranks. Indeed, this particular bus magnate was able to use his labour force on behalf of the UNP at both the 1947 and 1952 General Elections.

In 1947, the sole opponent Don Dip faced was from the LSSP. This candidate, a small-scale soap manufacturer, had few personal roots in the electorate. However, a long-time LSSP stalwart, he had earned a reputation as a 'freedom fighter'. He had been in jail with top leftist leaders during the early 1940s. More significantly, he had the solid backing of the urban-industrial sector. In 1947 he polled his votes largely from the western extremity of the electorate. His support was particularly marked amongst close-knit worker communities, such as those employed in the ports, railways, Dinosaur Brand Match Factory, and the manufacture of pots along the Red Town river, which had been exposed to LSSP influence for several years. It was less prevalent amongst the bus workers and others, who had not been so cohesive a group, or been organized by the party in quite the same way.

In 1952 the LSSP fielded the wife of a leading party figure. She again drew her votes largely from this area, though some of her party's support would have gone to Mrs Rou as the chief anti-UNP candidate most likely to defeat Don Dip. The LSSP failed both in 1947 and 1952 to campaign actively in the rural north-east, and did not therefore draw all the depressed caste votes there which it might have. In neither election was caste itself important as a basis for support. Where members of the *Vahumpura* and *Batgam* communities were bound by ties of dependence and obligation to the *Goigama* village elite in the east and north-east (and where they were constrained from exercising complete freedom), they voted fairly solidly for Don Dip in 1947, and to a lesser extent for Don Dip and Mrs Rou in 1952. However, in the urban industrial west, where they were closely bound by a community of economic interests (and not constrained by local elites), they tended to vote for the LSSP. This occurred in the case of the *Vahumpura* port workers, and the *Kumbal and Hunu* potters on the banks of the Red Town River. The phenomenon was especially marked where the labour force was closely knit and well organized, management weak and lenient, and the LSSP active for several years. So, both in 1947 and 1952, candidates drew votes from several castes. Thus, as in Greenville, caste cannot be said to have been important except in so far as it was congruent with class.

Conclusion

To summarize this chapter, then, Red Town in the period 1946–59 could be divided into two sectors: first, the agricultural east and north-east, where the patronage networks which prevailed were very similar to those operative in Greenville. However, the absence of a monopoly of *Muda-liyarships* by any one family or set of families (as in Greenville), and of candidates from this background, and the more egalitarian pattern of land ownership, enabled a relatively urbanized outsider, Don Dip, to penetrate the ranks of the village elite. This was done via contacts in the *Dayakaya-Sabha* of the Red Town temple. This was the only way in which the temple could have been termed as being politically important. The institution is unlikely to have had any moral influence in swaying the electorate. The second part of the electorate, confined to the western *peruwas*, was more urbanized and industrialized. Here there were concentrations of workers in different industrial occupations. Where these concentrations were closely knit and united, and management, weak or liberal, LSSP activity was greatest and most successful. The LSSP secured the votes of these groups at both the 1947 and the 1952 General Elections. On both occasions, the votes for these sectors were given on bases which cut across caste *per se*: a rudimentary form of class-consciousness in the industrial west, and a land based patronage network in the agricultural east and north-east.

8

Red Town: the growth of the State (1956–1982)

The 1956 Election: antecedent factors

Temples are popularly believed to have played a major role in the 1956 Election.[1] However, the actual effectiveness of priests in swaying the electorate is likely to have been small, or non-existent. This was because, first, for the reasons elaborated in Chapter 7, they wielded little, if any, 'moral influence' amongst the public. Secondly, there were more important socio-economic factors which explained the anti-UNP swing of 1956; in particular, their alienation of certain economically under-privileged groups. The anti-Western cultural tone the SLFP campaign of 1956 assumed merely provided the veneer for the articulation of their interests.

Nationally, the UNP regime of 1947–56 had done little to develop local industry. The implications of this were not felt so long as the Korean War boom lasted. Commodity exports fetched high prices, and the balance of payments and rupee remained strong. A high level of consumption could be maintained, with expensive welfare programmes, in particular, free education, health and consumer subsidies. All this changed with the collapse of the boom. World trade contracted, the payments situation worsened, and the rupee depreciated. The Government was forced to curtail its consumption and many of its welfare programmes. Most significant was its decision to reduce the rice subsidy, forcing the price up from 25 cents a measure to 70 cents a measure.[2] The move generated widespread ill-will, particularly in the urban areas. The *Hartal* of 12 August 1953, organized by the leftist parties to protest against the measure, led to a general closure of business establishments and Government offices, and the sabotage of public works.[3] A state of emergency had to be declared, and ten people are supposed to have died in clashes between the police and rioters.[4] In the event, the Prime Minister was forced to resign (September 1953), and a new Administration formed, under Sir John Kotelawala, in October that year.[5]

---

[1] See for instance Smith (1966), Chapter 22, and especially pp. 490–5.
[2] Kearney (1971), pp. 148–9.   [3] Ibid.   [4] Ibid.   [5] Ibid.

The *Hartal* revealed the intensity of the dissatisfaction with the growing economic malaise and the UNP's handling of the situation, especially in the urban sector. The resignation of the Prime Minister, Dudley Senanayake, may also have suggested to some of the more militant leftists the relative vulnerability of the Administration.

Sir John's Government, although maintaining an impressive parliamentary majority, seems to have drifted further from the masses. The new Prime Minister was regarded as even more westernized and inaccessible than his predecessor. In Red Town, his close associate, Don Dip, was seen in the same light. A popular story emerged that when headmen and such intermediaries went to see Don Dip about a problem he would feign interest in it, take up the telephone and pretend to attend to the matter, but that in reality he was only telephoning his wife upstairs, his telephone call merely being a ruse to create an impression of concern. Such stories are possibly distortions of the truth. But the fact that rumours of the above nature should have emerged about him, and then too amongst traditional intermediaries such as headmen, is indicative of dissatisfaction with the Government's work in the area. In the agricultural areas this dissatisfaction was largely amongst the traditional intermediaries of the village elites, those who delivered vote-blocs from their areas. In the urban region, however, dissatisfaction was amongst the public at large. It was prompted by the behaviour of some of Don Dip's own intermediaries in the areas.

This was very much the case in the Red Town Council. The chairmanship of this body had been monopolized by a notorious fish *mudalali*, Zip, since 1940. Zip and his supporters on the Council had treated the Red Town inhabitants and lesser bureaucrats almost as their personal servants. They would expect the AGA or lesser officials to see them on matters without prior appointments and, if their wishes were not met, abuse them. Zip himself would often stride into the AGA's office unannounced, sit on his desk, and expect to be attended to. Many were the instances when he would assault or bully those who displeased him. And it was well known that the best and most centrally located sales outlets in the area were reserved for himself and his closest associates. However, with the patronage of a powerful national politician, Don Dip, who may have been unaware of his general conduct, Zip seems to have survived. Moreover, for several years, the opposition to him and the UNP remained divided.

In the early 1950s, however, Teri Voo, a young activist, began to emerge in the area. He was of relatively humble origins, unlike most of the other candidates we have seen in earlier chapters. His mother had undergone great difficulty in securing his education. Voo had only begun to learn his alphabet at fourteen. When, later, his mother had tried to enter him into the relatively prestigious, assisted (Church) school, St Joseph's College, at a reduced rate, she had been refused. Eventually, after much difficulty, she managed to have him enrolled at Lorenz College (at half the usual rate), where he completed his education. Proceeding to work as a minor public servant, Voo had been subject to many of the pressures experienced by the ordinary inhabitants of the area; pressures the elitist candidates of Bluville and Greenville would not have undergone.

Indeed, on one occasion in 1942, he had been insulted and abused by Zip for being on the road during an air-raid. It was this incident, he says, which decided him to enter politics, and rid the area of the fish *mudalali*. In 1950 he helped organize a leftist anti-UNP youth front representing all the diverse opposition elements in the area. His contestant was a small-scale landowner of the region and part of the establishment. Voo was, however, defeated on this, his first, attempt to enter the Local Council. The other candidates of his front suffered the same fate.

Not to be deterred, however, Voo returned to the fray three years later. By then the removal of the rice subsidy and general rise in prices was engendering widespread public dissatisfaction with the governing party. Voo saw this, and regrouped his leftist forces. At the Council elections that year (1953), Voo was returned by 200 votes over his old rival. His alliance secured about two-thirds of the seats on the Council. The subsequent train of events leading to the election of the Council Chairman is worth recounting in some detail, as it reveals the lengths to which the establishment elite of the time would go to maintain itself in power.

Soon after his victory, Voo heard that some members of his alliance had been approached by Zip's associates with offers of gifts, in return for a switch over to their side. To forestall this, Voo invited his alliance members for dinner at his residence that Sunday, and asked them to bring the suits they would need for the Council's inaugural meeting on Tuesday. At dinner, he explained that they all faced physical danger at the hands of Zip's thugs. He persuaded them that the only escape from this lay in going into hiding at some unknown spot until the morning of the meeting, and to follow a plan he had prepared.

The party travelled south in the dead of night (following a circuitous route), where they lodged in two houses belonging to a friend of Voo. There they stayed in disguise until Monday evening, when they went to a film show in the centre of Colombo. Voo had tried to dissuade them from this, but to no avail. Unfortunately, they had been recognized at the cinema ticket office by an individual from Red Town. However, this person, being a close friend of Voo's, promised not to divulge the secret. He informed them that a frantic search was proceeding in Red Town for them. Voo's brother had been questioned, but had feigned ignorance of the whole affair. (Indeed, Voo, anticipating something of this nature, had borrowed his brother's car, leaving his own in Red Town, to give the impression that he was in the area.) Thus Monday evening passed off smoothly.

On Tuesday morning the party travelled back to Red Town along a circuitous little-known road. At the *Gansabhawa* building, where the election of the new Chairman and first Council meeting were to be held, there was a crowd of about five to six thousand. Voo, fearing trouble, advised his supporters to follow him in single file, with their eyes on the ground, and to enter the building through a side door. (This was to be a fortunate stroke, as will be seen later.)

Once in the Chamber they came face to face with Zip, his supporters, and the Assistant Commissioner of Local Government (who was to conduct the election for the Council chairmanship). Voo, still fearing that some of his alliance members may have been bribed, suggested that the vote be taken in public. Zip objected, saying that it should be taken by secret ballot. Eventually the Assistant Commissioner decided that the Council members should vote in public on how to conduct the election for the chairmanship. Voo and his eleven supporters voted for a public vote, and Zip and his four supporters for a secret ballot. At this Zip walked out in a huff, cursing and making a number of threats. The election for the chairmanship then took place, Voo being successful with twelve votes to Zip's two. (The latter had, as a result of his walk-out, lost his own vote and that of two supporters.) Thus ended the reign of Zip on the Red Town Council.

The incident reveals the lengths to which the establishment elite was prepared to go, as was suspected at the time, in order to maintain its position in the area. Indeed, it later became known that Zip had had some charms buried at the main entrance to the *Gansabhawa* building, in the hope that these would induce Voo's party members to switch to him as they entered (though as mentioned earlier, the party came in through a side door). The incident also illustrates some of the difficulties a relatively poor, and at that time insignificant, aspirant to political office, such as Voo, had to contend with. This was true even in an urban environment where the power of local influentials could be expected to have been less than in the rural areas. In particular, the need to hide the real purpose of the invitation to the Sunday dinner, till the dinner itself, the failure to prevent the alliance members from going to the film show in Colombo, and then the fear of them still being bribed and so the demand for a public ballot for Chairman, all point to Voo's lack of control over his supporters; a lack of control a rich person would not have experienced.

The loss of the Red Town Council to the Opposition in 1953 was part of a more general phenomenon. Throughout the electorate, Don Dip seems to have been losing support. In the agricultural areas, as mentioned, many traditional intermediaries grew dissatisfied with the extent of local development work. Not being as closely bound to Don Dip as their brethren in Bluville and Greenville were to their large-scale patrons (for the reasons elaborated in Chapter 7, pp. 139–41), it took little for them to switch over to Bandaranaike's SLFP. Bandaranaike himself had cultivated links amongst these sections during his period as Minister of Local Government (1936–47 and 1947–51). Moreover, with the help of the Rous and their contacts in the *Dayakaya-Sabha*, any Opposition candidate in Red Town had a base from which to begin.

Thus it was that, in 1956, Keni Voz emerged as an Independent candidate with SLFP support to challenge Don Dip. Keni Voz had a long-standing personal grudge against Don Dip. This enmity had been further accentuated by a certain degree of political jealousy.

In this context, prior to the 1956 General Election, Voo contacted Voz and suggested that he contest Don Dip in Red Town. Voz seems to have been reluctant, but Voo then asked him to address a few meetings in the area to gauge his strength. Voz eventually agreed to this. Voo then organized several meetings. All were well attended. At the final meeting, certain men, placed in the audience by Voo, publicly demanded that Voz contest the Red Town seat. This paved the way for the latter's entry as a candidate for Red Town at the 1956 General Election.

At this election Voz secured a staggering victory; nearly thrice Don Dip's total vote. He made major inroads into the latter's traditional base in the agricultural east and north-east, and also carried the urban-industrial west. The urban votes were easy to secure, as the socio-economic policies of the UNP had completely alienated this section. Moreover, there being no alternative leftist candidate, the SLFP/MEP having formed a no-contest agreement with these parties, Voz stood as the only anti-UNP figure in Red Town, and thus was the main beneficiary. He was helped by the fact that the Red Town poll was held on the last day of the election. The SLFP/MEP seen to be heading for a landslide victory, and Voz being known as a close associate of Bandaranaike and likely to hold a senior post in the incoming Administration, probably got a large number of floating votes. Nevertheless, as in Greenville and Bluville, it was not Don Dip's defeat that was surprising, but his relatively good performance with over a quarter of the total vote, when it was certain that he and his party would lose. These votes represented his traditional hard-core, and served as an index of the loyalty of this core to its candidate, despite the national swing.

Although the High Priest of the Red Town temple, had worked against Don Dip in 1956, this was probably of little consequence. He had worked against Don Dip as early as 1952, but to little effect. Indeed, in 1952, the Priest had not even been able to deliver the votes in his own temple area to his candidate, Mrs Rou, these going to another candidate. Moreover, the priests commanding very limited public esteem, exercised little, if any, moral influence over the electorate. Thus, the priests and their temple are unlikely to have been important in deciding the outcome of the 1956 election. It was the socio-economic and administrative factors, sketched above, which were more important than the religious. These took on an emotional and cultural flavour, with Bandaranaike's espousal of the alienated common Sinhala-Buddhist. A mistaken impression of language and religion being the major issues was thereby created, when in fact they were very much of secondary importance.

The extension of the State (1956–70)

In Red Town, as elsewhere, the election of 1956 ushered in a series of extensions of the State. Amongst the first of these was the nationalization of the transport service. This severely undermined the influence of men such as the premier bus magnate of the area. Still later came the takeover of the assisted schools. Red Town, with its large Christian population and several Catholic schools, became a major centre of controversy.

Most important, however, were the various industrial and commercial projects which began to emerge in the area, especially after 1960. Many of these were peculiar to Red Town (as opposed to Bluville and Greenville) as, being close to Colombo, it was strategically placed for such ventures. The period 1960–5 saw many local industries producing import substitutes and, encouraged by the SLFP's protectionist trade policies, developing in the area. Some important Government undertakings also emerged at this time. The UNP regime of 1965–70 did little to reverse the thrust of these measures, allowing the State sector to expand slowly, and the protected local industries to continue producing. Major industrial projects, the blueprints of which had been prepared during the earlier government's term of office, were allowed to emerge. Red Town therefore continued to industrialize and urbanize right through the period 1956–70, in a way Bluville and Greenville did not.

The dismantling of the old establishment, however, had begun in Red Town much earlier. As mentioned (and unlike in Bluville and

Greenville), certain vested interest groups had lost power in Red Town at the local authority level as early as 1953. Teri Voo's advent to prominence, as Chairman of the Red Town Council, was to usher in a number of reforms. Beef stall licences, which had previously been allocated to a few select favourites of Zip's, were now sold by tender to the highest bidder. (*Mudalalis* from outside Red Town thus started to secure lucrative sales in the area through successful bids, displacing local influentials.) This initially raised a furore amongst the latter group. One old *mudalali* favourite of Zip's even filed a writ of mandamus against Voo, but unsuccessfully. Meanwhile, a number of objections against the successful tenderers from outside Red Town were raised. No permanent licences could be issued by law so long as these objections remained pending. Therefore, Voo issued temporary licences to enable the successful tenderers to begin business. Immediately, five *mudalalis* of the old establishment filed action in the police court alleging that Voo had permitted certain individuals to begin business in the area without having issued proper licences. These objections were eventually dismissed. Nevertheless, the legal battles indicate the intensity of the resistance of the establishment elite to the new measures. This resistance has not always been confined to the court-room. One *mudalali* had approached Voo with his lawyer and attempted to browbeat him, but to no avail.

Meanwhile, the Council was strengthened by restructuring of its finances. On his election in 1953, Voo found the body to be deeply in debt, and his own powers circumscribed as a result. Rs 24,000 was due to the Electricity Board alone. With such arrears, local authority regulations dictated that the Council's budget and expenditure be controlled by the Assistant Commissioner of Local Government. Voo, as Chairman, found himself with no power to spend over Rs 25 per month without prior approval from the Assistant Commissioner. Voo also faced the threat of a cut-off in electricity supplies by the end of the month, if the bills remained unpaid. This was clearly an unsatisfactory state of affairs, and necessitated immediate remedial action. Voo therefore negotiated to settle the debt in instalments.

To meet this bill, and stabilize the Council's finances, he had to take some far-reaching revenue measures. Amongst these was the new tender system introduced for the allocation of beef stalls in the developing markets of the area. This helped raise Rs 28,000 at the first auction of five stalls in 1954; a considerable improvement on the Rs 50 per annum which had been raised previously. As time progressed and the area developed, bids and receipts from this source rose further. And, as the system began to be extended to other types of shopping stalls as well, the tender auctions became a major source of Council revenue. An entertainment tax was also introduced.

By such means the budget was balanced, Council finances freed of external control, and revenue raised for a number of ventures. Amongst these were the maintenance and extension of roads, bridges, culverts, community wells, *ayurvedic* dispensaries, street lamps, and conservancy and scavenging measures. New water services and scavenging services were also introduced to meet the needs of the local *perahera*. Thus, by 1958, Red Town was supposed to be one of the better run of local authorities.

However, many of these ventures merely represented a more efficient fulfilment of the usual duties of the local authority. There were no major new schemes launched to generate greater goodwill in the area. This was because the power of a local authority Chairman was limited at the best of times, so Voo's scope for using the office to become a major patron in the area was limited. It was not until he became the MP, in July 1960, that he was able to usher in major changes in the area. A study of his approach during the next ten years reveals a very careful manipulation of the State institutions at his command, with a consequent consolidation and extension of his support.

The first major project he was able to secure for the electorate was a tyre factory. When Bandaranaike as Prime Minister had negotiated the establishment of such a factory in the country, Voo had been Chairman of the Town Council. He had, on hearing this, proposed at a Council meeting that a small forty- to fifty-acre rubber estate in the area be taken over for the project, and the factory established on this site, in Red Town. Then, after corresponding with Bandaranaike, he was able to secure the latter's approval for his idea.

Following Bandaranaike's assassination in September 1959, however, and the subsequent changes of Government that month, and again in March and July 1960, this approval seems to have been forgotten. When Mrs Bandaranaike assumed the Premiership in July 1960, she faced a number of conflicting demands. One former Minister asked that the factory be located in his home town, eighty miles from Colombo, and not even a rubber-growing area. SLFP MPs from Ratnapura requested that it be located in their district, and those from Kalutara, in theirs.

Eventually, Voo (who had earlier promised his supporters the factory) was forced to see Mrs Bandaranaike, the new Prime Minister, and threaten to resign if it were not located in Red Town. He brought Mr Bandaranaike's letter approving this location, and was thus able to convince his widow that Red Town should be chosen. Official sanction was then given, and the factory was built by 1965, employing about 1,800 people from the electorate.

The incident reveals the tussle for State patronage, and the difficulties experienced by a relatively minor MP in securing it. Red Town was clearly the best location both from an ecological and a strategic point of view, being close to the major rubber-growing areas, and close to Colombo. Nevertheless, Voo had to show Bandaranaike's letter of approval, and threaten to resign, before he could secure the project for his electorate. Mrs Bandaranaike herself had to justify the decision to her MPs on the grounds that she was deferring to her late husband's wishes, which she said she held sacrosanct.

The next big State project to emerge in the area was an energy complex. This necessitated the takeover of approximately twenty-five acres or so of private land, belonging to about thirty to forty families. Protocol decreed that those affected be given cash compensation, assessed by the Government Valuer. However, this compensation was widely recognized as underestimating the true value and was inadequate to buy equivalent alternative land in the area.

The villagers concerned saw Voo about the matter. Voo, with the assistance of a senior Minister, was able to arrange the compulsory acquisition of a small block of rubber land in the area by the Government and its redistribution to the affected villagers in lieu of cash compensation. The villagers were also allowed to demolish their existing houses, and use the bricks, tiles and timber therefrom in the construction of new dwelling places on their new land. They were given free access to the jak and other trees in the area for such construction. They were also permitted to draw the proceeds from their vegetable plots and betel plantations (on their old land) to the very last possible moment, when construction on the new complex had to begin. Finally the road leading to their new land was widened, over a distance of three to four miles, at Government expense, and other infrastructural facilities, such as lights and water, were provided. Thus, the displaced inhabitants of the area were given every assistance to settle down comfortably in their new surroundings.

By such means Voo consolidated and extended his popular support in the area. His benign approach contrasted with that of the UNP regime of 1965–70, which acquired the land for an agricultural complex without giving the local villagers any sort of sympathetic hearing. The only exception seems to have been a delay of two days in demolition, granted to one individual to enable him to have his daughter married in his old home. Cash compensation was granted, but this was regarded as totally inadequate by the recipients. Bulldozers came and demolished their houses within days of the Government decision to acquire the land. The contractors in charge of the operation seem to have appropriated the building materials and timber themselves, leaving the villagers destitute. Several of these displaced inhabitants are supposed to be still in shanties.

Finally, there were certain administrative reforms Voo helped introduce, which resulted in better treatment at the local level for several areas in his electorate.[6] Nine wards in an eastern *peruwa*, although geographically in the Red Town electorate, were administratively placed under the jurisdiction of the Black Town Council. This latter body was expected to provide the amenities usually provided by a local authority. But the Black Town Council area fell within another electorate, Blackville. The MP for Blackville, although of the SLFP, naturally favoured those inhabitants who had a vote in his own electorate, and could help him secure re-election personally. He therefore seems to have meted out very stepmotherly treatment to those nine wards of the eastern *peruwa* in Red Town, the voters of which, although administratively under his area's jurisdiction, had no say in his election. Voo was able to arrange the amalgamation of these nine neglected wards with seven from the Red Town Council in the creation of a new Council wholly within the jurisdiction of his electorate. In this way he was able to secure better representation, and thus better treatment, for the villagers of these nine wards. Moreover, he also helped arrange the division of some of the larger and more cumbersome wards in the Red Town Council, with the same objectives in mind: better representation and better administration. Securing this, Voo of course earned further goodwill amongst the inhabitants of the area.

Nevertheless, in all these cases Voo was essentially responding to externally induced macro-economic measures. The tyre factory, energy complex, and even the administrative reforms of 1962, were initiated by the Government of the day. Voo's role was merely one of moulding these measures to suit his area. He was not initiating new measures himself, in quite the same way that the MP for Bluville (during the UNP regime) and that for Greenville (during the SLFP era) did. This was largely because he did not hold the same position nationally that these other two members did. He was neither a senior Cabinet Minister, like the Doctor, nor linked to the establishment family nexus, as certain others were. Thus, his scope for disbursing patronage, even as an MP and Deputy Minister, was severely circumscribed and constrained. Nevertheless, given these limitations, he could still act in such a way as to turn the State reforms initiated from above to his personal and political advantage. This was further facilitated by his generally kind and benign nature, which

[6] The administrative reforms described in this paragraph have been rechecked using GOC (1946), GOC (1959), Ordnance Survey Maps and GOC Lists of Villages (1946).

enabled him to assimilate opponents to a certain extent; a phenomenon we shall see more clearly in the next section.

The candidates and their campaigns (1960–70)

As outlined in the previous chapter, the delimitation of 1959 meant Red Town losing most of its agricultural eastern and north-eastern portions, and so becoming a very much more urban electorate than previously. Thus, by the March 1960 election, the urban-industrial vote in the west, the traditional core of leftist support, counted for a greater proportion of the total than in the past.

However, unfortunately for the left, it was severely divided at this time. No less than three leftist candidates vied for election at Red Town in March 1960. Teri Voo stood on the SLFP ticket. With a creditable record of social work and service as the Red Town Council Chairman, he polled from a wide spectrum of the west to secure just under a third of the total valid vote. A teacher at a local school stood on the MEP ticket. He secured fairly solid backing from many of his former students, and got a large part of the old LSSP vote from the port and railway workers in the extreme west of the electorate. Again, he polled just under a third of the total valid vote. Finally, the LSSP candidate managed about a tenth of the total valid vote, drawn from these latter areas, where the party had once been strong.

A product of Philip Gunawardene's VLSSP, the MEP had secured several seats at the 1956 General Election. More significantly, unlike the LSSP, it had already tasted the fruits of Government (in coalition with Bandaranaike between 1956 and 1959), its leader Philip Gunawardene holding the influential portfolio of Agriculture and Lands. It was therefore seen by many as a more viable alternative to the UNP than the LSSP, and thus the more appropriate leftist group to support. Moreover, in Red Town, its candidate being a better speaker than the LSSP's, he seems to have drawn larger crowds. This may have initiated a 'band wagon' effect in his favour, right from the start of the campaign. These factors help to explain the MEP candidate's better showing than the LSSP's.

Nevertheless, with the left vote divided between three candidates, Don Dip's re-election was facilitated. Polling just over a third of the total valid votes, he was returned once again as the MP for Red Town. He and his advisers, however, recognized this as an illusory victory. The left had, between its three candidates, polled nearly twice what he had been able to manage. In any future election, where they united behind a single candidate, Don Dip's chances of success seemed slim.

Moreover, the UNP, although returned as the largest single party, was, with 50 of the 151 seats in Parliament, without an overall majority. Its chances of remaining in office for any length of time seemed minimal. Another General Election loomed. Accordingly, Don Dip had to start seeking another, safer seat elsewhere. He was able to persuade a close associate of his to vacate a seat so that he could stand as the UNP candidate for this. Thus, in July 1960, Don Dip shifted away from Red Town.

When his decision to leave the area was announced several of his traditional supporters came to his residence weeping. They begged him not to leave them, but Don Dip was adamant. The traumatic scene bore some parallels to a similar occurrence in Bluville in 1956. Here, too, when a large scale patron from an aristocratic family (the Doctor) lost, several of his most loyal supporters came to his mother's residence, weeping. Some rolled on the ground, as a gesture of grief and abject humility. They vowed never to leave, and begged him not to give up politics in the area.

Both incidents indicate the depth and persistence of the emotional and personal ties binding such clients to their patrons, as well as the mainten-ance of private control, through private wealth over such individuals, at the time. By 1970 all this had changed. When the Doctor went, in May that year, in his official Minister's car to the *Kachcheri* to observe the counting of votes for the seat which he was then contesting, and lost the election, he came out to face a rude shock. His official car and chauffeur had gone. The chauffeur had told some bystanders that as the Doctor had lost the seat, and the UNP the General Election, he was leaving to serve his new masters in the SLFP. The old tie between patron and client had weakened.

In March 1960, however, it still remained. True, the adulation Don Dip received was dictated partly by his national stature. His prominence within the party and country had enabled him to do something for his clients. True, lesser intermediaries did not carry his weight. Indeed, Zip, the notorious fish *mudalali* and one time Chairman of Red Town Council, who stood as an Independent in March 1960, polled less than 1 per cent of the total valid votes. Nevertheless, it was not purely his national stature and access to Government which explained Don Dip's popularity in the area. Although Don Dip's family was not traditionally dominant in the region, he had built up a personal base in the east and north-east of Red Town; a base which was inherited by his successor as the UNP candidate, Erni Tou.

The July 1960 election saw a contest essentially between Voo and Erni Tou. Voo polled the bulk of the old left vote, securing over half the total valid votes. Tou inherited most of Don Dip's support, managing about two-fifths of the total valid vote. The third candidate in the fray, an Independent, was a beef staff *mudalali*. He had a personal grudge against Voo. An associate of Zip's, he had been severely hit by the vendor system, introduced by Voo in the mid 1950s. Indeed, he was the *mudalali* who had filed a writ of mandamus against Voo. Hoping to draw support away from the latter, he stood as an Independent. However, he managed less than a twentieth of the total valid vote (largely from the area in which he lived), and lost his deposit.

The next five years saw Voo gradually consolidating and extending his support base in the area, along the lines sketched in the preceding section. In the early 1960s, he was appointed a Deputy Minister. Unfortunately, for him, this office was a relatively junior one. His ability to initiate independent action was further circumscribed by his immediate superior, the Minister, who was extremely powerful and close to the Prime Minister. Thus, it was very much the Minister who set the tempo and Voo who had to follow. Moreover, Voo's personal relationship with the Minister and Prime Minister were not extremely close. All these factors meant that the appointment did not significantly increase his ability to secure State patronage for Red Town, a point recognized by Voo himself.

The March 1965 Election saw a nationwide swing against the sitting Government. The SLFP saw its seventy-five seats reduced to forty-one, with the UNP being returned to office once again. Red Town, however, was retained by Voo with a lesser majority. It seems that the bulk of Tou's increased vote may have been the result of urban workers, dissatisfied with the labour and prices record of the previous regime, switching against Voo. The SLFP's harsh handling of the strikes of 1961 and the General Strike of January 1962 led to a decline in its support amongst large sections of the working class, with defections from its own trade union ranks.[7] It had done little to curb inflation either. Most significantly, it had not expanded employment opportunities. All these factors hurt urban electorates, such as Red Town, most. Thus, the party lost some of its traditional support, whilst also failing to make any inroads into the youth vote. The bulk of this went to Tou. Nevertheless, Voo still managed to retain the seat.

The next five years saw Voo's influence severely circumscribed by his being an Opposition MP. His defeated rival, Tou, was appointed Chairman of an important corporation. It was believed that he would be able to give jobs to workers in Red Town, and generally help those already employed in the port residing there, through this office. Many began to

[7] Kearney (1971), pp. 65–6.

see him as a more influential patron than Voo, who had little access to Government or the higher reaches of Administration. Thus, when the villagers of a certain part of Red Town faced a takeover of their land for the construction of a corporation, it was Tou, and not Voo, they went to see. They asked that they be given the same benefits their neighbours had been accorded by Voo, when the energy complex project had been initiated, though their request could not be satisfied.

Voo has tended to act in a very broadminded and open manner, earning goodwill. In the early 1960s when some villagers, angry with Tou, sought revenge on him through a Government takeover of his land, Voo desisted from pursuing the matter. Again, when one of his bitterest opponents had urgently needed a car to take his pregnant wife to hospital, Voo himself drove them there. And yet again, as a Minister, Voo appointed another long-standing LSSP supporter to the post of Superintendent of a Government factory on his professional merits. And yet again he appointed several LSSP supporters to the Red Town Rent Conciliation Board on similar grounds.

In none of these cases was he able to persuade these opponents into his camp. The husband of the pregnant lady was a militant Christian who saw the SLFP as threatening his community, and the LSSP supporters were long-standing ideologists. Nevertheless, Voo's magnanimity earned him goodwill; goodwill which may partly explain why he and his properties in Red Town were left untouched in the 1965 and 1977 post-Election riots, when so many other outgoing Government members suffered physically and financially.

To conclude then, Voo's fairly benign approach enabled him to consolidate and extend his support in the area. His treatment of the villagers displaced by the energy complex earned him goodwill amongst this former UNP section. The various acts of charity and help extended to political opponents also won him goodwill. Eventually, one of Tou's sons was to join the SLFP.

In the disbursement of State patronage Voo seems to have generally acted in a very non-partisan way. This did not always result in opponents whom he had favoured switching over to his camp. Nevertheless, it blunted the intensity of political rivalry. In some cases, however, it certainly won him support in areas where he had not enjoyed much support. His *shramadana* in a depressed-caste village and his infrastructural schemes in the urban west helped him to break into these areas. In all this Voo was facilitated by the socio-economic nature of Red Town. As an urban electorate (especially after the 1959 delimitation), it was relatively easier for a candidate of his financial and social status to penetrate than a rural area.

Voo's main rival at the March 1960 Election was Don Dip, a major national figure. Don Dip's support had, however, not been 'inherited' (as that of the candidates in Bluville and Greenville), but cultivated by him during his tenure as MP and Minister. When he left, this support went to the next UNP candidate, Erni Tou, although the latter did not enjoy Don Dip's stature. Moreover, the support switched in spite of Don Dip not actively campaigning on his behalf. The party ticket, then, seems to have become the important factor in determining this behaviour.

Meanwhile, in the urban areas especially, the most important factor was the absence of bloc votes. In March 1960, a large part of the traditional LSSP vote went to the MEP candidate, as he was seen as the stronger of the two leftist figures. In July 1960, it switched to Voo of the SLFP, and remained with him at the next two elections as well.

National issues became more important, with a corresponding increase in the significance of the party ticket. Individual local notables, who contested as Independents, polled only a few hundred votes, largely centred around their residences. Others, such as one individual (contesting in March 1960) appealing on a communal basis to his own *Hunu* caste, lost to established leftist parties, which had become identified locally and nationally with these oppressed groups. The LSSP, for instance, had started schemes amongst the *Hunu* caste potters to improve their educational, health and living conditions, whilst also securing better markets for their products, and displacing exploitative middlemen. Their *Goigama* candidates in 1952 and March 1960 retained this *Hunu* support, against independent *Hunu* candidates.

Caste itself in Red Town, as elsewhere, was unimportant. Rather, it was economic factors, degree of class-consciousness, and identification of this with a party's (local) activities and programmes which determined voting behaviour. With the increasing urbanization of Red Town over the decade, these became even more important factors. It was to assume even greater importance in the next seven years of UF rule, which saw another major extension of the State. It is to this topic that we shall now turn.

The extension of the State (1970–7)

General

The May 1970 Election saw a landslide victory for the UF coalition. In Red Town, Voo retained his seat with an increased majority. His impressive showing can be attributed partly to his dedicated work in the area over the preceding years, but largely to the national swing in his party's favour.

As Red Town in 1970 was not an agricultural electorate, the scope for major State reforms in this sector radically to alter the local social structure was limited. Indeed, the Land Reform of 1972 hardly affected local properties, the largest estate being only 110 acres, and only a few others being of over fifty acres.

However, there were State takeovers in other sectors. The relatively rapid urbanization of the electorate seen in the 1960s had increased congestion. (By 1976, Red Town was seven times as densely populated as it had been in 1946.) A severe housing shortage emerged. Voo was forced to take over blocks of land to assuage this. Two such blocks, totalling about fifty acres, were appropriated for a self help scheme, whereby selected villagers were given plots to be developed by themselves.

Voo asserts that there was no element of partisanship in these matters. Although admitting that the individual who lost his land was a prominent supporter of the UNP, he says that this was not a factor in his being the victim of the takeover. Rather, he says that this individual, being a very rich man in the area, with several other sources of income and no children, was the least likely to feel its loss. Moreover, the land taken represented only a fraction of several such holdings he is supposed to have had in the electorate. In reallocating the land, too, Voo says that he followed the official guidelines, ignoring partisan loyalties and giving preference to landless, large families, resident in the area for at least five years, and with a monthly income of below Rs 300. The claim may be well founded because it seems that party branches were not asked to make recommendations regarding these allocations. We have also seen, in the preceding section, Voo's impartiality in the allocation of State offices to several non-SLFP individuals.

Meanwhile, he initiated about twenty-five to thirty handloom projects in the area, each employing about ten to fifteen girls. These were a success, so long as the stiff import controls of the SLFP remained in force. Voo was also able to persuade a well-known SLFP supporter and businessman to invest in the area. This businessman was representative of a wide section of newly rich businessmen, the products of the post-1956 closed economic policy of the SLFP. He had purchased a number of Tamil shops in Colombo at knockdown prices during the race riots of 1958, and then expanded into the field of production. He had first invested in Red Town during the early 1960s, producing various consumer goods, and expanded these interests in the 1970s to include textiles and retail outlets. By 1977 he was employing about 2,000 individuals in the electorate, and had earned the reputation of being a major Sri Lankan contributor to the SLFP's election fund.

In none of these instances, however, could the State be said to have expanded sufficiently to have afforded Voo the power significantly to consolidate or extend his support in the area. This was because, first, the scale of all these (State sector) operations in terms of investment, employment generation and markets was small, unlike that of the Land Reform projects in rural Bluville and Greenville. Secondly, they did not impinge on the day-to-day life of the majority of the electorate, as the Land Reform measures of the rural areas did. The only State sector which did was the Co-operative network, and it is this that we shall now focus upon.

The Co-operatives in Red Town (1970–7)

The Red Town electorate was serviced by three major Co-operatives. Two of these Co-operatives had about thirty branches each, and the other, about twenty. They were all very large institutions, one Co-operative alone having a turnover of about Rs 10 million per annum.

Voo seems to have exercised better supervision over these institutions than his colleagues in Bluville and Greenville. Consequently, the degree of mismanagement and corruption here seems to have been more limited than in the other two electorates. The Investigations Department of the Co-operatives, for instance, seems to have no record of Inquiries into malpractices in one of the three Co-operatives because no allegations were made. Indeed, Voo asserts that when he suspected an official of this body of misappropriating consumer goods, he refused to reappoint him for a second term. This official had also earned opprobrium by transporting Co-operative products in his own lorries on a private contract basis. (Such action had further fuelled rumours of misappropriation.) By refusing him reappointment, Voo was able to stifle such gossip.

Nevertheless, there were irregularities in the other two Co-operatives.[8] There were several cases of carelessness, one Co-operative having lost Rs 975 and another Rs 3,380.

Widespread inefficiency, incompetence and lethargy increased the scope for losses. When a senior official of one Co-operative was found to have misappropriated Rs 119,578.88, the inefficiency of another official in leading the prosecution had led to an award of only Rs 16,640.72 in the Society's favour. His failure to appeal against the decision further

---

[8] Commissioner of Co-operative Development (Investigations Department), Confidential Files of Inquiry into two of the relevant MPCS (1970–7) form the basis for this paragraph and the next eleven.

ensured that the Society had to lose the difference (of Rs 102,938.16), and earned him yet more chastisement in the Investigating Officer's Report. In another legal case, another Co-operative had foolishly appealed against a Court decision after a settlement had been reached, incurring unnecessary costs of Rs 2,047.75.

Meanwhile, one Co-operative was found to have overspent on the construction of two buildings to the extent of approximately Rs 30,000 and Rs 34,000. Such overspending, however, may have been dictated as much by the unforeseen widespread escalation in construction costs, as by general carelessness.

Meanwhile, at several outlets, insufficient precautions had been taken against burglary. This entailed losses through theft of Rs 658.57 in May 1972, Rs 29,114.45 in October 1974, and Rs 29,858 in November 1973. In this last case, the Insurance Corporation had refused to take liability because of shortcomings in the security arrangements. In all instances, the Investigating Officer noted that the officials concerned may have stolen the goods and feigned burglary thereafter, and not merely been careless.

Meanwhile, in one sales outlet, salesmen had been allowed to proceed with business without bothering to take prior stock verification. Pilfering by lesser officials seems to have resulted, for in a short time a loss of Rs 1,002.90 had been incurred.

There were also serious and blatant cases of favouritism and possible collusion in the misappropriation of official funds. In one Co-operative a favourite was re-employed after he had passed the retiring age of sixty, incurring unnecessary expenditure of Rs 5,463.15. In another Co-operative, too, several favoured workers had been paid unwarranted excess salaries, and an official had been allowed to leave owing the Society Rs 3,585.05.

There were several instances of the purchase of various items from favourites at inflated prices, and then resale at a subsequent loss. A senior official of one Co-operative had purchased excessive amounts of mustard and dried fish in 1972 and 1973 from favoured private traders. This had resulted in losses to the Society of Rs 2,952.60 and Rs 5,540.63 respectively. Similarly, in another Co-operative, an excessively large stock of condensed milk had been purchased and then resold at below the cost price to private traders, forcing the Society to bear a loss of Rs 7,670.40. Again, in one Co-operative, three officials had appropriated money from Society coffers for the purchase of seed-paddy, and then ordered less than warranted. Another thirty-one officials of the Society do not seem to have handed over a sum totalling Rs 32,643, which they are supposed to have raised through the sale of rice. In both cases, the Investigating

Officers did not rule out the possibility of the individuals involved having pocketed the proceeds themselves. Finally, the Society had paid Rs 100 as an advance to a certain trader for the supply of fibre goods to its bakery in February 1977. The goods had not been delivered, the money not received, and the Society forced to bear the loss.

In all these cases it is true that there may have been an element of carelessness, as well as of corruption. Nevertheless, there were more blatant instances of misappropriation and abuse of funds. A senior official of one Society had reduced the price of a bicycle for the purpose of selling it to another official of the Society, forcing the institution to bear a loss of Rs 192.85.

An official of one Society had rented a building of his to the Society, appropriated an advance of Rs 5,000 and requisitioned the building when Rs 450 was still outstanding, failing to return the balance. Again, he had rented another building to an associate of his, paid an advance of Rs 500 from official sources, but used the building for only six weeks (representing a rent of Rs 112.50), forcing the Society to bear a loss of Rs 387.50. Meanwhile, in another Co-operative a part of one depot had been rented to a favourite of a senior official's, who had not settled his dues. He had not been prosecuted or even apprehended, and the outstanding sum of Rs 2,290.20 was written off as a loss to the Society.

Society vehicles were freely used by officials for private travel. In one instance, no less than six such officials were found to owe the Society a total of Rs 10,839 in this respect.

There were also cases of Society funds being used for party-political purposes. In 1977, one particular Co-operative had erected a stage for an election meeting and spent Rs 300.74 from its coffers on the construction. Again, Rs 200 of Society funds had been donated to an SLFP branch in the electorate. Such contributions were totally unwarranted. Finally, Society vehicles had been used to transport SLFP supporters to election meetings, representing yet again an improper use of Government resources.

Thus, as in Bluville and Greenville, Society funds seem to have been squandered quite recklessly, and in many cases blatantly misappropriated. True, Teri Voo's supervision, especially over one particular Co-operative, seems to have been a moderating influence, leading perhaps to a greater incidence of malpractices on the grounds of carelessness, rather than of fraud. Nevertheless, malpractices there were.

However, many of these malpractices seem to have been in the lower reaches of the Societies. As such, they do not seem to have come to Voo's notice. He seems to have been unaware of them. Significantly, he was not charged, or even criticized in any of the Investigation Department's

Reports, as the MPs of certain areas were. His degree of conscious control over, and manipulation of, the Societies, being limited, it cannot therefore be said that he himself was manipulating these institutions inappropriately as some MPs did.

Nevertheless, as the incumbent Government's representative, Voo had to bear the brunt of the consumer ill-will caused by the mismanagement, and consequent shortages, in the network. Such shortages were particularly marked in Red Town. Being an urban electorate, with little paddy or vegetable agriculture, and no scope to feed itself, it was entirely dependent on outsiders, in a way rural Bluville and Greenville were not. The ban on the private transport of paddy, and the nationwide food scarcities which resulted, hit the urban areas hardest. The consumers of urban Red Town consequently suffered more than those of rural Bluville and Greenville, and the ill-will created was correspondingly higher.

This ill-will was further fed by rumours that Voo had blocked the development of a common market in the area to satisfy a few *mudalali* supporters of his. It was said that the creation of such a market, and the introduction of Marketing Department and CWE outlets, would have forced prices down, thus driving many of these *mudalalis* out of business, and that in deference to their wishes, Voo had opposed the move. A large part of this story may have been pure rumour. But, be that as it may, it gained wide currency in the electorate, undermining Voo's chances of re-election.

Moreover, by 1977, Voo was believed to favour only his own supporters in the allocation of jobs. Again, this may have been more an unsubstantiated rumour than fact. Nevertheless, it was widely believed, and undermined his popularity in the area.

Finally, Voo had been expected to do much more for the electorate (on being appointed to a key post) than he had done during his seven-year term. A post office, public conveniences, bus halts and improvements to schools and hospitals had been requested by some of his supporters, but little had materialized. When a major road was widened, a number of individuals had been displaced (with what they saw as insufficient cash and land compensation), and Voo had been unable to help them. In all fairness to him, he asserts that he took the matter up at Cabinet level, and arranged to have the widening limited. However, he was unable to stop it altogether.

This inability to meet the expectations of the electorate, on being appointed to a key post, may have been dictated by Voo's position within the national power structure. First, his position afforded relatively little potential to disburse State patronage. Secondly, unlinked by blood or marriage to the family nexus which controlled the SLFP and the country at this time, Voo does not seem to have enjoyed the close personal links with the Prime Minister (and her family), that some of her Cabinet Ministers did. His personal friendship with another senior Cabinet Minister, who was regarded as an upstart challenger to Mrs Bandaranaike, may have further weakened his links with the latter.

Indeed, according to Voo, it was a difference with the Prime Minister which prompted his withdrawal from politics. Doubtless, the anticipated swing against him and his party was another factor. But be that as it may, in February 1977 Voo announced that he would not be standing for re-election. Thus ended the career of one of the most colourful of Red Town's sons.

The 1977 Election and after

The new SLFP nominee for Red Town was Zami Voz, the widow of Keni Voz, who had represented the seat in the 1956–60 Parliament. Although having a few contacts in the temple, she relied almost wholly on the party ticket and national issues to draw her support, polling about four tenths of the total valid vote. At this election, especially, it became extremely difficult to isolate bloc votes from particular areas, even the urban west being very evenly divided in the support it gave the two chief candidates.

Zami's major rival, the UNP candidate, was a relative newcomer: Tali Gip, a wealthy businessman from the *Vahumpura* caste. Gip had a few relations in the area, and his community accounted for perhaps a third or more of the electorate. However, the support he drew was on a far wider basis. Several interviewees confirmed that the caste factor was unimportant, not operating in the manner Jiggins has supposed. Rather, it was again national issues and the party ticket which secured his election, with over half the valid votes.

The relative importance of these issues and the insignificance of the more traditional rural patron–client networks in Red Town, had been recognized by the party hierarchy, for, in choosing Gip, they were choosing an almost complete outsider. He had, as mentioned, a few distant relations in the area, but no significant land holdings, factories or other economic interests there. Moreover, he had never contested the seat earlier, having represented another seat in two earlier Parliaments. His victory in Red Town in July 1977 was almost entirely the product of the nation-wide swing in his party's favour.

Upon election, Gip was appointed a Minister. Like other Ministers, he tried to use his position to consolidate and extend his support in the area.

Various trade unionists, dissatisfied with the previous regime, who had helped him expand his party's own union, were rewarded. Many were given posts in corporations under his purview. When Opposition unionists at the Dinosaur Brand Match Factory struck during the 1979 disturbances, they were dismissed and their places filled by UNP union members. In such ways Gip attempted to strengthen the UNP trade-union base in the area.

At a more general level, about 6,000 new jobs were created for people in the electorate. A textile centre and a factory producing laboratory glassware, each employing fifty individuals, two pottery centres, each employing seventy-five individuals, and a weaving centre, employing twenty-five, were founded. In addition, a school for carpenters catering for about twenty-five a year, and another three for seamstresses, each providing for about twenty to twenty-five girls a year were formed.

Finally, two schemes to redevelop land in the area were drawn up. The first envisaged dredging about 2,000 acres to be reconstituted as paddy land holdings. The second was a UDA project, and involved dredging about 500 acres of marshy land, to be redeveloped as an industrial complex with provision for factories, warehousing and housing. The scheme was initiated in 1979, and the planners were hoping to sell leaseholds on a commercial basis to industrialists, to recover the costs. The villagers living in huts in the area were to be rehoused in better conditions on the site, on completion of the project.

Unfortunately, this, like so many other schemes, is seriously jeopardized by the constraints operating on the Sri Lankan economy, nationally and internationally. At present, the industrial project has been halted, for want of funds. Similarly, the paddy land redevelopment scheme exists merely on paper. The severe national budgetary constraints offer little hope of these very costly schemes materializing in the near future.

Meanwhile, the Government's free trade policy has exposed local producers to severe foreign competition. The textile centre, the weaving centre and the laboratory glassware project described earlier are all threatened. At present, they appear commercially unviable, and may even have to be closed down. This will of course adversely affect employment, and so, Gip's standing and popularity in the area.

Meanwhile, some projects over which he has greater control also undermine his popularity. The most noteworthy of these is the new Indplace approach road. Indplace, an industrial complex, is being developed in a neighbouring electorate, and the proposed road linking it to the capital runs through Red Town. This road will cross the properties of several UNP supporters and these properties are currently being appropriated by the Government. The compensation paid is regarded as inadequate, and the affected individuals seem to be switching their political loyalties as a result. The new railway line, also involving the takeover of UNP supporters' lands, is generating similar effects there.

In all these cases goodwill is being lost through what may seem to be an inappropriate manipulation of the State. But such manipulation is dictated, at least partly, by national considerations. The road and railway line are necessary for the industrialization of the area. It is hoped that the goodwill generated through the extra employment will outweigh the ill-will created amongst dispossessed land-holders.

Again, international constraints restrict the success of various development projects at the local level. By such factors, the MP's ability to generate goodwill and support is circumscribed.

The Elections of 1982

The Presidential Election of October 1982 was called suddenly. In Red Town Gip and the UNP secured over half the valid votes. This was only a small drop from the proportion secured in July 1977, and represented a median performance in the district.

The divisions within the Opposition were a major factor in the Government's victory. In Red Town these divisions were manifest in rival factions failing to co-operate. Zob Mudalali, who had organized party activities on behalf of one wing of the party, was deprived of this task by the party presidential candidate. Instead, this was entrusted to another individual, who had organized activities on behalf of the Sirima wing of the party. Consequently, Zob Mudalali worked against this latter individual until about two weeks before the election itself, when a superficial rapprochement between them was effected by the party leadership. Nevertheless, the issue undermined local confidence in the party's ability to win and robbed it of marginal support. It also meant that the party did not have Polling Agents to supervise its interests in several booths, and, even where it did, it could not always count on their reliability. This would have facilitated impersonation by the UNP, though this phenomenon was more marked at the Referendum Poll in December.

Meanwhile, Colvin R. de Silva, the LSSP presidential candidate and a noted constitutional lawyer, cast doubts on the SLFP candidate's legal ability to assume the Presidency.[9] De Silva suggested that being the representative of a party, the leader of which had been deprived of her civic rights, the SLFP candidate would face constitutional impediments

[9] Text of Speech broadcast over Rupavahini. Reprinted in *SLN*, 14 October 1982.

to assuming office even if he won the election. De Silva argued that a vote for the SLFP was therefore a wasted vote, and that all leftists should support him. In urban Red Town, with its relatively educated and politically aware electorate, this argument carried greater weight than in the rural areas. It lost the SLFP some marginal support in Red Town.

The SLFP campaign was also undermined from within, in various subtle ways. In one area, for instance, several families, the recipients of houses under the UNP's housing drive, discontented with galloping inflation, had been turning to the SLFP. The rival SLFP faction, hearing this, decided to act. They sent a senior party member to address a party meeting in that area. At this meeting the member warned the (UNP) recipients of houses that he knew they had been favoured, and that when his party was returned to power, their houses would be confiscated and reallocated to SLFP stalwarts. Attending the meeting, the innocent SLFP presidential candidate applauded. But, in such ways his campaign was, unknown to him, undermined by the rival wing of the party.

Thus the party lost Red Town, as it did the national election. In the Referendum which followed, malpractices were widespread. Although electoral legislation barred the advertising of the lamp symbol and use of party colours, this rule was openly flouted by Government supporters. Not only did they display flags and posters around their own homes and shops, but they pasted these around the homes of known SLFP sympathizers. In several cases the latter were warned against removing these banners.

At the Referendum Poll itself, there were numerous cases of thuggery and intimidation. One man, an LSSP agent in a neighbouring electorate, was so badly beaten that he died of a heart attack at the polling booth. Meanwhile, several SLFP supporters had been warned against turning up to vote. Impersonation was thereby facilitated. One garage worker claimed that he voted five times.

Nevertheless, in urban Red Town such impersonation and thuggery were less prevalent than in some of the neighbouring agricultural electorates. This was probably because the more urban, and so more atomized, nature of the electorate made for an absence of vote blocs. Thus it was less easy to identify, and concentrate resources upon, particular areas of party support.

These obstacles to impersonation and thuggery in Red Town may explain the Government's relatively poor showing in the electorate. It secured a significantly lower proportion than that secured in the entire electoral district, and the 55 per cent in the nation at large.

Conclusion: the importance of the urban context

To conclude then, the electoral redemarcation of 1959 made Red Town a far more urban electorate than before. Don Dip's largely rural-based network in the east and north-east was excluded, and he was forced to leave the area.

The new MP, Teri Voo, was from a relatively humble background. His rise had been facilitated by the relatively greater importance of State institutions in this urban context (when compared with rural electorates), even in the early 1960s. This, and the absence of traditional rural patron–client networks, meant that a poor individual with organizational talent and access to these State bodies could rise, in a way not possible in an agrarian context.

Voo was able to build up his support through the local State network and his post as Chairman of the Red Town Council area. On becoming MP, he was able to further consolidate and extend this. However, he was circumscribed in this by two factors. First, it was not until 1970 that he held a portfolio, and then too, it was one with relatively little scope for patronage disbursement. Secondly, his own non-elite background impeded his access to the Prime Minister and her inner circle, further limiting his ability to develop the electorate.

These factors, coupled with the poor economic performance of the UF regime, which hit urban areas such as Red Town particularly hard, meant a large swing to the Opposition UNP at the 1977 General Election. The new MP, Tali Gip, was an outsider. Since his election, he has been attempting to use his position as a Minister to develop the electorate and extend his support. However, he has been circumscribed in this by the non-availability of Government funds and the liberalized economic policy.

Thus, like Voo, Gip's ability to generate goodwill has been curtailed by factors outside his control. In Voo's case these were largely dictated by national politics, in Gip's, by international.

In this context national issues impinging on local structures have assumed greater prominence. In October 1982, for instance, the SLFP tended to get more support in the more rural paddy-growing parts of Red Town than elsewhere, for the same reasons that it did in Bluville (Chapter 4, p. 74).

However, major party candidates in the electorate have drawn support from a wide variety of castes and other social groups. As in Bluville and Greenville, the party ticket and national issues have become the key factors in explaining political success. And again, as in Bluville and Greenville, it has become increasingly difficult to speak of bloc votes.

However, in Red Town all these changes took place earlier, and to a greater extent, than in the other two electorates. This was because of the lesser presence and weaker effect of the traditional personalized patron–client relationships characteristic of rural areas here. Further, being an area that was not self-sufficient agriculturally, Red Town was particularly hit by the national food shortages and price rises in a way our two rural electorates were not, so that in the 1965, 1970, 1977 and 1982 elections these issues may have assumed a greater importance than elsewhere. Thus, in the last analysis, the greater significance of the party ticket in Red Town can be attributed to its relatively more urban nature.

9

Communal minorities, political dissidents and the JVP

General

In the preceding seven chapters we have looked at patronage networks, essentially confined to the Sinhala Buddhist population. However, certain racial and religious minorities have a distinct identity of their own and tend to vote en bloc, generally, for a particular party. In this chapter we shall first look at these minorities in the electorates we have studied. We shall then look at certain leftist groups operating outside the arena of formal electoral politics, and especially at the emergence and development of the 'Janatha Vimukthi Peramuna' (or 'People's Liberation Front'), better known as the JVP.

In Greenville in 1946 Buddhists constituted just over 90 per cent of the population, and the Sinhalese a similar proportion.[1] After the 1959 delimitation their proportions had risen,[2] and after the 1976 delimitation these proportions rose still further.[3] No one religious or racial minority accounted for more than 3 per cent of the electorate's population at any one time. The minorities, where they did exist, were dispersed, often in trading ventures, reasonably well assimilated with the majority Sinhala Buddhists, and electorally insignificant as a separate bloc.

In our other two electorates, however, the situation was different. In Bluville the Muslims formed a cohesive bloc, concentrated in the Zoville area. In 1946 they accounted for just under a twentieth of the electorate's population,[4] and for slightly higher proportions after the delimitations of 1959[5] and 1976.[6] In Red Town the Christians also constituted a distinct, self-conscious and somewhat insular group, concentrated in the urbanized western part of the electorate. In 1946 they accounted for about a seventh of the electorate's population,[7] and this proportion did not change significantly after the delimitations of 1959[8] and 1976.[9]

In Bluville no religious or racial minority, apart from the Muslims, ever accounted for more than 0.5 per cent of the electorate's population. In Red Town, however, Ceylonese and Indian Tamils accounted for

[1] GOC (1946). [2] GOC (1959). [3] GOSL (1976).
[4] GOC (1946). [5] GOC (1959). [6] GOSL (1976).
[7] GOC (1946). [8] GOC (1959). [9] GOSL (1976).

2 per cent of the total in 1946,[10] slightly more in 1959[11] and nearly 10 per cent in 1976.[12] A small proportion of these Tamils would have been Christians, but a larger proportion, Hindus. All Hindus are likely to have been Tamils, so that the rise in the proportion of this religious group from 1946[13] to 1959[14] and then to 1976,[15] mirrored the rise in the proportion of Tamils in the electorate. The proportion of Muslims in Red Town also rose from 1946[16] to 1959[17] and then to 1976.[18] Both communities, the Tamil-Hindus and the Muslims, were occupied largely in trading ventures in the urbanized west of the electorate. The increasing weight this area came to bear in the electorate, with successive delimitations and exclusion of the agricultural east, explains the gradually rising proportions of these communities in the electorate's population over time.

However, neither the Tamil Hindus nor the Muslims in Red Town were as concentrated, geographically, as the Muslim community in Bluville was. With their greater trading and other links with Colombo, they were more cosmopolitan and less insular than their counterparts in distant Bluville were. Thus, the phenomenon of bloc voting by these minorities for a particular party or candidate was probably less marked in Red Town than in Bluville. However, the Christians in Red Town formed a more cohesive, self-conscious group, and it is to them that we shall first turn.

The Christians in Red Town

The Christians in Red Town were largely Catholics. They were very staunch adherents of their faith, practising endogamy, attending Church regularly, partaking actively in Church sponsored functions and, before 1962, sending their children to exclusive, Catholic, assisted schools, where religious instruction was given pride of place. Geographical concentration and the fact that Church benefits were restricted to members of the congregation helped cultivate a community of economic interest. The Catholics thus formed a very self-conscious, closely knit group, insulated from other sections of the community.

They were influenced by their priests to a much greater extent than the average Buddhist layman was by his. This was because of their close daily involvement with the Church, which was not so characteristic of the Buddhists. Moreover, the Catholic priests seem to have enjoyed a reputation for better behaviour than their Buddhist counterparts, and so wielded correspondingly greater moral influence over their laity.

[10] GOC (1946).   [11] GOC (1959).   [12] GOSL (1976).
[13] GOC (1946).   [14] GOC (1959).   [15] GOSL (1976).
[16] GOC (1946).   [17] GOC (1959).   [18] GOSL (1976).

The Church, as a major landowner, had a vested interest in maintaining private property. Not surprisingly, in 1947 and 1952, it supported the UNP, both financially and ideologically. Local priests urged their congregations to support the party which would 'guard Catholic interests best', a clear reference to the UNP. The LSSP and CP, representing as they did a threat to the Church's wealth and privileges, never received this sort of backing. With the emergence of the chauvinistic Sinhala Buddhist SLFP, the Church was forced even closer into the arms of the UNP. In 1956, and subsequently, the entire Catholic coastal belt from Chilaw to Colombo could be taken to be solidly for the UNP. In Red Town, even when the Catholic Teri Voo stood on the SLFP ticket in March and July 1960, he failed to secure his community's support.

Indeed, Voo had a serious dispute with the Church authorities over the assisted schools takeover in 1962. The incident is worth recounting, as it illustrates the intensity of the religious passions prevailing at this time.

The Catholic Church had founded, endowed and continued to maintain a number of schools throughout the country. These were some of the largest and richest on the Island. Being well financed and having some of the best educational facilities in Ceylon, the institutions were regarded as citadels of privilege; this, especially as entry was restricted partly or wholly to Catholics. The schools were also seen as agents of proselytization. Ill-will was generated amongst sections of the Buddhist majority. Thus, the takeover of the schools became a major plank in Bandaranaike's election platform. By the early 1960s the idea of takeover was being mooted in Government circles, and in 1962 legislation was prepared. It was proposed that the Government take over responsibility for the entire financing of these schools, whilst simultaneously controlling the appointment of staff, curricula and administration. This would have meant the Church losing the influence it had traditionally exercised over the populace via these institutions.

Only two of the seventy-five Government MPs at this time were Catholics, one of whom was Teri Voo. The Church tried to approach them via three UNP Catholic MPs. The latter tried to persuade the two SLFP MPs to oppose the move, but to little avail. Thereafter, several hundred Catholics barricaded themselves within the largest of their schools, eating and sleeping within the premises. Four such schools were affected in Red Town. The object of the exercise was to prevent physically the takeover.

Catholic animosity towards Voo in Red Town was marked. When his father and sister visited a local church in January 1963, to attend the annual festival and confession, they were driven away by the local priest. This priest, who was a foreign national, was subsequently asked to leave the country. Thereafter, the local inhabitants of the area named the approach road to the Church after him. They dubbed Voo 'Judas', and several unflattering portraits and effigies of him were burnt in public.

Meanwhile, a leading Catholic figure in the country asked Voo to visit him. Voo did so as a matter of courtesy. He pointed out that he himself, although a Catholic, had not been able to enter St Joseph's, one of the most exclusive of Church schools, due to financial constraints. He argued that his support for the takeover was based on grounds of socio-economic egalitarianism, rather than religious spite. The Catholic leader, however, remained unconvinced. Indeed he is alleged to have insulted and abused Voo, and even threatened him with excommunication. The meeting ended in a state of mutual ill-will and distrust.

Meanwhile, a vast meeting of Catholics, called from many parts of the country, was held at the local church, which the Voos normally attended. A resolution was adopted, banning Voo and his entire family from Church functions. They were not to be invited to weddings, funerals or any Church occasions.

At the same time, a local thug was found to be observing Voo's house. The local members of the SLFP were able to help Voo guard his residence, until a Government bodyguard was provided. The police subsequently arrested the thug for trespass. In the Inquiry which followed, it transpired that he had been hired by the local church school authorities to harass Voo.

Despite such pressures, the takeover proposals were passed. In Red Town four schools, all of primary standard, were taken over. Three of these were expanded into *Maha Vidyalayas*, providing a secondary education as well. They received more and better qualified staff and improved laboratory and games facilities. The fourth remained a primary school, though it too received better facilities.

Entry to these schools was opened to a far wider section of the public than previously. Yet Catholic distrust of Voo and the SLFP remained as deep rooted as ever. Thus, although he gave several Catholic opponents jobs and favours, and on one notable occasion, recounted in a previous chapter, he even drove the pregnant wife of a long-standing foe to hospital, he was unable to win them to his cause, politically. He may have earned some personal goodwill, but these men continued to work against him at every election. To them, he, and his party, represented a threat to the religion and values which they held so dear.

The Muslims of Bluville

The Muslims of Bluville were descended from Arab traders who came and settled there in the thirteenth century and subsequently. They initially congregated in the centre of the town. Later they spread out towards the periphery. By Independence they were concentrated in the north-eastern part of the urban council area, Zoville, with smaller pockets towards the north of the electorate.

Being traders, they were closely knit, perhaps even more so than the Catholics in Red Town. A Muslim shopowner tended to favour his own relations in granting employment, so that Muslim-owned enterprises were staffed almost wholly by Muslims. Geographical concentration, strict endogamy and fairly regular Mosque attendance reinforced this community of economic interests and, thus, communal solidarity.

Having very clear cut trading interests, the Muslims have generally favoured the conservative UNP against leftist forces. In 1947 and 1952 they voted for the Doctor, en bloc. But this was not only due to their identity with the party's economic philosophy. It was also because the areas they inhabited, lying close to *Mudaliyar* Coo's residence, had been patronized by the family. During the floods of 1889 the *Mudaliyar* had provided food, clothing and provisional shelter to the affected victims in a village, many of whom were Muslims. He had subsequently constructed a bridge to help preclude such a disaster again. This again had benefited the Muslims resident there, as much as the Sinhalese. The community had therefore tasted the *Mudaliyar*'s largesse.

However, the Muslims cannot be said to have fallen into the Doctor's patronage network in the early period (1947–56) in quite the same way that the fish *mudalalis* and agricultural village elites in eastern Bluville did. This was because they were not 'tied' to the Doctor in the way these latter groups were. They were a relatively independent trading community, conscious of their own identity, operating outside the mainstream of political activity.

This can be more clearly seen by the way in which the Doctor secured their votes. He did not operate through the five or so leading traders in the area, trying to satisfy their own particular economic interests. Rather, he appealed to the community as a whole, on the grounds that he and his party were the most capable of protecting the minority's distinctive trading and religious interests. The message was repeated by some leading Muslims from Colombo. These men, who had endowed some large Muslim schools and institutions in the country, were regarded as national leaders of the community. Their support and talk of the threat which 'irreligious leftism' represented to their religion fuelled the Doctor's campaign. This, the trading interests of the community, and the history of the Coo benefactions, were the probable factors in the Muslims' support of the Doctor in 1947 and 1952.

In 1956, however, the community switched en bloc to Dee Foo and the SLFP. This was probably because the polls in Bluville being held on the second day of the General Election, when it was certain that the SLFP would form the next Government, a vote for the UNP Opposition seemed a wasted one. A Government MP, and especially one who was closely related to the incoming Prime Minister, seemed more capable of safeguarding the minority's interests and securing patronage for the area. This, and the relative 'independence' of the group (when compared to the Doctor's traditional clients), explains the shift in support.

However, the SLFP Government of 1956–9 was not particularly favourable to Muslim trading interests. Its policies of import substitution encouraged production, at the expense of consumption and distribution. Thus, the returns from Muslim and other trading ventures fell. The '*Swabasha*' scheme, providing for the greater use of Sinhalese in education and administration, threatened the non-business members of the Muslim community. These members, whose main language was Tamil, now found avenues of employment increasingly blocked. Finally, the communal tensions which the SLFP Government had stimulated, and the 1958 race riots in particular, spread unease amongst all minorities, including the Muslims.

Thus, in March 1960 and succeeding elections, the Muslim vote switched back to the Doctor and the UNP. The SLFP was to find it increasingly difficult to break into this bloc. Indeed, one of Dee's most prominent supporters observed that he could hardly find an election agent from amongst the Muslim community itself to man his candidate's polling booth. Where such agents were occasionally secured, their loyalties were always suspect. This reflected the widespread distrust Muslims throughout the country felt for the party.

The SLFP made one notable attempt to rectify this and broaden its support amongst the community. It attempted to build up a Colombo-based Muslim and a founder of the Islamic Socialist Front as a national Muslim leader. In 1970 he was appointed to an important position. He in turn appointed a Muslim from Bluville as his Private Secretary.

The latter, a one time Principal of the Zo *Maha Vidyalaya*, a Muslim school in Zoville, now sought to widen his base in the area. He arranged the construction of a large school with the best facilities in the electorate. This was to cater exclusively to the Muslim community. The Sinhalese believed that the existing Zo *Maha Vidyalaya* already catered adequately to the minority, and that it was their own needs which were neglected. A new school exclusively for Muslims, with no corresponding institution for themselves, aroused their ill-will. Many of these Sinhalese, who had supported Dee in the past, switched to the UNP in 1977, partly as a result. Meanwhile, the school, although benefiting the Muslims, did little to induce them to change loyalties.

The Private Secretary's reputation for considering financial priorities in granting favours to his fellow Muslims further militated against his building up a support base amongst the community. Moreover, there were the general factors of the SLFP's restrictive trade policy and parochial stand on language and religion, which undermined its potential to win Muslim support. In July 1977 the Muslim vote went yet again, en bloc, to the Doctor and the UNP.

Since then the community has benefited from several of the projects launched in the area. The new coir factory and fertilizer complex have provided employment for some of their youth. A new post office as well as improved road and water facilities represent some of the more general infrastructural improvements effected. Such improvements have not been aimed specifically at the Muslim community, and are merely part of the more general attempts to develop the electorate. Indeed, the Muslims, being concentrated in the urban sector of the electorate, have always been relatively privileged in terms of services, enjoying piped water, electricity and good roads for far longer than those in the rural hinterland. Thus schemes such as the rural electrification projects have not had the same impact that they have had in the rural interior. Indeed, this has generated some mutterings amongst the community, some members of which say that their lights are not as strong as those in the interior now. This shows the difficulties in satisfying all communities in an electorate.

Nevertheless, by not explicitly favouring the Muslims, the Doctor has not antagonized the Sinhalese Buddhist majority (as the Private Secretary of the SLFP official did). At the same time, where the Muslims have specific needs which do not clash with those of other groups, these have been sympathetically considered. For instance, a Muslim police officer was given a transfer in 1982, so that he could be close to a mosque and more easily attend prayer services. By such means Muslim support has been consolidated, but not at the expense of antagonizing (or losing the goodwill of) the Sinhala Buddhist majority. This has made for communal harmony. Not surprisingly, Bluville was unaffected by the Sinhala–Muslim troubles in early August 1982.

The UNP has managed to secure and retain the Muslim vote in Bluville largely through its pluralistic nature, liberal social policies, and the fact that the major Opposition party, the SLFP, is regarded as chauvinistically Sinhala Buddhist. The trading interests of the community are also better served by the more conservative UNP. The community has voted en bloc for the Doctor at every election, save that of 1956. Although there are some rich traders, they have not acted as intermediaries as in the Sinhalese areas. Indeed, when one such trader worked against Zee, the Doctor's replacement in 1970, he could not even carry his own kinsmen with him. Thus, the community has voted as a community (as the Catholics have in Red Town), and not as the clientele of one or more intermediating patrons. National factors of economic self interest seem to have been the key considerations in this behaviour.

We have so far looked at the patterns of allegiance of groups operating within the arena of formal electoral politics. We shall now look at the activities of certain leftist factions operating outside this framework, and especially the emergence and development of the JVP.

Some leftist groups and the emergence of the JVP

As argued earlier, the LSSP and other leftist parties have traditionally required two important conditions to draw electoral support. First, there had to be a certain group or set of groups with a self-conscious identity or rudimentary sense of 'class consciousness', which felt oppressed by the intermediary and large-scale patrons of the UNP (and later the SLFP). The depressed castes in Greenville and the *Hunu* potters in Red Town are classic examples of such groups. Secondly, they had to have enjoyed sufficient freedom to cast their votes as they wished. Such freedom seems to have been more marked where these groups were in a numerical majority, with their own headmen, and administratively independent. It also seems to have increased over time, especially with the electoral reforms of 1956–65.

In addition, the leftist party candidates have been able to draw some traditional personal support where they have come from established *Mudaliyar* or landowning backgrounds. However, although operating within a parliamentary framework, not all such candidates seem to have accepted its legitimacy. Several have spoken at various times of using extra-parliamentary means in securing office.

Meanwhile, at the local level, several groups have emerged from time to time, seeking to challenge the status quo. In Bluville the most notable of these was the 'Progressive Youth League'. In 1942 several of the larger Colombo schools had closed in view of the War, and the students dispersed to their homes in the outstations. Some teenagers from Bluville, too, had been sent back to their homes as a result. Some of these students formed a leftist social service organization dubbed the

'Progressive Youth League'. With an annual membership fee of one rupee per entrant, they were able to raise sufficient funds to establish and maintain a reading room and library and hold political discussions and meetings. Several leftist leaders opposed to the CNC were invited to speak at its functions.

In 1943 S. W. R. D. Bandaranaike, then Minister of Local Administration, was invited to speak. After the meeting, which was attended by over a thousand people, Bandaranaike called the organizers together. He explained that he was sympathetic to their views, and tried to persuade them to join his '*Sinhala Maha Sabha*'. At the same time he asked them what specific problems the people of Bluville faced, and whether he could be of any assistance in helping them to solve them. The organizers explained that the local fishermen found it extremely difficult to secure kerosene oil because of the wartime restrictions on its supply. They pointed out that the local agent (to whom the kerosene oil distribution monopoly had been given) was restricting supply to his favourites, and selling the surplus at black market prices to the general public. Bandaranaike, under whose Ministry kerosene distribution came, promised to look into the matter. Within a week of his return to Colombo he had effected the cancellation of the local agent's licence and the transference of this to the organizers of the Youth League.

The organizers had never asked for the licence. Many of them were only sixteen or seventeen and they were surprised and flattered by the trust placed in them. They decided to meet the challenge and bought barrels, printed cards and distributed the kerosene at the official price. In this way they earned local goodwill. However, with the end of the war in 1945, they had to return to their schools in Colombo. The kerosene distribution ceased and the movement died down.

The Youth League had, at one stage, attempted to secure financial support from the Doctor, who was just emerging in local politics as the Bluville Urban Council Chairman at this time. Its leaders had gone to see him at his residence to explain their policies. The Doctor seems to have been very accommodating. He explained that he was sympathetic to many of their ideals, and that there was a radical section in the CNC (comprising himself and others of the younger generation), which would strive for what they wished. He contributed generously towards their reading room and library, though later when he found them working against him, he naturally became less free with his resources. However, the fact that he was so encouraging initially is indicative as much of the fluidity of party and ideological dogma at this time, as of his own tact, diplomacy and generosity.

The League atrophied, eventually, due to the dispersal of its members and their inability to maintain control over a period of any important patronage disbursing agency. There were other minor attempts by members of the CP to live with fishermen in Bluville and Okerville and penetrate these communities, which failed for similar reasons.

In Red Town the attempts by the LSSP to nurture the support of the *Hunu* potters were not pursued for as long as they might have been. In Greenville no leftist group tried to penetrate any area over a period and build up support. The pattern, then, seems to have been one of sporadic and half-hearted attempts to capitalize on grievances, with no consistent work over a long period. This lack of perseverance, coupled with the overwhelming patronage, private and public, judiciously disbursed by the established patrons, ensured that the networks of the latter, by and large, remained intact.

Meanwhile, successive splits within the leftist movement meant that it did not provide a nationally credible alternative to either the UNP or the SLFP. As such, its members were not seen as likely candidates for State office and State patronage-disbursing agencies. A vote for them began to be seen increasingly as a wasted vote. This further compounded their electoral failures.

Nevertheless, there were certain groups which could have provided the bases for leftist support. These groups, largely from the depressed communities, had failed to benefit under both the UNP and the SLFP. This was because their interests were diametrically opposed to those of the *Goigama* village elites, through which candidates of the two major parties operated. As such, their interests invariably received a priority second to that of the elites. Indeed, any benefits, which threatened to advance their interests at the expense of the elites and break their dependence on the latter, were blocked. This failure to benefit was the result of the way in which the system of patronage disbursement and political intermediation operated. It meant that in many areas large sections of the depressed groups remained depressed and dissatisfied with the prevailing system. It was these dissatisfied depressed groups which were to provide a major base for the JVP, as we shall see in the next section.

The JVP: its development and social bases (1965–71)

The JVP was the product of the failure of the established leftist parties to satisfy certain oppressed rural groups. The LSSP, founded in 1935, had subsequently split into various factions. In the early 1940s, the Stalinists within the movement had been expelled, and went on to form the

Communist Party in 1943. In 1945, a leading LSSP figure, Dr Colvin R. de Silva, left to form the Bolshevik-Leninist Party, though he rejoined in 1950. Later, Philip Gunawardene left to form the VLSSP, and in 1956 this party allied with the SLFP to form the MEP coalition. In 1958 Gunawardene left the coalition. His party, which had acquired the label of the MEP, contested elections separately in March and July 1960, though by 1965 it had allied itself with the UNP. Meanwhile, 1960 saw the CP split into a 'Moscow wing' and a 'Peking wing'.

A 'United Left Front' (ULF) of all these diverse groups was formed in early 1964, but within six months differences emerged. The decision of the LSSP and CP (Moscow wing) to enter into a coalition with the SLFP generated opposition from within their ranks. Two leading members of the LSSP left the party and the ULF to form the LSSP (Revolutionary Wing). The CP (Peking wing) also left the ULF. As time progressed, various splinter groups emerged within the CP (Peking wing). One of these, led by Rohana Wijeweera, was later to form the nucleus of the JVP. It was subsequently joined by two other such factions, one led by Mahinda Wijesekere and the other by Dharmasekere.

The JVP leadership bore two important characteristics. First, it was authoritarian in its control of party members. Secondly, the two highest bodies, the Politbureau and the Central Committee, were not formed in a democratic manner. Individuals were appointed to these and other bodies on the bases of personal contacts with the leaders.[19] Indeed, appointments were essentially made by fiat by Wijeweera himself. It was this, in our view, which explains the social homogeneity of a large section of the Politbureau. Those appointed had been known to Wijeweera since his childhood. Eight of the fourteen members of the Politbureau were from Wijeweera's own Kalutara District, and six from his Ambalangoda Urban Council area. As many as five had been educated at his own school 'Dharmasoka *Vidyalaya*'. It was this shared background and long history of friendship with the leader which helped secure their appointments to the Politbureau. The fact that these members were from Wijeweera's *Karave* caste was merely indicative of the community's predominance in the area. It was certainly not indicative of any conscious favouritism shown to the community *per se* in appointment. Neither was it indicative of any *Karave* dissatisfaction with the *Goigama*, as Jiggins has suggested.[20]

A fairly detailed study of the 10,192 arrested insurgents (more representative of the movement at the grass-roots level) confirms this picture. According to this, the *Goigama* and *Karave* were under-represented by about 40–50 per cent in the sample, and the *Vahumpura* and *Batgam*

[19] Keerawala (1980).   [20] Jiggins (1979).

communities over-represented.[21] Moreover, the heaviest fighting occurred in the Kegalle and Ratnapura Districts and the interior portions of the Southern Province; all areas of *Vahumpura* and *Batgam* concentration.

It seems that it was these largely depressed-caste groups which formed the local backbone for the insurrection. These groups, the clients of the *Goigama* village elites, had, as argued in earlier chapters, generally failed to benefit under either the UNP or the SLFP. Both parties had tended to draw candidates from the families of large-scale patrons. These patrons, in turn, had tended to favour their immediate clients and intermediaries when in office, in return for their mobilizing political support. These intermediaries, who formed the village elites, mobilized support by virtue of their economic control over poorer clients. They strove to ensure that no Government reform prejudiced this control. Consequently, they manipulated policies to protect, and sometimes even enhance, this control. Thus, the welfare of the poorest groups was not significantly improved.

However, with the advent of free education, many of these groups were able to send their children to good schools, and sometimes even university. Here, these children, facing a future of unemployment and frustration, fell within the JVP nexus. Often the student would get to know of the party through a friend or relation. He would then attend four of the five classes which a senior member of the local branch conducted. At the fifth class, if regarded as reliable, he would be inducted into the movement and taught basic military skills.

The student would then be incorporated into a 'cell' of five members, which met regularly for military training and the discussion of political affairs. In each village a number of such cells generally existed. Each such cell generally sent one member to the Police or Area Committee, whose jurisdiction spanned that of a Police Area. Each Police Committee sent a member to a District Committee, of which there were twenty-two in the entire island. Above the District Committee came the Central Committee of about twenty members, and above this the Politbureau.

There was a certain dislocation in organization, as the entire Politbureau and Central Committee and several members of the District Committees were appointed from above, and those at the village cell and Police Committee levels had little influence over them. Indeed, the latter were merely expected to carry out the orders of the leadership. And this was how the insurrection developed.

Wijeweera had been expelled from the Peking wing of the Communist

21 Obeysekere (1974).

Party in April 1966. After discussions with several colleagues he decided to form a militant activist organization, and in April 1968 the first educational and military training session was conducted. By May 1970 the movement had attracted students from a wide cross-section of localities. Wijeweera requested that his members vote the United Front into office, seemingly in the belief that his organization would be more leniently tolerated than it had been in the past. However, it is unlikely that he or the other leaders believed that such an electoral victory would usher in the socialist state they dreamed of. Several of his colleagues allege that the decision to support the United Front electorally was a mere tactic, and that the JVP, even at this stage, contemplated an eventual violent seizure of power.

Throughout 1970 and 1971 preparations for some such attempt seem to have been underway. A number of robberies occurred, allegedly to finance the movement.[22] Attempts were made to infiltrate the armed forces.[23] The Government, suspecting some uprising, began to monitor the movement's meetings and activities more closely, apprehending leaders where evidence of robbery or some such crime existed. In March 1971 Wijeweera and some others were arrested and confined to jail. The remaining leaders, realizing that their activities were being circumscribed, decided that an attempt to seize power would have to be made soon. On 2 April 1971 the Politbureau met. It decided to strike on the night of 5 April, by seizing police stations throughout the Island, arming its members, and then marching on key towns in the country.[24]

However, a premature attack on the Wellawaya Police Station, at 5 a.m. on 5 April, aborted the surprise in this attempt. By 5 p.m. that day police throughout the Island had been alerted, and a nationwide curfew proclaimed. Thus, when the insurgents struck on the fifth evening, the larger police stations, forewarned, had been reinforced and remained impregnable. It was only the smaller, more isolated, and less well-equipped stations which fell into JVP hands.

In the district within which Bluville fell, all six police stations in the interior were attacked and captured. None of the coastal police stations, one of which was Bluville, were captured in this way. Two coastal police stations, reinforced, held out throughout the insurrection. Another repulsed the attack it faced. Bluville station suffered a slight attack and was abandoned after some days, only for strategic reasons. It saw little fighting in its area of jurisdiction and remained undamaged.[25]

The pattern, then, seems to have been one of greater insurgent success in the interior than along the coast. In our view there were two reasons for this. First, the depressed castes were concentrated in the interior, so that

[22] Alles (1976).   [23] Ibid.   [24] Ibid.   [25] Ibid.

the social structure was more inegalitarian there and more similar to that in Greenville. There was a greater element of coercion and oppression in the hold of the *Goigama* village elite patrons over these groups in the interior, than along the coast. Thus, ill-will and social friction was more marked in the interior villages.

Many depressed-caste clients took advantage of the uprising to settle old scores. In one village north of Bluville, they marched on the *Goigama* village elite supporters of the Government MP of the area, and attacked them first. The latter held key posts in the local Co-operatives. They were believed to have used these for self-aggrandizement, neglecting the needs of the poorest sections. The manager of the local Co-operative had purchased a relatively large holding of twenty-five to thirty perches for the construction of a new house. As his monthly salary was only Rs 300, many suspected him of having financed the purchase through the misappropriation of official funds. His new house was burned during the insurrection by aggrieved members of the *Vahumpura* caste.

In another town, two brothers, both members of the Communist Party, wielded a lot of influence through their contacts with the local MP. One brother was the President of the local Co-operative branch and Principal of the local school. He was believed to favour his own relations in the distribution of essential commodities, job recommendations and the like. He was also suspected of misappropriating Co-operative fertilizer for use on his own, and his brother's, land. The poorest sections drawn largely from the *Vahumpura*, *Berawa* and *Hena* communities, but also including the *Goigama*, felt themselves ignored. They took advantage of the uprising to attack both brothers, one of whom was shot dead.

In Bluville electorate itself, there was less activity. This was partly due to the more benevolent patron–client relations prevailing there. But even then, tensions were more marked amongst the ostracized communities in the western paddy-growing parts of the electorate (which had provided the base for Dee's support) than elsewhere. There, the *Oli* community had been despised and ostracized by the *Goigama* village elites. Their alleged habits of killing turtles and cows and scavenging for a living were regarded as socially degrading. The *Hena* caste to the north (which traditionally washed for the *Salagama*), the *Rada* (or *Dhobi*) and the few *Vahumpura* there were in this area, formed the rest of the core of the JVP support.

Significantly, the depressed castes which geographically fell within the patronage network of the Doctor's family, and had directly benefited from his largesse, did not help the JVP. The *Kumbal* potters and the *Nekathi* (or *Berawa*) were prominent in their non-involvement in the insurrection. This was because their geographical proximity to the

Doctor had enabled them to bypass the *Goigama* village elites and the *Mudaliyar* system, and secure benefits directly from his family. They had been able to secure personal, and later State, patronage, on a scale not known by their counterparts elsewhere. They therefore bore correspondingly greater goodwill towards the prevailing system. They did not share the grievances of their brethren elsewhere, so that the JVP message had relatively little effect upon them.

The second factor explaining the greater incidence of activity in the interior of the district than within the coastal belt within which Bluville fell was logistical. The interior was more remote, less well serviced by roads, railways and telecommunications, and had poorly equipped police stations. After the police stations serving the area fell, there was no force to maintain law and order. Thus the situation invited further agitation by oppressed groups. In the more urbanized coastal belt, however, army and police reinforcements were rushed to the scene after the first attack. Thus, Government authority was maintained in a way it was not in the interior.

In Greenville too, proximity to Colombo and good communications helped ensure the maintenance of order. Two police stations in the electorate, although attacked, were reinforced and remained securely manned throughout the insurgency. Good roads and proximity to the capital meant easier patrolling and a more thorough implementation of the curfew. Thus, although there were large sections of the depressed communities in certain areas with strongly developed senses of self-identity, they did not have the opportunity to revolt. In Red Town, which was even closer to Colombo, this was even more true.

Thus, two factors can be distinguished in explaining the relative intensity of insurgent activity in 1971. First, support for the JVP was more marked in areas where patronage systems were more oppressive. Secondly, activity was logistically facilitated in the remoter areas, which were less easily supervised by the police and armed services and fell under insurgent control after the first attack on 5 April 1971. Thus, those areas which were both remote and had long histories of oppressive patronage networks were those which saw the greatest activity; Kegalle and Ratnapura Districts and the interior of the Southern Province, in particular.

However, whether all those partaking in such activities were ideologically committed to the movement's goals *per se* is doubtful. In several regions individuals merely took advantage of the breakdown in law and order to secure revenge upon oppressive patrons. These patrons did not necessarily come from any particular party. Indeed, in parts of the Southern Province, they were from the Communist Party, which had controlled the area for several decades and formed a constituent of the sitting Government. In some areas the JVP was even assisted by supporters of the UNP. Thus, the insurrection, as it operated at the local level, can be seen as essentially anti-establishment in character, and not necessarily as anti-right or ideologically motivated.

Conclusion

In this chapter we have pursued two important exercises. First, we have studied the role of two major religious minorities in Bluville and Greenville. We have seen how their particular economic interests have reinforced a strong sense of communal solidarity, and how both factors have led them to prefer the more liberal and pluralistic UNP to the more chauvinistic SLFP. Secondly, we have studied certain leftist groups operating outside the arena of formal electoral politics. We have paid particular attention to the development of the JVP and the social bases for the insurrection of 1971. We have shown that these lay in the grievances of certain oppressed groups; grievances which had not been redressed by either the UNP or the SLFP. We have argued that this was due to the nature of the patron–client relationships underlying rural society, and the manner in which they impeded benefits from percolating down to all sections of the community. Thus, we have shown that aspects of Sri Lankan politics outside the framework of formal elections can be understood in these terms of patronage disbursement.

10

Conclusion

In this study we have examined the economic and social bases of political allegiance in low-country Sinhalese Sri Lanka. We have done this by focussing on three representative electorates in the Sinhalese Low Country, and on the families there which produced the candidates for election to Parliament from 1947 onwards. These families, from more than one caste, came from a given social stratum. They were almost always large landowners, with holdings spanning two or more districts. Their families intermarried with those of equivalent status, often from other districts, and sometimes from other provinces as well. They were often major philanthropists, and had also held *Mudaliyarships* in the British Provincial Administration.

The landholdings, wealth and administrative offices they monopolized enabled them to emerge as the major dispensers of local patronage. Such patronage took several forms: employment and fringe benefits offered to workers on estates; the construction of infrastructural facilities such as schools, hospitals and temples; private acts of charity and help extended especially to village elites and, most important, the protection offered to the latter and the opportunities given them to amass wealth and influence.

This patronage was dispensed primarily to local influentials and village notables. This was largely determined by structural factors. The schools, hospitals, roads and bridges constructed by the Doctor's family in Bluville benefited the richer villagers first. They were the ones best placed to afford the books, sandals and clothes needed to send their children to school. They were the ones who were most amenable to using Western medical facilities. And they were the ones who were involved in the fish and paddy transport trades, and so, well placed to take the greatest advantage of the better road facilities. For similar reasons the private patronage disbursed by the Mous and the Nous of Greenville benefited the village elites first. Again, the administrative protection afforded the lesser headmen in these two rural electorates, by the *Mudaliyar* families of the areas helped this particular social stratum. The lesser headmen were, as demonstrated, invariably drawn from the ranks of the village elite.

Thus, in this process of patronage disbursement, a bond developed between the leading patrons of the area and these village elites. The village elites, in turn, had a hold over the ordinary, poorer, inhabitants of their localities. This hold was partially economic, as in the case of the fish *mudalalis* of Bluville and the richer paddy landowners of Greenville. It was often buttressed by an administrative hold as well. Many members of the village elites held headmanships and were thereby able to coerce and favour the other inhabitants.

With the introduction of universal adult suffrage in 1931, and the emergence of parliamentary politics from 1947 onwards, these patronage networks were to provide the bases for electoral support. This was especially so in the rural areas. The leading patrons of each area, the Coos and the Foos in Bluville, the Mou/Nous and the Pou/Kous in Greenville, and, to a lesser extent, the Dip/Rous in rural Red Town, appealed to the village elites whom they had traditionally patronized, who delivered them blocs of votes.

The strength of the patron–client bond and the geographical spread of the patronage network were major determinants of the electoral success of candidates. In the fishing villages and estate sectors of Bluville the village intermediaries' hold over their clients tended to be stronger than in the paddy-growing interior. It also survived the demise of the village headmen's system better. The support these intermediaries gave the Doctor was therefore more reliable than that afforded by the headmen towards Dee Foo. Moreover, the Doctor's own hold over these intermediaries was stronger than Dee's over his, as he controlled land and capital resources in a way the latter did not. The patronage network underlying the Doctor's support was therefore more fundamental and enduring than that underlying Dee's. This was a major factor in his political dominance of the area after 1947.

In Greenville both sets of patronizing families counted on qualitatively very similar networks of support. The differences in the electoral strengths of the Mou/Nous as opposed to the Pou/Kous can then be explained largely in terms of the former having had a more extensive set of intermediaries and clients in the electorate until the Delimitation of 1959, and a lesser set thereafter. The Kous' dominance of this electorate after 1959 can be seen in terms of their dual monopoly of *Mudaliyarships* and land in the area. This dual monopoly by any one family, or set of families, was absent in Bluville, Red Town and most other parts of the country. Thus, few patronizing families dominated their areas quite as

easily as the Kous dominated Greenville, and the Pous dominated Greenville and neighbouring electorates.

In Red Town the absence of a monopoly of *Mudaliyarships* by any one
family or set of families, as in Greenville, and of candidates from this
background, and the more egalitarian pattern of land-ownership led to
looser patronage networks. This enabled a relatively urbanized outsider,
such as Don Dip, to penetrate the ranks of the village elites in a way he
would not have been able to in a more rural electorate with more
institutionalized patronage networks. It also helped a fairly poor man,
such as Teri Voo, to rise in the Red Town Council, through organizational talents and access to State patronage. In the urban sector, moreover, the industrial structure made for a state of affairs which helped the
LSSP to successfully make an appeal to interests of class.

In the rural areas, then, the nature of the patron–client bond, and the
hold of a major family upon intermediaries and of these intermediaries
upon their clients, was fundamental in explaining the electoral performances of candidates. This patron–client bond was, itself, largely determined by the agro-ecological and socio-economic backgrounds of the
areas.

The agro-ecological background influenced first, the extent of patronage disbursed, and so potential political support cultivated. The tea and
rubber in Bluville, for instance, afforded permanent employment which
could be controlled, and this on a larger scale acre for acre than the
coconut in Greenville did. It was quantitatively more important in
generating electoral support than was the latter crop. Secondly, the
agro-ecological background also influenced the type of patronage disbursed, and so the qualitative nature of the support generated. Tea and
rubber afforded more scope for the extension of fringe benefits, and left
less room for theft and therefore friction. The Doctor, cultivating tea and
rubber, was therefore better placed to use this land source to generate
genuine goodwill than his counterparts cultivating coconut in Greenville
were.

The economic activities pursued in an area were also important in
explaining the type of patronage disbursed, and so the qualitative nature
of support generated. In the fishing villages, for instance, fishing was the
only economic activity pursued. The ordinary inhabitants had no alternative sources of income, as those in the agricultural interior did. As
such, their dependence on the village elites tended to be greater than in
the latter areas, so that the patron–client bond was stronger. Moreover,
kin networks sometimes reinforced this bond in the fishing villages, so
that it was more paternalistic and less exploitative than that between a
Goigama headman and depressed-caste client in, say, Greenville. For

these reasons support from the fishing villages was more reliable than that from the agricultural areas of Bluville or Greenville. This explains the greater incidence of bloc voting in the fishing villages than in the farming ones.

In the urban areas of Red Town there were no formalized patron–client bonds of this nature. However, the degree of population congestion and shared poverty and insecurity of employment were important in explaining the emergence of a rudimentary form of community consciousness amongst the dock and railway workers there. The relative cohesion of management, workers, and the latter's indispensability, were variables explaining the extent to which this consciousness was translated into successful industrial action and active support for leftist parties.

Caste *per se* was unimportant in Red Town and our other two electorates. True, in the rural areas of each electorate, the caste tie was often congruent with a patron–client tie. Yet this was a geographical co-incidence, dictated by the fact that in the single caste village structure of the Low Country, a patron tended to live surrounded by members of his own community. The support these caste members rendered their patron was on the basis of his being their patron, and not as a member of their caste. Where the patron came from a different community he could just as easily draw on their support, as the Doctor could in parts of Bluville, and the leading families of Greenville and rural Red Town could on the depressed-caste clients of *Goigama* village elites. Thus, the caste vote in politics was only a special case of a more fundamental client vote.

In some cases this client bloc was congruent with an oppressed caste bloc, as in the case of the *Batgam* and *Vahumpura* in Greenville, and the *Hunu* potters in Red Town. In such cases, where the patron–client bond was particularly exploitative and oppressive, a community consciousness developed, sometimes fostered as a rudimentary form of class consciousness by leftist parties and candidates. Then, where the electoral administration permitted it, the oppressed client caste or class voted as a bloc against the candidates favoured by the *Goigama* village elites. But in such cases, what seemed a caste vote was really a client-class vote.

Nevertheless, a caste had a class interest only in certain special cases. It is difficult to isolate class interests in Sri Lankan politics. Even if they did exist in certain special circumstances, they were not always perceived as existing, and still less often was any such perception acted upon.

To sum up so far, electoral allegiance at Independence could be explained essentially in terms of the patronage networks of particular local notables, and their effective mobilization of these networks at the polls. These patronage networks, in turn, were greatly influenced and conditioned by the particular agro-ecological and socio-economic backgrounds of the areas they prevailed in.

With the growth of the State after 1956, the nature of these patronage networks changed. Nationalization of the bus services in 1957, and of the schools in 1962, eroded the potential for private disbursement of patronage through these channels. This was especially so in Bluville and Red Town where they had been important sources of support for the UNP candidates. The demise of the village headmen's system (1958–63) undermined the influence of these local intermediaries, and so, of the candidates from the *Mudaliyar* families whom they traditionally backed in all constituencies. Land Reform (1972–5) undermined the influence of landowners in Bluville and Greenville. Finally, at the grass-roots, the Paddy Lands Act of 1958, and the new People's Bank and Fisheries Corporation went some way towards reducing the power of local influentials in both the agricultural and coastal areas. However, their importance has, as argued, been exaggerated, and they do not seem to have radically altered the composition of the village elites.

Meanwhile, the electoral reforms of 1956–64 reduced the intermediaries' power to supervise polling, and thereby deliver a candidate blocs of votes. However, the effective implementation of these reforms required a well-organized Opposition, able to supervise its interests at each and every polling booth. This condition, satisfied in the period 1965–77, was not met in December 1982.

Meanwhile, the growth of the State also meant new institutions and programmes emerging. These afforded discerning candidates the opportunity to make inroads into the patronage networks of their rivals. Dee attempted to use the Government's fisheries mechanization and harbour construction programmes of 1956–64 to break the power of the *madel* fishing elites in Bluville, and cultivate a new basis of support amongst the poorer fishermen. The *madel* owners' entry into deep sea fishing, and the technological constraints impeding the dissemination of benefits amongst the poorer fishermen, constrained the success of his plans. Meanwhile, the various public works undertaken by the Doctor in Bluville (1965–70 and 1977–82), by Napi Nip in Greenville (1977–82), and Teri Voo and Tali Gip in Red Town (1960–77) were important in explaining their ability to consolidate support in existing strongholds, and extend it in weaker areas.

At the same time, an inappropriate manipulation of the State could just as easily lose support. The Doctor's construction of Beach Way in 1968 lost him so much support amongst traditional clients in Bluville town that he was forced to withdraw from the electorate and contest another seat in 1970. Teri Voo's widening of a major road in 1975 and the dislocation this caused families generated similar ill-will in Red Town. Again, Zela Kou's failure to reward certain depressed-caste loyalists in Greenville in the distribution of land and jobs meant their switching support to the rival candidate in 1977. Finally, the mismanagement of the Co-operatives in all three electorates helped lose the SLFP so much support that it contributed significantly towards their loss of these seats at the July 1977 General Election.

State institutions therefore had to be appropriately manipulated in order to generate political support. Such appropriate manipulation, however, was not always practised. There was, and is, a (growing) tendency for those in State bodies to treat them as the means for personal material enrichment. Such enrichment has been at the expense of political goodwill, as the SLFP learnt to its cost in 1970, and certain UNP candidates did in October and December 1982.

But, even with appropriate manipulation, candidates faced important constraints. Some of these were externally determined. The completion of the Cocos River Basin Scheme and electrification projects in Bluville were held up by the slowdown in foreign aid disbursements. The two land redevelopment projects earmarked for Red Town were similarly stalled by the cutbacks in public investment imposed in 1981. Meanwhile, in late 1982, the textile centres in all three electorates as well as certain other minor export industries faced closure with the adverse trade climate abroad. In all these cases investment, income and employment generation were threatened, and political goodwill sacrificed. And in all these cases this was largely beyond the control of the local MP.

Given such constraints on the manipulation of State bodies, the local MP's national stature and connections are also important in determining the benefits secured for an electorate and the goodwill generated. The Doctor was able to do more for Bluville over the last five years by virtue of his being a senior Cabinet Minister, than Napi Nip was for Greenville. Teri Voo was able to do less for Red Town than was expected, by virtue of his holding a relatively minor portfolio and enjoying a poor personal rapport with the then Prime Minister. Access to the State is therefore now crucial in the effective disbursement of patronage, and the generation of political support.

Meanwhile, the various restrictions on private wealth have meant few individuals retaining the personal resources to create and maintain large personal clienteles. This can only be done by seizing control of the all-important State network. With the curbs on Independent candidates, their deteriorating electoral performance and, most important, the need for links with Government Ministers and the Colombo Administration for the implementation of popular local projects, the party is seen as the main or only vehicle by which such control can be achieved. Thus, the premium placed on securing the party ticket in any electoral contest has grown. This helps explain the increasing importance of parties in electoral politics in Sri Lanka.

Intra-elite conflict at the national level led to S. W. R. D. Bandaranaike leaving the UNP in 1951. Having a strong base in the Colombo District and a widespread network of contacts amongst other local patrons and village elites, Bandaranaike was able to build his party as an alternative to the UNP. Although several other patrons subsequently formed parties of their own, they did not have the large landholdings *and* widespread administrative contacts which he did. Neither had they been able to cultivate and strengthen links amongst the village elites in the way Bandaranaike had during his tenure as Minister of Local Government (1936–51). As such, their parties never developed as national alternatives to the UNP, in the way the SLFP was able to. Thus, a two-party system came to be established in Sri Lanka.

At the same time, the growth of the State at the expense of private wealth has made for more equality of opportunity in politics. This equality had always been more marked in urban areas such as Red Town (where private landed wealth was insignificant), as our study of Teri Voo's rise shows. But now, even in rural electorates such as Bluville, many of the new intermediaries rising to prominence hail from very poor backgrounds. Their present wealth and position is largely the result of their access to the Doctor, and through him, to the State.

The basis on which patronage is disbursed has therefore changed, as has the composition of personnel. At the same time, the links binding a client to his patron have become far more temporary and loose than in the past. The links tend to exist only so long as the patron retains control of a State post, as Tyrrel Ay's relationship with his chauffeur shows. Moreover, as this incident again reveals, as the client's links are with the State body they can survive the exit of any one patron. This looser relationship has made for a greater atomization of villages, and the gradual atrophy of bloc voting.

The Insurgency of 1971 can be seen in terms of these patronage networks. It found greatest support in the depressed-caste areas of the Sabaragamuwa and Southern Provinces.[1] This was because the depressed-caste clients of *Goigama* village elites here had failed to benefit under either the UNP or SLFP, due to the way in which (as in Wun) the patronage network operated. Benefiting under neither party, they sought redress in armed insurrection. They tended to be more successful in their activities here as well, as these areas are geographically remote,

---

[1] See Jiggins (1979), Chapter 7.

inaccessible and distant from Colombo, and therefore offered logistic advantages in guerrilla-type activity. As such, the districts north of Greenville and Bluville witnessed more activity and destruction than our two rural electorates.[2]

Meanwhile, in the urban areas, the absence of links based on private landed wealth made for a lesser incidence of the patronage networks as they operated in the rural context. The religious minorities congregating in these areas, such as the Christians of Red Town and Muslims of Bluville town, traditionally voted for the party they believed to be most tolerant of their views, and most likely to protect their particular interests: the UNP. In the more industrial areas of Red Town, a more class-based form of politics prevailed as early as 1947.

To sum up then, this study seeks to explain political allegiance in Sri Lanka in terms of patronage networks, as influenced by the agro-ecological and socio-economic contexts they operated in. These networks, especially in the rural areas, were initially based on private (often landed) wealth. After 1956, as the State expanded, they came to be based on control of State institutions. Such control was best realized through affiliation with a governing (or potentially governing) party, and so, competition for the party ticket grew. In the process a more open and egalitarian form of politics emerged.

This study is the first detailed comparative analysis of electorates in Sri Lanka over time. As such, it sheds new light on the bases of political support, in a way some of the more aggregative and national,[3] and detailed village level studies,[4] described in Chapter 1, do not. In particular, it demonstrates that caste was unimportant except in so far as it was congruent with a patronage network; that the patronage network was the fundamental explanatory variable, and that where it cut across the caste tie, it was decisive. In this context, this study seeks to displace Jiggins' explanation of caste in politics,[5] and also this presumption as it appears in so many general works on the subject.[6] The study also substantiates, with reference to Sri Lanka, some of the ideas Washbrook and certain students of the Indian scene have propounded.[7] The importance of ideological factors, and especially of Buddhist priests in electoral contests in Sri Lanka, suggested in so many works,[8] is also reassessed, and found to be minimal.

[2] Alles (1976).   [3] See Chapter 1, footnote 11.
[4] See Chapter 1, footnote 12.   [5] Jiggins (1979).
[6] See Chapter 1, footnote 19.   [7] See Chapter 1, pp. 1–3.
[8] Smith (1966), Phadnis (1976).

GLOSSARY OF SINHALESE TERMS

amunam   measure of land (equivalent to about two acres)

ande   form of paddy land tenure

arrack   alcoholic beverage distilled from *toddy*

arrack-renter   individual who had purchased the right (from the Colonial Government) to levy and retain the tax on *arrack* within a particular district

Atapattu-Mudaliyar   *Mudaliyar* working in a *Kachcheri*

ayurvedic   form of native herbal medication

Basnayake-Nilame   chief lay trustee of a *devale*

Batgam   underprivileged and numerically large Sinhalese caste

Berawa/Nekathi   underprivileged and numerically small Sinhalese caste

bulat-hurulle   Betel leaf offering

Chief-Dayakaya   chief lay trustee of a Buddhist temple

Constable-Arachchi   minor native headman of a similar rank to a *Police-Vidane*

Dalada Maligawa   temple of the (Lord Buddha's) tooth relic in Kandy

Dayakaya   lay trustee of a Buddhist temple

Dayakaya-Sabha   council of lay trustees of a Buddhist temple

devale   (Hindu and/or Buddhist) shrine to a deity

Dharma   Buddhist doctrine of righteousness

Durave   economically privileged and numerically small Sinhalese caste

Gansabhawa   council meeting place

Gate Mudaliyar   honorary *Mudaliyar* attached to the Governor personally

Goigama   economically privileged and numerically large Sinhalese caste

Gramodaya Mandalaya   local-level popular institution representing different rural interests

Guard Mudaliyar   honorary *Mudaliyar* attached to the Governor personally

Hamu-Mahatmaya   deferential form of address somewhat akin to 'Revered Sir'

hartal   form of strike

Hena   underprivileged and numerically small Sinhalese caste

Hunu   underprivileged and numerically small Sinhalese caste

Huwandiram-Rent   tax levied on the paddy harvest

Kachcheri   chief government administrative office in a district

Kamma   South Indian caste found chiefly in Andhra Pradesh

kangany/kanganies   labour supervisor/supervisors, generally on a tea estate

Karave   economically privileged and numerically small Sinhalese caste

Kayastha   North Indian caste

Kinneriya   underprivileged and numerically small Sinhalese caste *kootu-ande*   form of paddy land tenure whereby the tenant works alongside the paddy landowner

korale   administrative area supervised by a *Mudaliyar*

Korale-Mudaliyar   *Mudaliyar* supervising a *korale*

Korale-Muhandiram   *Muhandiram* supervising a *korale*

Kumbal   underprivileged and numerically small Sinhalese caste

madel   type of fishing net

Maha-Mudaliyar   chief *Mudaliyar*

Maha-Nayakaya   chief Priest

Maha Vidyalaya   secondary (vernacular) school

Maha-Vihare   great Buddhist temple

Malwatte Chapter/Malwatte Vihare   one of the two Chapters of the Siam *Nikaya*

maravenu   form of service tenure

mathini   mother

mudalali   small-scale trader or entrepreneur

Mudaliyar   highest ranking native headman in the Colonial Administration

Muhandiram   second-highest ranking native headman in the Colonial Administration (after the *Mudaliyar*)

Navandanna   relatively privileged and numerically small Sinhalese caste

Nekathi/Berawa   underprivileged and numerically small Sinhalese caste

nikaya   (Buddhist) sect

palate   administrative area generally covering a few villages and smaller than a *korale* or *pattuwa*

Panna(ma)   underprivileged and numerically small Sinhalese caste

pansala   colloquial Sinhalese term for temple

paravenu   form of service tenure

Patabendi-Arachchi   minor native headman of about the same rank as a *Vidane-Arachchi*

Pattu-Mudaliyar   *Mudaliyar* supervising a *pattuwa*

pattuwa   administrative area generally smaller than a *korale*

perahera   Buddhist religious procession in which a casket containing relics is generally taken around

peruwa   administrative area generally covering a few villages and smaller than a *korale* or *pattuwa*

pirivena   training centre for novice Buddhist monks

Police Duraya   minor native headman

Police-Vidane   minor native headman

Rada/Dhobi   underprivileged and numerically small Sinhalese caste

raja-kariya   form of feudal service tenure prevalent in the Kandyan districts in the pre-twentieth-century era

Ramayana-Nikaya   one of the three Buddhist sects in Sri Lanka

Ratemahatmaya   Kandyan equivalent of *Mudaliyar*

Reddi   South Indian caste found chiefly in Andhra Pradesh

Ruvanvelisaya   major edifice (supposedly containing relics of the Lord Buddha) constructed in Anuradhapura about 2,000 years ago

Sabha   Council

Salagama   economically privileged and numerically small Sinhalese caste

Sangha   Buddhist clergy

shramadana   voluntary work performed for the community: form of social service

Siam Nikaya   one of the three Buddhist sects in Sri Lanka

Sinhala Maha Sabha   Sinhala Great Council

Suriyamal Campaign   LSSP campaign to sell *suriyamal* (or sunflowers) to raise funds for local causes and counteract the sale of poppies for the war dead of England

swabasha   native language

toddy   mildly alcoholic syrup derived from the coconut flower

Vahumpura   underprivileged and numerically large Sinhalese caste

Vellalla   South Indian caste found chiefly in Tamil Nadu and also in northern Sri Lanka

Vel-Vidane   minor native headman in charge of overseeing irrigation canals

Vidane-Arachchi   middle-level native headman ranking below a *Muhandiram* but above a *Police-Vidane*

vidyalaya   school

vihare   Buddhist temple

vihare-stupa   edifice in a Buddhist temple within which a relic or relics are interned

walauwwa   residence of a local influential

Warnasinghe Eksath Peramuna   United Youth Front

Wesak   anniversary of Lord Buddha's birth, enlightenment and death

yaya   paddy field

REFERENCES

Published sources

Abeysooriya, S. (1928) *Who's Who of Ceylon, 1928*, Colombo, privately published

Alexander, P. (1982) *Sri Lankan Fishermen: Rural Capitalism and Peasant Society*, Canberra, Australian National University Monograph on South Asia, Number 7

Alles, A. C. (1976) *Insurgency 1971*, Colombo, Colombo Apothecaries

ARTI (1975) *The Agrarian Situation Relating to Paddy Cultivation in Five Selected Districts of Sri Lanka*, Part 5, *Colombo District*, Colombo, ARTI

Baker, Christopher J. (1976) *The Politics of South India 1920–1937*, Cambridge, Cambridge University Press

Breman, J. (1974) *Patronage and Exploitation: Changing Agrarian Relations in South Gujarat, India*, Berkeley, CA, University of California Press

Carroll, L. (1975) 'Caste, Social Change and the Social Scientist: A Note on the Ahistorical Approach to Indian Social History', *Journal of Asian Studies*, Volume 35, pp. 63–84

Carroll, L. (1978) 'Colonial Perceptions of Indian Society and the Emergence of Caste(s) Associations', *Journal of Asian Studies*, Volume 37, Number 2, pp. 233–50

Carter, A. T. (1974) *Elite Politics in Rural India: Political Stratification and Alliances in Western Maharashtra*, Cambridge, Cambridge University Press

CDN (1947) *Parliament of Ceylon, 1947*, Colombo, Associated Newspapers of Ceylon

CDN (1952) *Parliament of Ceylon, 1952* (Sinhalese Version), Colombo, Associated Newspapers of Ceylon

CDN (1956) *Parliament of Ceylon, 1956*, Colombo, Associated Newspapers of Ceylon

CDN (1960) *Parliament of Ceylon, 1960*, Colombo, Associated Newspapers of Ceyon

CDN (1965) *Parliament of Ceylon 1965*, Colombo, Associated Newspapers of Ceylon

CDN (1970) *Parliament of Ceylon, 1970*, Colombo, Associated Newspapers of Ceylon

CDN (1977) *Parliament of Ceylon, 1977*, Colombo, Associated Newspapers of Ceylon

Eisenstadt, S. N. and Roniger, L. (1980) 'Patron–Client Relations as a Model of

Structuring Social Exchange', *Comparative Studies in Society and History*, Volume 22, pp. 42–77

Eisenstadt, S. N. and Roniger, L. (1984) *Patrons, Clients and Friends*, Cambridge, Cambridge University Press

Evers, H. D. (1972) *Monks, Priests and Peasants: A Study of Buddhism and Social Structure in Central Ceylon*, Leiden, E. J. Brill

Farmer, B. H. (1963) *Ceylon: A Divided Nation*, London, Oxford University Press

Ferguson's *Ceylon Directories* (1880–1958), Colombo, Ceylon Observer Press

Fernando, S., Devasena, L., Ranaweera Banda, R. M. and Somawantha, H. K. M. (1984) 'The Impact of Buddhism on Small Scale Fishery Performance and Development in Sri Lanka', *Marga Quarterly Journal*, Volume 1, Numbers 2 and 3, pp. 110–62

Gellner, E. (1977), 'Patrons and Clients' in E. Gellner and J. Waterbury (eds.) *Patrons and Clients in Mediterranean Societies*, London, Duckworth, pp. 1–6

Government of Ceylon/Sri Lanka (GOC/GOSL)

(a) *Official Documents*

GOC *Blue Books (1849–1954)*, Colombo, Government Press

GOC *Census of Agriculture (1946)*, Colombo, Government Press

GOC *Census of Agriculture (1952)*, Colombo, Government Press

GOC *Census of Agriculture (1962)*, Colombo, Government Press

GOC *Civil Lists (1849–1954)*, Colombo, Government Press

GOC *Hansards (1931–1981)*, Colombo, Government Press

GOC *Lists of Villages (1928, 1946)*, Colombo, Government Press

GOC (1922) *Report of the Headmen's Commission*, SP 2 of 1922, Colombo, Government Press

GOC (1935) *Report of the Headmen's Commission*, SP 27 of 1935, Colombo, Government Press

GOC (1946) *Report of the Delimitation Commission*, Colombo, Government Press

GOC (1956) *Report of the Commission on the Tenure of Lands of Viharagam, Devalagam and Nindagam*, SP 1 of 1956, Colombo, Government Press

GOC (1959) *Report of the Delimitation Commission*, Colombo, Government Press

GOC (1962) *Report on the Parliamentary General Elections, 19 March and 20 July 1960*, SP 2 of 1962, Colombo, Government Press

GOC (1966) *Report on the Sixth Parliamentary General Election of Ceylon, 22nd March 1965*, SP 20 of 1966, Colombo, Government Press

GOSL (1972a) *Reprint of the Ceylon Parliamentary Elections Order in Council 1946 (Chapter 381), as amended by Act 4 of 1959, 11 of 1959, 26 of 1959, 2 of 1960, 72 of 1961, 8 of 1964, 10 of 1964, 9 of 1970, and by Rule published in Government Gazette 14,569 of 26 November, 1965*, Colombo, Government Press

GOSL (1972b) *Results of Elections to the Parliaments of Ceylon, 1947–1970*, Colombo, Government Press

GOSL (1976) *Report of the Delimitation Commission*, Colombo, Government Press

GOSL (1983) *Report on the First Presidential Election in Sri Lanka held on 20th October 1982*, SP 8 of 1983, Colombo, Government Press

GOSL (1987) *Report on the First Referendum on Sri Lanka*, SP 2 of 1987, Colombo, Government Press

(b) *Acts of Parliament*

Agrarian Services Act 58 of 1979, Colombo, Government Press

Estates (Control of Transfer and Acquisition) Act 2 of 1972, Colombo, Government Press

Land Reform Law 1 of 1972, Colombo, Government Press

Paddy Lands Act 1 of 1958, Colombo, Government Press

Hardgrave, R. (1969) *The Nadars of Tamil Nad*, Berkeley, CA, University of California Press

Hawthorn, G. P. (1982) 'Caste and Politics in India since 1947' in D. McGilvray (ed.) *Caste Ideology and Interaction*, Cambridge, Cambridge University Press, pp. 204–20

Jayawardene, V. K. (1972) *The Rise of the Labour Movement in Sri Lanka*, Durham, NC, Duke University Press

Jeffrey, R. (1974) 'The Social Origins of a Caste Association, 1875–1905: The Founding of the SNDP Yogam', *South Asia*, Number 4, pp. 39–59

Jeffrey, R. (1976) *The Decline of Nayar Dominance: Society and Politics in Travancore, 1847–1908*, Sussex University Press

Jennings, Sir Ivor (1948) 'The Ceylon General Election of 1947', *University of Ceylon Review*, Volume 6, Number 3, pp. 133–95

Jennings, Sir Ivor (1952) 'Ceylon 1952 Elections', *Eastern Survey*, Volume 21, pp. 177–80

Jennings, Sir Ivor (1953) 'Additional Notes on the General Elections of 1952', *Ceylon Historical Journal*, Volume 2, Numbers 3 and 4, pp. 193–208

Jiggins, J. (1974) 'Dedigama 1973: A Profile of a By-election in Sri Lanka'. *Asian Survey*, Volume 14, Number 11, pp. 1,000–14

Jiggins, J. (1979) *Caste and Family in the Politics of the Sinhalese 1947–1976*, London, Cambridge University Press

Jupp, J. (1978) *Sri Lanka: Third World Democracy*, London, Cass

Kearney, R. N. (1971) *Trade Unions and Politics in Sri Lanka*, Berkeley, CA, University of California Press

Kearney, R. N. (1973) *The Politics of Ceylon (Sri Lanka)*, London, Cornell University Press

Keerawala (1980) 'The Janatha Vimukthi Peramuna and the 1971 Uprising', *The Social Science Review*, Number 2, pp. 46–7

Kurushetra (1977) *Caste Papers*, Volumes 1–3, Colombo, privately published

Moore, M. P. (1978) 'Caste and Family in the Politics of the Sinhalese: A Review Article', *MARGA Quarterly Journal*, Volume 5, Number 4, pp. 77–82

Moore, M. P. (1981a) 'Politics in Sri Lanka: A Review Article', *Modern Asian Studies* Volume 15, Number 1

Morrison, Moore *et al.* (1979) *The Disintegrating Village*, Colombo, Lakehouse Investments Ltd

Obeysekere, G. (1967) *Land Tenure in Village Ceylon*, London, Cambridge University Press

Obeysekere, G. (1974) 'Some Comments on the Social Backgrounds of the April 1971 Insurgency in Ceylon (Sri Lanka)', *Journal of Asian Studies*, Volume 33, Number 3, May 1974, pp. 367–84

Phadnis, U. (1969) 'Agalawatte By-election: A Case Study of the Political Behaviour of Rural Ceylon', *International Studies* 10(3), pp. 321–8

Phadnis, U. (1976) *Religion and Politics in Sri Lanka*, New Delhi, Manohar

Rees, F. (1955/6) 'The Soulbury Commission 1944–45', *Ceylon Historical Journal*, Volume 5, Number 1–4

Roberts, M. (1979a) 'Meanderings in the Pathways of Collective Identities and Nationalisms' in Roberts, M. (ed.) *Collective Identities, Nationalisms and Protest in Modern Sri Lanka*, Colombo, MARGA, pp. 1–98

Roberts, M. (1979b) 'Elite Formation and Elites, 1832–1931' in Roberts M. (ed.) *Collective Identities, Nationalisms and Protest in Modern Sri Lanka*, Colombo, MARGA, pp. 153–213

Roberts, M. (1982) *Caste Conflict and Elite Formation: The Rise of a Karava Elite in Sri Lanka, 1500–1931*, Cambridge, Cambridge University Press

Robinson, M. S. (1975) *Political Structure in a Changing Sinhalese Village*, London, Cambridge University Press

Ryan, B. (1953) *Caste in Modern Ceylon: The Sinhalese System in Transition*, New Brunswick, NJ, Rutgers University Press

Seneviratne (1978) *Rituals of the Kandyan State*, London, Cambridge University Press

Smith, D. E. (ed.) (1966) *South Asian Politics and Religion*, Princeton, NJ, Princeton University Press

Tressie-Leittan, G. R. (1979) *Local Government and Decentralized Administration in Sri Lanka*, Colombo, Lakehouse Investments Ltd

Wanigaratne, Gooneratne and Shanmugaratnam (1979) *The Policies and Implementation of Land Reform in Selected Villages of Sri Lanka*, Colombo, ARTI

Washbrook, D. (1975) 'The Development of Caste Organization in South India 1880–1925' in C. J. Baker and D. A. Washbrook (eds.) *South India: Political Institutions and Political Change 1880–1940*, New Delhi, Macmillans, pp. 150–203

Washbrook (1976) *The Emergence of Provincial Politics: The Madras Presidency 1870–1920*, Cambridge, Cambridge University Press

Weerawardene, I. D. S. (1952) 'The General Elections in Ceylon, 1952', *Ceylon Historical Journal*, Volume 2, Numbers 1 and 2, pp. 111–78

Weerawardene, I. D. S. (1960) *Ceylon General Election, 1956*, Colombo, Gunasena

Wilson, A. J. (1975) *Electoral Politics in an Emergent State: The Ceylon General Election of May 1970*, London, Cambridge University Press

Wilson, A. J. (1979) *Politics in Sri Lanka, 1947–79*, London, Macmillan

Woodward, C. A. (1969) *The Growth of a Party System in Ceylon*, Providence, RI, Brown University Press

Wriggins, W. H. (1960) *Ceylon: Dilemmas of a New Nation*, Princeton, NJ, Princeton University Press

Unpublished sources

Asiriwatham (1981) 'People's Participation in the Co-operative Movement', Colombo, MARGA Mimeo

Census and Statistics Department, Census Returns of Villages, 1946

Commissioner of Co-operative Development (Investigations Department).
   Confidential Files of Inquiry into the Taluville Multi-purpose Co-operative Society (MPCS) (1970–7)
   Confidential Files of Inquiry into the Red Town Central Multi-purpose Co-operative Society (MPCS) (1970–7)
   Confidential Files of Inquiry into the Greenville Multi-purpose Co-operative Society (MPCS) (1970–7)
   Confidential Files of Inquiry into the Purville Korale Multi-purpose Co-operative Society (MPCS) (1970–7)

Land Reform Commission (LRC) (1972–9) Confidential Files on the Use and Distribution of Alienated Land

Moore, M. P. (1981b) 'The State and Peasantry in Sri Lanka', unpublished Ph.D. thesis, University of Sussex

Peebles, P. (1973) 'The Transformation of a Colonial Elite: The *Mudaliyars* of Late Nineteenth Century Ceylon', unpublished Ph.D. thesis, University of Chicago

Sri Lanka National Archives (SLNA) Records: In the footnotes, where appropriate, the lot and file number of each file used is given, in that order. Thus, if file 748 of lot 26 is used, this is denoted by the abbreviation SLNA 26/748. The list below only covers some of the broad subjects and lots referred to in the footnotes:
   Dutch Records (including the Land and School Tombos) (SLNA Lot 1)
   Matara *Kachcheri* Records (including the *Huwandiram-Rent* Records) (SLNA Lot 26)
   Colombo *Kachcheri* Records (SLNA Lot 33)

Tennekoon, M. U. A. (1980) 'Towards a Pragmatic Rural Credit Policy in Sri Lanka', Paper presented at the *Ceylon Studies Seminar*, University of Peradeniya, Ceylon, 19 December 1980

Newspapers

Ceylon Daily News
Ceylon Sunday Observer
Island
Sun
Sri Lanka News

Ordnance Survey Maps

INDEX

CAMBRIDGE SOUTH ASIAN STUDIES

These monographs are published by the Syndics of Cambridge University Press in association with the Cambridge University Centre for South Asian Studies. The following books have been published in this series: